THE
HISTORY OF
TURKEY

ADVISORY BOARD

THE
HISTORY OF
TURKEY

Douglas A. Howard

The Greenwood Histories of the Modern Nations
Frank W. Thackeray and John E. Findling, Series Editors

Greenwood Press
Westport, Connecticut • London

Library of Congress Cataloging-in-Publication Data

Howard, Douglas A. (Douglas Arthur), 1958–
    The history of Turkey / Douglas A. Howard.
      p. cm.—(The Greenwood histories of the modern nations, ISSN 1096–2905)
    Includes bibliographical references (p.) and index.
    ISBN 0–313–30708–3 (alk. paper)
    1. Turkey—History. I. Title. II. Series.
  DR441.H69   2001
   956.1—dc21   00–061720

British Library Cataloguing in Publication Data is available.

Library of Congress Catalog Card Number: 00–061720
ISBN: 0–313–30708–3
ISSN: 1096–2905

First published in 2001

Greenwood Press, 88 Post Road West, Westport, CT 06881
An imprint of Greenwood Publishing Group, Inc.
www.greenwood.com

Printed in the United States of America

The paper used in this book complies with the
Permanent Paper Standard issued by the National
Information Standards Organization (Z39.48–1984).

10 9 8 7 6 5 4 3 2 1

For Elizabeth, Graham, Steven and Geoffrey

Contents

Series Foreword

The Greenwood Histories of the Modern Nations series is intended to provide students and interested laypeople with up-to-date, concise, and analytical histories of many of the nations of the contemporary world. Not since the 1960s has there been a systematic attempt to publish a series of national histories, and, as series editors, we believe that this series will prove to be a valuable contribution to our understanding of other countries in our increasingly interdependent world.

Over thirty years ago, at the end of the 1960s, the Cold War was an accepted reality of global politics, the process of decolonization was still in progress, the idea of a unified Europe with a single currency was unheard of, the United States was mired in a war in Vietnam, and the economic boom of Asia was still years in the future. Richard Nixon was president of the United States, Mao Tse-tung (not yet Mao Zedong) ruled China, Leonid Brezhnev guided the Soviet Union, and Harold Wilson was prime minister of the United Kingdom. Authoritarian dictators still ruled most of Latin America, the Middle East was reeling in the wake of the Six-Day War, and Shah Reza Pahlavi was at the height of his power in Iran. Clearly, the past thirty years have been witness to a great deal of historical change, and it is to this change that this series is primarily addressed.

With the help of a distinguished advisory board, we have selected nations whose political, economic, and social affairs mark them as among the most important in the waning years of the twentieth century, and for each nation we have found an author who is recognized as specialist in the history of that nation. These authors have worked most cooperatively with us and with Greenwood Press to produce volumes that reflect current research on their nation and that are interesting and informative to their prospective readers.

The importance of a series such as this cannot be underestimated. As a superpower whose influence is felt all over the world, the United States can claim a "special" relationship with almost every other nation. Yet many Americans know very little about the histories of the nations with which the United States relates. How did they get to be the way they are? What kind of political systems have evolved there? What kind of influence do they have in their own region? What are the dominant political, religious, and cultural forces that move their leaders? These and many other questions are answered in the volumes of this series.

The authors who have contributed to this series have written comprehensive histories of their nations, dating back to prehistoric time in some cases. Each of them, however, has devoted a significant portion of the book to events of the past thirty years, because the modern era has contributed the most to contemporary issues that have an impact on U.S. policy. Authors have made an effort to be as up-to-date as possible so that readers can benefit from the most recent scholarship and a narrative that includes very recent events.

In addition to the historical narrative, each volume in this series contains an introductory overview of the country's geography, political institutions, economic structure, and cultural attributes. This is designed to give readers a picture of the nation as it exists in the contemporary world. Each volume also contains additional chapters that add interesting and useful detail to the historical narrative. One chapter is a thorough chronology of important historical events, making it easy for readers to follow the flow of a particular nation's history. Another chapter features biographical sketches of the nation's most important figures in order to humanize some of the individuals who have contributed to the historical development of their nation. Each volume also contains a comprehensive bibliography, so that those readers whose interest has been sparked may find out more about the nation and its history. Finally, there is a carefully prepared topic and person index.

Readers of these volumes will find them fascinating to read and useful in understanding the contemporary world and the nations that comprise it. As series editors, it is our hope that this series will contribute to a heightened sense of global understanding as we enter a new century.

Frank W. Thackeray and John E. Findling
Indiana University Southeast

Preface

Since 1989, it has become somewhat easier to think of the history of Turkey apart from the categories imposed by the cold war. The events of that year across east central Europe have stimulated fresh thinking about the history of Turkey in the twentieth century. With the other states of east central and southeastern Europe, it is possible to begin assessing the impact of the Ottoman past, of the authoritarian interwar years, and of the Cold War on Turkish society.

The Republic of Turkey was established through a War of Independence that freed the country from foreign domination after World War I. In the interwar years, the first president of Turkey, Mustafa Kemal Atatürk, directed the reconstruction of the Turkish economy and Turkish society through the authoritarian means of a single-party state. The formal structures of a new model of Turkish public life had been erected when World War II erupted. Almost immediately after the conclusion of that conflict, Turkey, threatened by the Soviet Union and the descending Iron Curtain, was drawn into the alliance system being built by the United States. During most of the next forty years, Turkey held the ironic position of a military-dominated parliamentary democracy with a planned economy in the North Atlantic alliance.

This book attempts to interpret the modern history of Turkey in these terms. After an introductory chapter in which the current geographic, economic, and political circumstances of the country are summarized, the book presents the history of Turkey from the Neolithic age to the industrial age. The emphasis is on events of the twentieth century, beginning with the period of the late Ottoman revolution of the Young Turks. If there is a main character of the story, it is Atatürk, whose legacy is at the center of public discussion in modern Turkish life.

While writing, I tried to keep in mind the needs of readers who might be like the ones in my own family a generation ago. Eagerly anticipating an assignment to Turkey, we checked out the books on the history of Turkey from our local library. At that time, the books available to us included Geoffrey Lewis's *Turkey*, Lord Kinross's fine biography *Atatürk*, and Roderic Davison's *Turkey; A Short History*. Those books inspired us for the adventure ahead. Though I cannot hope to equal the elegance and erudition of those classics, if current readers find the present book half as useful as a starting point for understanding Turkey today, and are motivated to read and learn more, I will have accomplished my purpose.

Several people helped see this project to fruition. I owe thanks to Frank Thackeray, series editor, for his feedback on drafts of the chapters. Barbara Rader at Greenwood Press patiently accommodated the needs of a full-time college teacher. Colleagues in the Turkish Studies Association gave encouragement. A paper by John M. Vander Lippe helped clarify my views of post–World War II developments, and Aygen Erdentuğ's comments stimulated my thinking about important issues in contemporary Turkey. The insightful remarks of my students in class discussions invariably made me see the subject more clearly. My colleagues and friends in the History Department at Calvin College, and especially my chairman James Bratt, were unfailingly supportive in the project, and David Diephouse responded to a draft of a difficult section.

My wife, Sandy, and our children, to whom the book is dedicated, were gracious, forgiving, and good humored during long evenings while the work proceeded slowly. Finally, I owe special gratitude to my parents, Frank A. Howard and Theodora Howard, who led me to the subject in spite of myself. Errors and failings that remain are, naturally, my own.

Timeline of Historical Events

1097–1099	First Crusade
1176	Battle of Myriokephalon
1204	Fall of Constantinople in Fourth Crusade
1219–1236	Reign of Alauddin Kaykubad, Seljuk Turkish ruler in Konya
1243	Mongols defeat the Seljuks at the Battle of Köse Dagh
1300	Defeat of Byzantine forces by Osman
1327	Orhan captures Bursa
1330–1331	Ibn Battuta in Anatolia
1395	Ottoman province of Anadolu organized
1402	Tamerlane defeats Ottoman Sultan Bayezid at the Battle of Ankara
1402–1411	Ottoman interregnum, and civil war and reconquest of Anatolia
1453	Fall of Constantinople (Istanbul) to Ottoman Sultan Mehmed II
1466–1478	Reign of Uzun Hasan, Akkoyunlu ruler
1507	Shah Ismail invades Anatolia
1514	Ottoman Sultan Selim I defeats Shah Ismail at the Battle of Çaldıran
1516	Sultan Selim I conquers the Ramazanoğlu state in Cilicia
1517	Sultan Selim I conquers Syria, Egypt, and Arabia
1520–1566	Reign of Sultan Süleyman Kanuni
1578–1590	War with Iran in Armenia, Azerbaijan, and the Transcaucasus
1630–1672	Evliya Çelebi's career of travels
1656	Appointment of Mehmed Köprülü as Grand Vezir
1768–1774	War with Russia; Treaty of Küçük Kaynarca

1789–1807	Reign of Sultan Selim III
1808–1839	Reign of Sultan Mahmud II
1826	Destruction of the Janissaries
1832	Egyptian invasion of Anatolia; Ottoman armies defeated at Konya
1839	Rose Garden reform decree initiates the Tanzimat
1839–1861	Reign of Sultan Abdülmecid
1856	Imperial Rescript reform decree
1861–1876	Reign of Sultan Abdülaziz
1864	Provincial reorganization
1869	Promulgation of the *Mecelle* code
1875 July	Bosnian peasant revolt breaks out; Serbia and Montenegro declare war on Ottomans
1876 May–August	Reign of Sultan Murad V
1876–1909	Reign of Sultan Abdülhamid II
1876 December	Promulgation of the Ottoman constitution; first Ottoman elections
1877 March	War with Serbia and Montenegro ends; Russia declares war on Ottomans
1878 February	Russian armies take Edirne; Sultan Abdülhamid prorogues parliament indefinitely
1878 March	Treaty of San Stefano
1878 June	Congress of Berlin
1881	Creation of the Ottoman Public Debt Administration
1881	Birth of Mustafa Kemal in Salonika
1889	Formation of the Committee of Union and Progress in Paris
1908 July	Mutiny of Ottoman Third Army in Macedonia begins the Young Turks Revolution; Sultan Abdülhamid II restores the constitution

1908 December	National elections for parliament
1909 April	Counterrevolution suppressed in Istanbul
1909–1918	Reign of Sultan Mehmed V Reşad
1912–1913	First and Second Balkan Wars
1913 January	CUP coup in Istanbul led by Major Enver
1914–1918	World War I
1915 April	British military landing at Dardanelles repulsed; deportations and massacres of Armenians begins in eastern Anatolia
1919 May	Mustafa Kemal Pasha lands at Samsun
1919 July–September	Nationalist congresses at Erzurum and Sivas; adoption of the National Pact
1919–1922	Turkish War of Independence
1920 August	Treaty of Sèvres
1923 July	Treaty of Lausanne
1923 October	Declaration of the Republic of Turkey
1924 April	Ratification of the Constitution of the Republic
1925	Kurdish revolt of Shaykh Said
1925 November	Law banning the fez
1925 December	International calendar and clock adopted
1927 October	Mustafa Kemal's six-day speech at the RPP congress
1928 November	Romanized alphabet adopted
1934	First five-year plan adopted
1934	Family name law adopted; women receive the suffrage
1938 November	Atatürk dies; İsmet İnönü becomes second president of the Republic
1940	Village Institutes opened nationwide
1942	Capital tax

1950 May	Democrat Party wins landslide victory in national elections; Celal Bayar elected third president of the Republic; Adnan Menderes becomes prime minister
1952 February	Turkey joins NATO
1959 February	Republic of Cyprus declared as an independent state
1959 September	Turkey applies for associate membership in EEC
1960 May	Junior officers seize power in Turkey's first military coup; form National Unity Committee (NUC)
1961 June	New constitution adopted in a national referendum; beginning of Second Republic
1961 September	Former Prime Minister Adnan Menderes and other Democrat Party leaders executed
1963 December	First Cyprus war between Turkish and Greek Cypriots
1967 November	Second Cyprus war between Turkish and Greek Cypriots
1971 March	Military forces Demirel's resignation in the Coup by Memorandum; Nihat Erim made prime minister
1973 October	RPP wins postcoup national elections; Bülent Ecevit becomes prime minister; Fahri Korutürk becomes sixth president of the Republic
1974	Coup in Cyprus; Turkish invasion
1978 November	PKK founded in Ankara by Abdullah Öcalan
1980 September	Turkish military seizes control of the government, suspends constitution, and closes parliament
1982 November	National referendum on new constitution; Kenan Evren elected seventh president of the Republic; beginning of Third Republic
1983 November	Motherland Party wins national elections; Turgut Özal becomes prime minister

1988 June	Özal survives an assassination attempt at a party congress
1989 November	President Kenan Evren retires; Turgut Özal becomes eighth president of the Republic; Yıldırım Akbulut becomes prime minister
1993 April	Death of President Turgut Özal; Süleyman Demirel becomes ninth president of the Republic
1994 April	Welfare Party wins local elections, including mayorships in Istanbul and Ankara
1995 December	Welfare Party wins national elections
1996 June	Necmettin Erbakan becomes prime minister
1996 November	Auto accident at Susurluk brings to light extensive government corruption scandal
1997 February	Military forces Prime Minister Erbakan to agree to measures limiting influence of Islam in public life
1997 December	European Union rejects Turkey's bid for membership
1998 November	Prime Minister Yılmaz resigns amid charges of corruption; Bülent Ecevit becomes prime minister
1999 February	PKK leader Abdullah Öcalan captured
1999 April	Democratic Left Party of Bülent Ecevit wins national elections
1999 August	Massive earthquake strikes northwestern Turkey; more than 17,000 people die
1999 December	EU readmits Turkey to candidate status
2000 May	President Süleyman Demirel retires; Necdet Sezer becomes tenth president of the republic

Turkish Spelling and Pronunciation Guide

Modern Turkish uses a modified Roman alphabet of 29 letters, pronounced approximately as follows:

A, a	a, as in *father*
B, b	b, as in *bad*
C, c	j, as in *joke*
Ç, ç	ch, as in *chimney*
D, d	d, as in *dad*
E, e	e, as in *egg*
F, f	f, as in *final*
G, g	g, as in *gallon*
Ğ, ğ	"soft g," in eastern dialects this is a gh, but in the standardized İstanbul dialect it is softened. It elongates the previous vowel, something like the slur between the two i's in the first word of the song "Silent Night."
H, h	h, as in *hello*
I, ı	an unrounded back vowel, something like the io in the second syllable of *cushion*

İ, i	i, as in *pit*
J, j	like the French j, or the s in *measure*
K, k	k, as in *kind*
L, l	l, as in *lament*
M, m	m, as in *mother*
N, n	n, as in *never*
O, o	o, as in *obey*
Ö, ö	like the German ö, or the French eu, as in *bleu*
P, p	p, as in *pine*
R, r	flap r, as the tt in *batter*
S, s	s, as in *son*
Ş, ş	sh, as in *shimmer*
T, t	t, as in *time*
U, u	u, as in *put*
Ü, ü,	like German ü
V, v	v, as in *vote*
Y, y	y, as in *yellow*
Z, z	z, as in *zebra*

1

Turkey Today

TURKEY AND THE TURKS

High on a bluff overlooking the city of Ankara, the capital of Turkey, stands the final resting place of Mustafa Kemal Atatürk, first president of the Republic of Turkey and one of the most important world figures of the twentieth century. If indeed a country can be said to be the creation of a single individual, then Turkey is a new country, the creation of Mustafa Kemal Atatürk. Emerging out of the momentous changes brought to Europe and southwestern Asia as a result of the violence and suffering of the First World War, Turkey established its separate destiny through a bloody war of independence between 1919 and 1922. In World War I, the great Ottoman Turkish Empire had collapsed. The Republic of Turkey became one of the successor states of the Ottoman Empire when General Mustafa Kemal led a movement of national resistance to an imposed peace settlement that included the division of Anatolia into foreign occupied zones. As a result of the War of Independence, the foreign armies of Great Britain, France, Italy, and Greece withdrew or were driven out, the Ottoman sultan was deposed, and in 1923 a republic was established.

Atatürk's mausoleum, called *Anıtkabir*, or "The Memorial Tomb," is

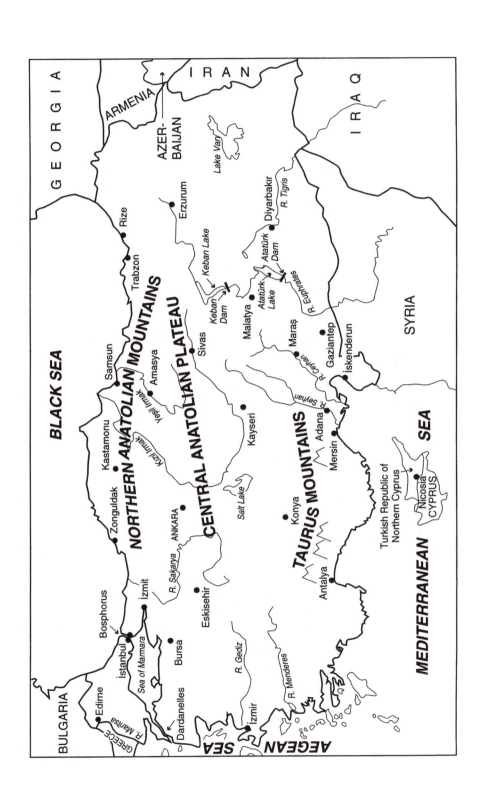

much more than a mere tomb. The mausoleum functions as a national shrine, where the epic events of the nation's founding are commemorated, where the nation comes together in honoring the memory of those times. Standing in the middle of Ankara, in the middle of the country, it sums up the nation. Its structures, especially the stately, columned Hall of Honor, together with the Turkish flag—a white crescent and star on a red background—and the bust of Mustafa Kemal, are almost ubiquitous national symbols.

The mausoleum is approached by a long drive, guarded on either side by stone lions. Entirely covering the hillside, the mausoleum, in its immensity, impresses the visitor into respectful silence. Its stones were quarried from sites all over Turkey. The huge, rectangular central court, paved in white stones and surrounded on three sides by a colonnaded ambulatory, stands quietly empty. The gaze is directed toward the Hall of Honor, which sits on a raised plinth and is approached by wide steps. The steps are flanked on either side by limestone bas-relief murals depicting episodes in the story of the national struggle. Inscriptions quote excerpts from the speeches of Atatürk. The Hall of Honor itself is only a room with a marble box, which stands over the crypt containing the remains of Mustafa Kemal Atatürk.

Outside again, strolling between rows of Hittite lions down the long, straight, stone-paved corridor off the main courtyard, the visitor's vision is directed outward, over the edge of the hillside to the city of Ankara spread out in the basin below, to Anatolia, to the heart of the nation itself. Perhaps better than anything else, Ankara epitomizes both the newness and the antiquity of Turkey. Although its roots reach to before the classical age, in a sense the city itself is, like the country, largely the creation of Atatürk. At the end of World War I, Ankara was a provincial city with a population of perhaps 75,000, but during the Turkish war of independence (1919–1922) Mustafa Kemal had made it his headquarters, and in 1923 the city was made the capital of the new country. Today Ankara is a metropolis of more than three million people, and is dotted by modern government offices, crossed by wide boulevards, and surrounded by the suburbs of the affluent and slums of the poor. On a prominent hill in its ancient center stands the citadel, which dates from before the Romans. Not far away, a lengthy Latin inscription of the best known copy of Augustus Caesar's Deeds—a decree written about A.D. 13—survives on a wall of the temple of Augustus. The Roman historian Suetonius wrote that Augustus had had the original decree inscribed on bronze tablets for permanent deposit in his own mausoleum. In the final paragraph of the decree, Caesar Augustus notes with pride that the Roman Senate and the Roman people bestowed on him the title "Father of My Country," a title recalled in Mustafa Kemal's chosen family name, Atatürk, meaning "Father Turk," or "Father of the Turks."

The ancient town of Ankara became the capital of the new Turkey for many reasons, not least because it was not Constantinople, the old imperial capital. But also, Ankara lay in the midst of Anatolia and stood for the nation's reoriented memory and symbols, now directed away from the most recent Ottoman imperial past and toward the ancient Anatolian past and toward the new nation and the future. Turkey's past is older than the Ottomans, Ankara seems to say, older than the memory of the citizens of the new nation; it is as old as history itself. But it is also brand new, like a city where one had not existed before. Ankara is a Republican city. The house of parliament is there, as are the headquarters of government departments, the embassies of foreign nations, the presidential palace built for Atatürk in the suburb of Çankaya, and the mausoleum of the father of the country.

The modern Turkish identity rests in a shared sense of community among the citizens of the new nation, an identity formed out of ties of language and ethnicity, of custom and folklore, of religion, of local geographic and cultural identifications, of loyalty to the ideals of the Turkish state, and the like. These overlapping elements of the shared sense of identity are not necessarily common to all citizens of Turkey, of course, and as in most countries, some of the most important episodes of Turkish history in the twentieth century arise from the conflicts, negotiations, agreements, and compromises surrounding the ongoing national discussion of identity and belonging.

THE PEOPLE OF TURKEY

The Turkish identity is partly built out of ties of language and ethnicity. The nation was founded on a common sense of Turkishness that is shared by most, but indeed not by all, citizens of the nation. About 75 percent of the current population of 64 million are Turks, which is to say that they speak Turkish and identify themselves as Turks.

Turkish is a language of the Turkic group of the Altaic language family, a family of languages spoken by about 110 million people living in Europe, Asia Minor, the Transcaucasus region, and across the central Eurasia steppe zone from the Black Sea to the Gobi Desert. The Turkish spoken in modern Turkey is a southern Oghuz dialect of the Turkic family and is mutually intelligible with related western Turkic languages such as Azerbaijani and Turkmen. It is more distantly related to Tatar, Uzbek, Kazakh, Uygur, and the other Turkic languages spoken in Russia; Ukraine; the Central Asian republics of Uzbekistan, Kazakhstan, and Kyrghyzia; and in China, especially in the province of Sinkiang. The other principal modern representative of the Altaic language family is Mongolian. Turkish is therefore linguistically completely unrelated to the other major languages of the Middle East—Arabic and Hebrew belong to the Semitic language family, while Persian (also called Iranian), Kurdish, Greek and Armenian are Indo-European.

But Turkish is not the first language of all citizens of Turkey. An especially important non-Turkish language in Turkey is Kurdish, which is spoken by approximately 15 to 25 percent of the population—estimates vary widely. Kurdish is an Indo-European language. The main dialects spoken in Turkey are Zaza and Kirmancı. Kurds form a majority of the population in some southeastern provinces and a significant minority in many large cities. Other non-Turkish languages spoken by minority populations in Turkey include Armenian and Greek. The numbers of current speakers of Armenian and Greek in Turkey are not large, but the importance of these populations for the history of Turkey is considerable.

RELIGION IN TURKEY

Another important ingredient in the shared national identity is religion. The nation of Turkey has no official state religion except the secularism declared in the constitution. In some respects, allegiance to the nation has taken on appearances of a civic religion in Turkey, shown through veneration of its symbols, respect for its sainted historical figures, especially Atatürk, and observation of the cycle of national holidays, especially October 29, the anniversary of the declaration of the republic. Every town prominently displays a sculpture or a bust of Atatürk, and a photograph or painting of him hangs in all government and most private offices. It is unlawful to publicly demean Atatürk, and the day of his death is commemorated annually on November 10 with a nationwide period of silence lasting two minutes, during which all activity, including even traffic, comes to a complete halt. It has already been seen to that his mausoleum functions as a national shrine.

It must be noted immediately, however, that the religion of the vast majority—an estimated 99 percent—of Turkish citizens is Islam. Turkish citizens differ in the importance they place on religious belief and practice, the amount of attention they give to religious observances, and the role they might ideally give religion in the public life of the nation. This issue remains at the front of the ongoing public discussion of the legacy of Atatürk and the nature of the Turkish revolution, and takes a central place in national political discourse.

Large numbers of Turkish people, perhaps the majority, are religiously devout Muslims and to some degree observant, attending prayers at the mosques, particularly on Fridays, making an effort to keep the Ramadan fast, and keeping the various holy days. Very sizable groups are not religiously observant, however, especially in the major urban centers. Among Muslims, the majority in Turkey is Sunnite, but a large minority, an estimated one-fourth to one-third of the entire population, is Alevi, or Shiite. And not all Turkish citizens are Muslims. Approximately 100,000 are Christians, and about 25,000 are Jews. An important historical Jewish community is the Spanish Jews of Istanbul, descendants of those who fled the Spanish Inquisition in the late fifteenth century. The landscape of Turkey, moreover, contains significant remains of the cultures of all three of these great monotheistic religions—Judaism, Christianity and Islam—as well as of earlier paganism.

THE REGIONS OF TURKEY

A third element of the shared identity of the nation is rooted in the land of Anatolia, in its distinct regions, cultures, and customs. The English term *Anatolia*, and the Turkish term *Anadolu*, derive from the Greek word *Anatole*, meaning "rising, the quarter of the sunrise, the East," or in other words, "the land of the rising sun." A peninsula bounded by the Black Sea on the north, the Aegean Sea on the west, and the Mediterranean Sea on the south, Anatolia appears to be a single geographic unit, with a high central plateau surrounded by mountains. At closer inspection, however, Anatolia contains at least seven distinct regions, each having slightly different climates, agricultural and industrial products, cuisines, local artistic styles and folk traditions, and regional dialects of spoken Turkish. Even within these regions, great variety can be found, and local loyalties may still tie residents to a village, a town, a valley, or a set of hills. A local area may be recognized throughout Turkey by a variety of cultural artifacts, for its type of roasted meat (*kebap*), for example, or for a typical design or color used in its woven carpets or woolen stockings, or for its folk dances or music. This regional variety continues to be important, at the same time as the nation's growth propels the development of a homogeneous, national Turkish economy, language, historical tradition, and culture, even a popular culture of national movie stars, rock bands, fashion trends, and soccer and basketball leagues.

The plateau of central Anatolia, of which Ankara (population 3.1 million) is the main city, extends from the mountains and river valleys of the Aegean coast to the mountains of the Anti-Taurus range in the east. This semiarid plateau, its elevation gradually increasing from about 2,000 feet in the west to about 4,000 feet in the east, is broken by basins such as the Konya plain and the marshes of the Tuz Gölü (Salt Lake), and by massifs and unusual volcanic rock formations such as those in the Cappadocian valley. The climate is continental, with hot, dry summers and cold, snowy winters. Parts of the plateau receive less than ten inches of rainfall annually. The main crop grown on the plateau is wheat, although irrigation makes barley, corn, fruits, poppies, beets, and tobacco cultivable. Much land on the plateau is also devoted to the grazing of cattle and sheep and goats. Copper has been mined in Anatolia since antiquity, and today the plateau also produces other important minerals, such as bauxite, chromium, manganese, and sulphur. Besides Ankara, other major cities of central Anatolia include Konya (population 1 million) in the south, Kayseri in the southeast, and Eskişehir in the northwest.

Not even geographical identification with the land of Anatolia, however, is shared by all Turkish citizens. The land area of Turkey is 300,947 square miles (779,452 square kilometers), about the size of the state of Texas. Approximately 3 percent of this land area lies in eastern Thrace, in the Balkan Peninsula of Europe, separated from the rest of Turkey by the Bosphorus, the Sea of Marmara, and the Dardanelles. In this southeastern tip of the Balkan Peninsula, Turkey also borders Bulgaria. Edirne, on the Maritsa River, is the major urban center in this heavily cultivated, grain growing region. The fact that this portion of Turkey lies in Thrace has led to the observation that Turkey straddles Europe and Asia, symbolically having a foot in each and literally bridging the two at the Straits. This geographical observation leads some to suggest that culturally, too, Turkey's heritage is ambiguous, having roots in both Europe and Asia. Attempts to define what exactly is meant by a "European" culture and what is meant by an "Asian" culture turn out not to be easy, and the geographic reality on which it is based is itself somewhat artificial, since Europe is nothing but the western part of the great Eurasian land mass. The issue of geographic and cultural identity, however, is real enough and forms part of the story of Turkish history.

The distance across Turkey, from the Maritsa River in the west where Turkey borders Greece and Bulgaria, to the southeastern corner where Turkey, Iran, and Iraq come together, is approximately 1,000 miles "as the crow flies," or about the same distance as from Des Moines, Iowa, to the Chesapeake Bay. The distance between the Black Sea on the north and the Mediterranean Sea on the south is about 450 miles, or about the same as from Chicago, Illinois, to Nashville, Tennessee.

The Marmara region of northwestern Anatolia is dominated by the Straits, the famous water passage that flows north to south from the Black Sea to the Aegean, by the city of Istanbul, and by the heavily industrialized corridor running along the eastern shore of the Sea of Marmara. The climate of the Marmara region is temperate. Istanbul, the largest city in Turkey with a population of more than ten million, is the former capital of the Ottoman Empire and before it of the Byzantine Roman Empire, and remains today a cosmopolitan city at the center of national commercial and cultural life. Kocaeli is a major port and industrial center. The Kocaeli valley and the Bursa plain are rich agricultural areas, producing olives, nuts, fruits, and tobacco. Bursa (population 1.3 million), Turkey's fifth largest city, is significant for its manufacturing and as a historical center.

The Aegean region of the western coast has been a heavily populated, richly agricultural area since antiquity and is today the most densely populated region of the country. İzmir (population 2.4 million), the main port of this region, is Turkey's third largest city and a major manufacturing center. The climate is Mediterranean, having hot, humid summers and mild, rainy winters. A series of parallel mountain ranges running east to west, broken by the broad valleys of the Gediz and the Greater and Lesser Menderes Rivers, the region produces cereals, citrus, and other fruits, cotton, and tobacco. Its numerous classical sites and beautiful beaches give the Aegean coastal area a significance in the tourism industry.

The Mediterranean region of the south consists of the Taurus Mountains and the coastal plain, which is quite narrow or nonexistent in the western half of the region, where the mountains run right down to the sea, and then widens out into the Çukurova plain (Cilicia) in the eastern part of the region. The Taurus, a formidable mountain chain reaching 6,000 to 9,000 feet, is rugged and sparsely populated. In the coastal plain, the climate and the vegetation are nearly tropical; temperatures exceed 100 degrees Fahrenheit in the summer, and palm trees and cacti are prominent, especially in the east. Winters are mild and wet. A variety of fruits, including grapes, bananas, and figs, grow here, as well as barley, wheat, and rice, and in the Çukurova plain, cotton. A few large cities are to be found along the coast, including Mersin, an important Mediterranean port, and Antalya, important in the tourism industry. The Çukurova is an agrarian plain whose main city is Adana (population 1.5 million) on the Seyhan River, Turkey's fourth largest city. Two rivers whose sources lie in the Anti-Taurus range, the Seyhan and the Ceyhan, wind a flat route across the Çukurova to reach the Mediterranean. Mountainous Hatay Province, with its chief city, the major port of İskenderun, occupies Turkey's eastern Mediterranean shore.

Eastern Anatolia is a relatively sparsely populated, mountainous area stretching from an area east of Sivas and Kayseri to the borders of Georgia and Armenia in the northeast and of Iran, Iraq and Syria in the southeast, the region known as Kurdistan. The only major city in the region is Erzurum (population 250,000). Agriculture, especially cereals, and grazing are important industries. Virtually all of Turkey's iron ore is mined at Divriği, between Sivas and Erzurum. Winters in eastern Anatolia are harsh, summers short and mild. The waters of Lake Van, Turkey's largest lake, lie at an elevation of more than 5,000 feet. The highest peak in Turkey, the volcanic cone called Ağrı Dağı, or Mt. Ararat, and the headwaters of two great rivers, the Tigris and the Euphrates, are situated in this region.

In southeastern Anatolia, the mountains gradually give way to rolling hills that form the northernmost segment of the Jazira plain. Wheat is the main crop grown on this relatively dry plain. Turkey's modest production of crude petroleum comes mostly from the Batman area. The Tigris River flows through Diyarbakır, the major city of this region, and the Euphrates flows by the town of Birecik, as both rivers descend toward their ultimate destination in the Persian Gulf, some six or seven hundred miles to the southeast. Several dams interrupt the flow of the rivers, the largest being the great Atatürk Dam on the Euphrates northwest of Urfa.

The Black Sea region of the north, from just west of Zonguldak to Rize, consists of the heavily forested northern slopes of the Pontic ranges, which reach as high as 13,000 feet at points in the east, and a narrow coastal plain. Two major Anatolian rivers, the Sakarya and the Kızılırmak, and several minor rivers break the long mountain chains to empty into the Black Sea. This is a prosperous agrarian region, supporting a relatively heavy agricultural population and numerous important towns. The tobacco of the Samsun area is famous. Around Trabzon, hazelnuts are prominent, and the Rize area produces much of Turkey's tea. Zonguldak is a center of coal mining and heavy industry.

THE ECONOMY OF TURKEY

Turkey's gross domestic product (GDP) of about $350 billion ranks eighteenth in the world. The economy of Turkey is built on some fundamental strengths. It possesses a large, mostly literate labor force. Most of its land is fertile and has a long history of supporting successful agriculture. Its strong manufacturing sector works off of a robust identity based on traditional products such as cotton cloth, leather goods, cigarettes, carpets, and ceramics, and a rapidly expanding industrial sector is fed largely by domestic raw materials. Although Turkey conducts most of its trade now with OECD (Organization for Economic Cooperation and Development) states, the country's location gives it relatively easy access to substantial regional markets for its goods in the Middle East and North Africa, in east central Europe and the Balkans, and in the new central Asian and Caucasus states.

The main weaknesses of the Turkish economy arise from structural problems that are exacerbated by political instability. Communications difficulties, the result of a challenging geography and of slow progress in infrastructural development, have hindered the full realization of Turkey's economic potential. In the late 1990s, Turkey continued a transition begun in the 1980s from a heavily state-directed, planned economy focused on import substitution to an export-oriented, free market economy. The effort has culminated in some economic successes, but the transformation has not been accomplished without difficulty, as political corruption and nagging financial problems clearly attest, and it has generated a national debate about economic policy and its consequences. The history of state planning and state ownership of major economic enterprises during most of the twentieth century has left a legacy of economic inefficiency.

Turkey's rate of population increase has averaged well over 2 percent annually since the mid-1980s. The wealthiest 20 percent of these citizens earn about $8,037 per capita, while the poorest 20 percent earn $717, making for the worst income distribution among countries in the OECD, with the exception of Mexico. High budget deficits have fueled inflationary pressures, and balance of payments deficits have resulted in a weak currency. The main causes of the budget deficits have been interest on the national debt, subsidies to state enterprises, and an estimated $7 billion spent annually on the Kurdish war.

About one-third of Turkey's labor force is employed in industry. The industrial sector accounts for about 30 percent of the GDP. The country's main industries are textiles and food processing. The textiles industry, especially cotton and processed leather products, makes up about one-third of manufacturing employment. Textiles and leather goods form the largest part of manufactured goods, which make up almost three-fourths of Turkey's approximately $26.2 billion of exports (1997 figures). Turkish cotton textiles and processed leather goods enjoy an outstanding world reputation. Glass and ceramic products are two other traditional manufactured commodities.

Foodstuffs account for another 20 percent of exports. Agriculture employs about 45 percent of the labor force and accounts for about 15 percent of the GDP. Cereals and sugar are the largest agricultural industries. About half of Turkey's arable land is given to cereals, of which wheat is the most important. Other grains grown include barley, corn, rye, oats, and rice. Cotton, grown in western Anatolia in the İzmir area and in Cilicia, is the most important export crop. Besides sugar beets, oilseeds, including sunflower, cotton, sesame, linseed, and olives, are important cash crops. Turkish tobacco is world renowned. The area along the Black Sea coast from Giresün to Trabzon produces more hazelnuts than any region in the world. A variety of fruits and vegetables are cultivated both for domestic consumption and for export, including potatoes, grapes, citrus fruits, tomatoes, melons, and bananas.

Other major national industries are metals, chemicals, and cement. Turkey produces bauxite, borax, chromium, copper, iron, manganese and sulphur. Although Turkey has very little domestic petroleum, the manufacture of petrochemicals at four major refineries (in Mersin, İzmit, Batman and Aliağa) is another important industry. The lengthy oil pipeline that crosses southeastern Turkey from Batman to Dörtyol, near the port of İskenderun, provides a significant source of hard currency. Before 1990, this pipeline carried two-thirds of Iraq's exported crude oil. Turkey imports about $48.5 billion of goods annually (1997), more than half of which consists of machinery and equipment.

Turkey's principal trading partners are the countries of the European Union, the United States, and the states of the former USSR. Germany alone purchases almost one-fourth of Turkey's exports and supplies

more than 15 percent of its imports. Turkey's second largest single trading partner is the United States, followed by Italy and then Russia, which
has since 1995 surpassed France and the United Kingdom in the amount
of goods both exported to Turkey and imported from Turkey. An important Turkish export is labor, in the form of an estimated 1.4 million
Turkish people who live and work abroad. More than half of them live
in Germany. The total number of Turkish workers abroad has risen only
slowly during the 1990s, with the increase going mostly to countries of
the former USSR, especially Russia. The percentage of Turkish workers
living in countries of the European Union has fallen, and the total remittances to Turkey of all workers abroad, an important source of hard
currency, has also dropped.

The Turkish economy also earns significant hard currency through its
tourism sector. More than eight million tourists visit Turkey annually,
mostly from other European countries and the United States. During the
peak summer months, from May to October, more than a million visitors
arrive each month. Among the favorite destinations are the classical cities
of the Aegean region, particularly the remains of Troy, the spectacular
ruins of the ancient Roman city of Ephesus, and the sandy beaches of
the Aegean and Mediterranean shores. The Byzantine and Ottoman imperial monuments in Istanbul are also favorites, and the remains of the
ancient Christian community of the Cappadocian valley in central Anatolia, where unusual rock formations have been shaped by ancient volcanic activity and erosion over the centuries, attract thousands of visitors.

Turkey's main revenue sources, for purposes of its national budget,
are income taxes, import taxes and duties, taxes and fees on services,
some continued revenues from state monopolies, and a national value-
added tax. Its major expenditures include general public services, which
account for about one-third of all expenditures; national defense, which
accounts for about 10 percent of expenditures; and education, health, and
welfare, which together make up about 20 percent of budgeted expenditures.

Labor Unions

There are two major labor union confederations in Turkey. The largest,
the Confederation of Turkish Trade Unions (*Türkiye İşçi Sendikaları Konfederasyonu*, or Türk-İş), is also the only one involved in large-scale collective bargaining. Türk-İş, founded in 1952, has historically taken a

moderate political stance and survived the 1980 military coup while others were closed. The other major confederation, which reopened by the mid-1980s, is the leftist Confederation of Revolutionary Workers' Trade Unions of Turkey (*Türkiye Devrimci İşçi Sendikaları Konfederasyonu*, or DİSK), formed in 1967.

Transportation and Communications

The Turkish highway network consists of more than 60,000 kilometers of paved roads. Carrying the bulk of Turkey's automobile transport, six major highways spread out from Ankara to the far reaches of Anatolia like spokes from the hub of a wheel. One highway goes northwest to Istanbul and Edirne, connecting to the old route through the Balkans, via Nish in Bulgaria and Belgrade on the Danube in Serbia, to central Europe. Another highway heads west, towards the port of İzmir. One branch turns northward, leading to Bursa, via Eskişehir. A third highway proceeds south, one fork going to Konya and the other crossing the Taurus Mountains at the Cilician Gates to reach Adana and the Mediterranean port of İskenderun. A fourth highway leads southeast, via Kayseri and Malatya, one branch then going on via Elazığ to Diyarbakır and Lake Van, and another south to Gaziantep and crossing the border toward Aleppo in Syria. A fifth highway heads due east across the plateau, via Sivas and Erzincan to Erzurum, and beyond that to Kars and the Armenian border. A final highway leads northeast to the Black Sea port of Samsun and follows the coast eastward to Trabzon.

Most Turkish cities have organized mass transit networks, usually in the form of bus systems. The municipality of Ankara has recently constructed a more extensive light rail and "metro" system. Mass transit in Istanbul has for centuries meant mostly ferry traffic along and across the Bosphorus. This traditional means of transit has in the twentieth century been supplemented by an extensive bus and trolley system. In 1973, the first bridge across the Bosphorus opened; since then, another Bosphorus bridge has given Europe and Asia vastly improved connections across this international waterway. Istanbul now also has added an underground and a metro line linked to an older light rail system, which connected the harbor to the international airport southwest of the city. The press of dramatically increased automobile traffic in both Istanbul and Ankara threatens to squeeze out a uniquely Turkish transportation institution, the *dolmuş*. This "stuffed" taxi system provided service between fixed points in a metropolitan area on an as-needed, regular schedule and gave employment to scores of transportation entrepreneurs. It continues to operate in major cities.

About 10,000 kilometers of rail lines serve Turkish freight and passenger needs. Direct rail lines link Turkey with Bulgaria, with Iran, and with Syria. Although the Turkish railway system is a national monopoly owned by the state, important state monopolies over other communications systems, including air transport, ended in the 1980s. Airports at four cities—Istanbul, Ankara, Izmir and Trabzon—handle scheduled domestic and international airline flights. Airports at Adana, Dalaman, and Antalya offer international charter service in addition to domestic scheduled flights, and fifteen other airports provide domestic service.

Over fifty daily newspapers are published in Turkey, as well as numerous weeklies, biweeklies, and monthlies. The leading mass circulation daily papers are without exception based in Istanbul. Among the leading national dailies, *Milliyet* (The Nation), *Hürriyet* (Freedom), and *Sabah* (The Morning) have a circulation of more than half a million. Although *Cumhuriyet*, established by Atatürk in 1924 as the first daily newspaper in the Republic, has a smaller circulation, it wields influence beyond its numbers as a paper read widely by intellectuals and by the economic and political elite. The main news agency in Turkey, Anadolu Ajansı, the Anatolian News Agency, was founded by Atatürk in 1920.

The first radio broadcast in Turkey occurred in 1927. The state public broadcasting company, Turkish Radio and Television (*Türk Radyo Televisyonu*, TRT) was established in 1964 and began television broadcasts from a station in Ankara in 1968. After the appearance of satellite television dishes in the early 1990s, constitutional amendments have permitted the establishment of private radio and television broadcasting stations. By the late 1990s, there were 16 national, 15 regional and some 300 local television stations; in addition, there were 35 national, 109 regional, and about 1,000 local radio stations. By the mid-1990s, the number of television sets surpassed radios, with an estimated 11 million TV sets and radios combined.

Although there is no prepublication censorship of the press in Turkey, the government restricts publication of material concerning subjects deemed important to national security and prohibits any promotion of "separatism."

Education

Primary education through age fourteen is free, coeducational, and compulsory in Turkey, and attendance rates run at about 97 percent (they are somewhat lower in rural areas, where it seems that prejudice against the education of girls is still felt). One result of the education policy has been a national literacy rate of over 82 percent. More than 80 percent of the school-age population (about 88 percent males and 71 percent females) is enrolled in 10,500 general *lises*, which offer a college preparatory curriculum and more than 3,500 vocational and technical schools. About 300 of the latter are schools of religious education, called *İmam-hatip* schools, which have flourished since the early 1980s and now enroll an estimated 10 percent of students attending high schools. The most prestigious *lises* in the major cities offer a kind of bilingual education, with humanities courses being taught in Turkish and other courses being taught in English, French, or German.

About 450,000 students are enrolled in various institutions of higher education. Higher education in Turkey falls under the jurisdiction of *Yüksek Öğretim Kurumu* (YÖK), the Higher Education Council. Under the leadership of the Higher Education Council, the number of universities has increased from nineteen in the 1981–1982 academic year to seventy-two today, and standards of admission and curriculum have been somewhat regularized. Of the currently existing seventy-two universities, fifty-three are public and the remaining nineteen are private. More than half of these universities opened during the decade of the 1990s, and several have not actually begun offering classes, being still in the process of constructing a campus and recruiting staff. The best and most prestigious universities in Turkey are much older. They include Boğaziçi University in Istanbul, which became a university in 1973 but is the continuation of Robert College, founded in 1863; Istanbul University opened in 1900 as the Ottoman Darülfünûn, and was reorganized in 1933; Istanbul Technical University was formed in 1944 from a school whose origins reach back ultimately to the naval technical academy established in 1773. Ankara University and Middle East Technical University, also in Ankara, are two excellent universities with more recent origins. Ankara University was organized in 1946 from several smaller faculties, all founded in the Republican era, and Middle East Technical University was one of four new universities founded in the 1950s. An interesting new development since the 1980s has been the emergence of several private universities, the first of which, Bilkent University, opened in Ankara in 1984.

Sports

Republican Turkey placed such emphasis on sports and recreation that Atatürk declared May 19 to be Youth and Sports Day, a national holiday. National programs are coordinated by a General Directorate of Youth and Sports, which for a time during the 1970s became a cabinet-level government ministry.

Undoubtedly, soccer ranks as the favorite of sports-minded Turks. Some of Turkey's largest television audiences watch the international quadrennial World Cup competition. The Turkish national team once reached the final tournament in 1954, but in recent years it has not succeeded in making it out of the qualifying round. Professional soccer is well developed in Turkey, with three leagues operating. The first, or elite, league, which currently fields eighteen teams, has since its inception in 1950 been dominated by three powerful Istanbul teams, their colors becoming nationally recognized: Galatasaray's yellow and red, Fenerbahçe's blue and gold, and the black and white of Beşiktaş.

Turkey has participated in the Olympic Games since 1936. In the past decade, the Turkish National Olympic Committee has made an effort to bring the summer Olympic Games to Istanbul by submitting bids to the International Olympic Committee and working to update and improve athletic, residential, and press and communications facilities in the city. Turkey owns a strong international reputation in wrestling and in weight lifting, winning a number of Olympic medals in these sports.

THE GOVERNMENT OF TURKEY

The Turkish constitution of 1982 specifies that the Turkish state is a republic, a "democratic, secular and social state governed by the rule of law." Sovereignty is vested by the constitution "without reservation or condition" in the Turkish nation, which exercises its sovereignty through authorized organs of legislative, executive, and judicial power for the constitutional purposes of safeguarding the independence and integrity of the nation and its democracy, insuring the peace and prosperity of individuals and society, removing obstacles that restrict individual freedoms, and promoting the conditions for the citizens' material and spiritual existence. The Turkish government can be understood as the interrelated activities of these judicial, legislative, and executive branches. It is a parliamentary democracy, headed by a prime minister and a president, with an independent court system.

The Judicial Branch

Turkey's legal system consists of three courts—judicial, military, and administrative—each having lower courts and appellate courts.

The judicial court system includes justices of the peace, single-judge courts, three-judge courts, and the Court of Appeals. This system comprises the greatest number of courts and takes up the bulk of civil and criminal cases involving common citizens. Justices of the peace handle minor complaints and civil cases. Every organized municipality (of a population of 2,000 or more) must have at least one single-judge court, the actual number varying according to the population. These courts deal with minor crimes and misdemeanors, while major crimes and civil cases are tried in three-judge courts. Judges hear the cases and decide the verdicts; there is no jury system. The military courts have jurisdiction over the personnel of the armed forces. Administrative courts have jurisdiction over administrative affairs; the court of appeals of the administrative court system is the Council of State, which hears disputes over administrative legislation and may, when requested by the prime minister or council of ministers, render an opinion on draft legislation.

An eleven-member Constitutional Court, appointed by the president of the Republic, functions as the court of judicial review, holding final jurisdiction over the constitutionality of laws and decrees. Its members are nominated for consideration by the president by the lower courts and by the High Council of Judges and public prosecutors. This body has responsibility for judicial appointments, transfers, and promotions and oversees the professional conduct of all judges and prosecutors. It is headed by the Minister of Justice.

The Legislative Branch

Legislative power is exercised through a unicameral national parliament called the *Büyük Millet Meclisi*, the Grand National Assembly.

The 550 seats in parliament are filled by national elections held every five years, or more often under certain circumstances. Each of the seventy-nine provinces of Turkey make up a legislative district, with the three largest cities being further subdivided. Each of these eighty-three legislative districts sends at least one representative to parliament. The more populous districts send more than one representative, the numbers of representatives being determined by the size of the population. Nationally organized political parties contest the elections, submitting a slate of candidates in each electoral district and winning seats based on a system of proportional representation: The seats in each electoral district are distributed to the parties in proportion to the percentage of the popular vote received. All Turkish citizens twenty years old and older have the right to vote (except prisoners, military cadets, and men performing their obligatory military service). Political parties must be truly national in scope; they are required to have an organization in every province and in two-thirds of the municipalities of each province. Party success depends, moreover, on national appeal, since parties failing to receive 10 percent of the popular vote nationally receive no representation in parliament.

The constitution gives parliament the power to supervise a Council of Ministers and authorizes it to issue laws, to approve the budget of the republic, to print money, to declare war, to ratify international treaties and agreements, to confirm death sentences passed by the courts and to proclaim amnesties and pardons, and to exercise other responsibilities such as are outlined in the constitution. The assembly opens session each year on September 1 and may be in recess for a maximum of three months in a legislative year.

The Executive Branch

Executive power in Turkey is exercised primarily by the president of the Republic, but the Council of Ministers of parliament and the chief of the general staff and the National Security Council also perform important executive functions. In the complex interrelationship of these executive authorities lies much of the distinctive character and personality of the Turkish system.

The president of Turkey is the head of state, elected by a two-thirds majority of the parliament for a single term of seven years. The president calls new elections for parliament, summons parliament to meet, and delivers the opening address on the first day of the legislative year. He appoints the prime minister and accepts his resignation, appoints and dismisses ministers on the Council of Ministers at the proposal of the prime minister, and may call, and presides over, meetings of the Council of Ministers when he deems it necessary. He promulgates laws, may issue and sign decrees that carry the force of law in accordance with the decisions of the Council of Ministers, may return laws to the parliament for reconsideration, and may appeal to the Constitutional Court for the annulment of laws that he deems unconstitutional. Additionally, the president receives foreign ambassadors, appoints ambassadors from Turkey to other countries, and ratifies and promulgates international treaties. As commander in chief of the Turkish armed forces (on behalf of the Grand National Assembly, according to the constitution), the president appoints the chief of the general staff, calls and presides over meetings of the National Security Council, and proclaims states of emergency or martial law.

The president appoints numerous high judicial officials, including members of the Constitutional Court, one-fourth of the members of the Council of State, the Chief Public Prosecutor and Deputy Chief Public Prosecutor of the High Court of Appeals, the members of the Military High Court of Appeals, the Supreme Military Administrative Court, and the Supreme Council of Judges and Public Prosecutors. The president also manages a General Secretariat of the presidency; he appoints members and the chair of the State Supervisory Council, a body that investigates and inspects public bodies, organizations and institutions, labor unions, professional associations and the like; and the president appoints members of the Higher Education Council and rectors (presidents) of universities.

The Council of Ministers is headed by the prime minister. The head of the party with the largest number of seats in the parliament becomes prime minister and is invited by the president of the Republic to form the Council of Ministers, subject to his approval and that of the parliament. The departments headed by the Council of Ministers include the Ministry of National Defense, the Ministry of Foreign Affairs, the Ministry of the Interior, the Ministry of Finance, the Ministry of Industry and Trade, the Ministry of Agriculture and Rural Affairs, the Ministry of Energy and Natural Resources, the Ministry of Environment, the Ministry of Forestry, the Ministry of Health, the Ministry of Public Works and Resettlement, the Ministry of Communications and Transport, the Ministry of Justice, the Ministry of Labor, the Ministry of Education, the Ministry of Culture, and the Ministry of Tourism.

As in most countries, the constitutional structure of government does not fully account for the actual operation of the political system. The American Constitution, for example, says nothing about political parties or congressional committees, but it would be virtually impossible to understand the working of the American system of government without an awareness of those institutions. Similarly, in Turkey it is crucial to be aware of the existence of political parties and of informal but powerful networks of political patronage, both personal and associated with political parties, to understand the operation of the Turkish system of government. The political parties currently represented in parliament are the Virtue Party (*Fazilet Partisi*, abbreviated FP), led by Recai Kutan, the Motherland Party (*Anavatan Partisi*, often abbreviated ANAP) led by Mesut Yılmaz, the True Path Party (although its name *Doğru Yol Partisi*, abbreviated DYP, might better be translated "The Party of the Right Way," or the Straight Way) led by Tansu Çiller, the Democratic Left Party (*Demokratik Sol Partisi*, abbreviated DSP) led by Bülent Ecevit, and the Republican People's Party (*Cumhuriyet Halk Partisi*, abbreviated CHP) headed by Deniz Baykal.

The Military

Through the National Security Council, the constitution defines a role for the Turkish military in the exercise of executive authority. This is a significant fact when it is remembered that on three occasions, in 1960–1961, in 1971–1973, and again in 1980–1983, the Turkish army has taken over control of the government by coups d'état. Indeed, the Turkish military has played, since the beginning of the republic, a complex and ambiguous political role in Turkish public life, aptly illustrated by the fact that most presidents of the republic, beginning with Mustafa Kemal himself, have been former career military officers. The three most recent presidents, Turgut Özal (1989–1993), Süleyman Demirel (1993–2000), and Necdat Sezer (since 2000), however, have been civilians.

The National Security Council, composed of both military and civilian members, sets national security policy and oversees national defense. Besides the president of the Republic, who chairs it, the National Security Council is made up of the chief of the general staff, the commander of the army and of the gendarmerie, and the ministers of defense, interior, and foreign affairs. The present chief of the general staff is Army General Hüseyin Kivrikoğlu.

The Turkish military comprises the army, air force, and naval branches and includes about half a million active duty personnel—the second largest force in NATO, of which Turkey has been a member since 1952—and another 900,000 reserves. Another 70,000 active duty personnel and 50,000 reserves form the gendarmerie, a force placed under military command during time of war or martial law. Fifteen months of military service are required of all male citizens. The Turkish military budget is the equivalent of 9.4 percent of the GNP (1994 figures); its per capita military spending places Turkey lowest in NATO.

The central issues of modern Turkish history continue to be the meaning of the Turkish revolution, the legacy of Mustafa Kemal Atatürk, and the nature of Turkish culture under the conditions of modernity. In political life, in the workings of the economy, and in the everyday life of Turkish citizens, these issues continue to predominate. The origins and development of this Turkish nation will be examined in the chapters that follow.

2

Ancient Anatolia

In Turkey, as elsewhere, the study of ancient history is inseparable from the politics of the modern nation so that the modern nation grew up alongside the academic study of antiquity. At the same time that people evinced the greatest awareness of and interest in their ancient past, the modern nation was forming; nations and their leaders have always been keenly interested in the potential uses of ancient history for modern purposes. It is not coincidental that during the 1870s, while Heinrich Schliemann conducted his celebrated excavations at the site of Troy, searching under Ottoman soil for the oldest layers of European civilization, the Ottoman Empire was fighting a war for its survival, and European statesmen were planning the Empire's political destiny. During the next three decades, the discovery of the previously little known Hittite civilization of Anatolia slowly became public at the same time as Ottoman patriots and expatriates grappled with the meaning of their Turkishness and secretly planned the destiny of a Turkish nation. When the Turkish Republic was founded in the 1920s, its first president, Mustafa Kemal Atatürk, harnessed this study of Anatolian antiquity to the project of building a national consciousness, concocting, and forcing on the public and universities alike fantastic theories about the relationship between the nationalist Anatolian present and the ancient Anatolian past.

PREHISTORIC ANATOLIA

The Anatolian plateau has been inhabited by human societies since the Neolithic period (about 10,000 B.C.), when settled agriculture first began to be practiced and animals domesticated. At the end of the last glacial age, three human cultural zones developed in southwestern Eurasia; in the Zagros Mountain region; in a zone along the eastern Mediterranean coast in Syria, Lebanon, and Palestine; and north of the Taurus Mountains on the Anatolian plateau. The earliest datable excavated settlements in Anatolia are a group of agricultural villages in the southern plateau, the oldest of which, Hacılar, dates from before 7000 B.C. But Hacılar was inexplicably abandoned after about a thousand years, and the main center of Neolithic culture in Anatolia developed at Çatal Hüyük.

The spectacular settlement at Çatal Hüyük, discovered in 1961 southeast of Konya, dates from approximately 6500 B.C. Covering thirty-two acres, Çatal Hüyük is one of the largest and richest Neolithic settlements ever found. It is a town of contiguously built houses and other structures made of sun-dried mud brick. Grain agriculture formed the basis of its economy. Luxury items such as obsidian mirrors, daggers, and smelted lead and copper jewelry testify to its prosperity and social complexity. Its numerous shrines contain plaster wall reliefs, painted murals, and male, female, and animal cultic figurines. The religious attention of the community seems to have been directed toward commemoration of control over the natural forces, thereby ensuring prosperity through the hunt, through agriculture, and through fertility.

Less is known of the next three thousand years of Anatolian history. The development of Çatal Hüyük was not sustained. The site at Hacılar was reoccupied after about 5500 B.C., during the Chalcolithic period, and beautiful pottery was produced there. A walled fortress at Mersin, dating to about 4500 B.C., is one of the best examples of Anatolian craftsmanship, bridging the Chalcolithic period, when copper and stone tools predominated, with the early Bronze Age, when advances in metallurgical technology made it possible to mix copper and tin to produce the more durable bronze. The earliest architectural remains at Troy also date from this period. But the next extensive architectural remains come from the middle Bronze Age. These include the second level of Troy and Alaca Hüyük, east of Ankara on the central plateau, where a royal cemetery containing thirteen richly supplied tombs was discovered, dating to approximately 2400 B.C. During this time, Anatolia was inhabited by a people called the Hattians and was known by the Mesopotamians and Egyptians as the Hattian land. The Hittites, who later built a kingdom in central Anatolia, got their name because they were known as "kings of the Hattian land." The Hattian language, which is unrelated to other known languages, survives only in fragments, but Hattian culture left a deep impression on subsequent layers of Anatolian history.

THE HITTITES

Sometime before 2000 B.C., diverse tribes of people speaking Indo-European languages began migrating into Anatolia. Some of the migrants established city-states in former Hattian cities. Indeed, recorded history in Anatolia begins with a collection of clay tablets, the business records of an early Assyrian commercial colony, uncovered in a Hattian city—modern Kültepe, east of Kayseri—that had been taken over by Neshite immigrant kings. The new Neshite rulers borrowed the cuneiform writing system of the Assyrian merchants and began keeping their own records. The discovery in 1906 of an archive of more than 10,000 tablets at Boğazköy showed that the new rulers, the Neshites, were the same kings whom the Egyptian Amarna documents called simply "Kings of the Hattian Land" and whom the Old Testament referred to as *Hittites*. Boğazköy, or Hattusas, where the archive of tablets was found, was the capital of a large central Anatolian kingdom in which Hittite kings gradually displaced the rulers of the old Hattian cities.

The age of the Hittite kingdom corresponds to the Late Bronze Age in Anatolia, about 1700 to 1200 B.C. The Hittite kingdom was not the only state in Anatolia at the time. The Hittites shared the plateau with Luwians and Palaians, other contemporary Indo-European immigrants; between the Tigris and Euphrates Rivers, the Hurrian kingdom of Mitanni controlled the southeast and threatened the central plateau. Around 1600 B.C., the Hittite kings took Aleppo and Babylon, ending the dynasty of Hammurabi. The most powerful Hittite king, Suppiluliumas (1375–1346 B.C.), conquered western Syria, took Carchemish, and defeated the Mitanni. After Suppiluliumas, the Egyptian pharaohs contested Hittite control of Syria until the Hittites defeated them at the Battle of Kadesh (1286 B.C.). A narrative description and artistic depictions of this battle survive, as do copies of the peace treaty reached afterward between Pharaoh Ramses II and the Hittite king Muwatallis. The Hittite kingdom collapsed, however, around 1200 B.C., victim of a political system that left it unable to tie its vassal states to a centrally conceived imperial project and unable to solve the great disparity of wealth between a few major cities and the comparatively impoverished countryside.

AFTER THE HITTITES

Migrations of new Indo-European peoples from southeastern Europe had already begun by the time the Hittite kingdom fell. Several centuries of warfare, invasion, and political uncertainty followed, in which apparently no substantial urban settlements existed in the formerly Hittite country. Egyptian documents speak of the depredations of the "Sea Peoples," but obviously not all the migrations were on the seas. The Trojan War also belongs to this time of troubles.

When reliable records become available again, around 750 B.C., a Phrygian state existed on the Anatolian plateau made up of two confederations of cities, one in the west centered at Gordium and the other in the east, at what is today Kayseri. The most impressive Phrygian monument is a mausoleum known as the Tomb of Midas, the rock facade of which has a niche for the mother goddess Cybele. The cult of the mother goddess, which reconfigured elements of indigenous religious fascination with control of the physical environment and the forces of nature into potent and original new forms, dominated life in Phrygian central Anatolia.

In the southeast, between Cilicia and the Euphrates, contemporaries of the Phrygians included a group of cities ruled by "neo-Hittite" kings; Carchemish, Zincirli, and Malatya. In the river valleys of the Aegean shores, Greek migrations had begun around 1000 B.C. At first these settlements were poor agricultural villages with single-room, mud-brick houses. By the seventh century, these eastern Greek settlements grew more prosperous, expanding northward along the coast, and took the lead in building a powerful Greek civilization in the Aegean.

At the same time, a great state appeared in mountainous eastern Anatolia with its capital near Lake Van. This was the Urartian kingdom, perhaps descended from the Hurrians. Its culture was strongly influenced by Assyria. Tribal federations of Urartians are mentioned in Assyrian documents as early as the thirteenth century B.C., and the Assyrian kings describe numerous campaigns in the eastern Anatolian mountains. By the eleventh century, an Urartian state structure existed. At its largest extent, Urartu covered all of eastern Anatolia north of the upper Tigris-Euphrates region, including large parts of Transcaucasia. The Urartian kingdom lasted until the final years of the seventh century, when its northern cities were raided by semi-nomadic Scythian tribes from central Eurasia, and the Medes, who had destroyed Assyria in 612, expanded northward into Anatolia. At this time, the Armenians appear. The Greek historian Herodotus says that the Armenians were a branch of the Phrygian kingdom. By Herodotus's time, Armenia was a province of the Persian Achaemenid empire. In the trilingual inscription left by the Persian king Darius I at Behistun (495 B.C.) two of the sections call the region Armenia, while in the Old Babylonian section it is still called Urartu.

When the Phrygian state in central Anatolia disintegrated about 650 B.C., raided by Cimmerian nomads, the new state of Lydia absorbed much of its western portions. The powerful Mermnad dynasty ruled Lydia at the city of Sardis in the Meander valley. Neighbors of the Lydians were the Lycians, whose capital was Xanthos in southwestern Anatolia, and the Carrians. The Lydian and Lycian languages are Indo-European; the undeciphered Carrian script resembles these and Phrygian and Greek, suggesting that Carrian may be Indo-European as well. Herodotus writes that the Carrians, however, considered themselves natives of Anatolia. The Lydian and Lycian languages too preserve numerous non-Indo-European elements of the indigenous Hattian. All three of these cultures can be considered a reassertion of the ancient, indigenous culture of the Hattian cities of Anatolia.

Lydia was a powerful state where, according to Herodotus, coins were first used. The Halys River (the Kızıl Irmak) became the rough boundary between Lydia and Median Armenia. In the middle of the fifth century, Lydia's greatest king, Croesus, clashed with Cyrus, founder of the Persian Achaemenid dynasty that displaced the Medes. In 547 B.C., Cyrus raided eastern Anatolia, and the two generals fought indecisively. Cyrus, however, surprised Croesus by pursuing his army and catching the Lydians when they had begun to demobilize. Cyrus captured Sardis, the Lydian capital, including the citadel, and western Anatolia submitted to the Persians. Sardis became the center of Persian administration in Anatolia. Native states survived along the Black Sea and in various temple city-states.

HELLENISTIC ANATOLIA

The Persian invasions of Greece, which form the subject of Herodotus's book, aimed to root out Balkan support of the revolt of the Anatolian Greek cities. The Greeks repelled the Persians and liberated the Aegean coast of Anatolia. The majority of the Anatolian interior remained under Persian rule until the campaigns of Alexander the Great a century and a half later. The vacuum left by Alexander's victories over Darius III at the Granicus River (334 B.C.) and at Issus in Cilicia (333 B.C.), the collapse of the Persian Empire, and Alexander's death was filled by several new states. Along the Aegean, the Greek cities evolved into states with fiercely independent civic traditions. Thriving commerce grew on the bedrock of a slave economy, funding a prodigious scholarly and scientific achievement that mapped out the work of the next thousand years throughout the Mediterranean basin. In the north, native Anatolian states ruled the Black Sea coast and the Marmara, while the kingdom of Armenia emerged in eastern Anatolia. The bulk of Anatolia formed several provinces ruled by the Seleucid dynasty in Iraq, but the tendency for these to evolve into independent kingdoms is illustrated by the case of Pergamum, which became a powerful state by the middle of the second century B.C.

The sudden disappearance of the Persian empire, and the conquest of virtually the entire Middle Eastern world from the Nile to the Indus by Alexander the Great, caused tremendous political and cultural upheaval. Working out vague notions of the fundamental commonality of the human spirit, summed up in the ideal of the "brotherhood of man" attributed to Alexander himself, statesmen throughout the conquered regions attempted to implement a policy of Hellenization. For indigenous elites, this amounted to the forced assimilation of native religion and culture to Greek models. It met resistance in Anatolia as elsewhere, especially from priests and others who controlled temple wealth. More important than the superficial impact of official policy was the growing popularity among Greek settlers and in the established Greek cities of religious movements, whose roots lay in traditional Anatolian religions, and of philosophical ideas that responded to the profound sense of personal moral dislocation caused by Alexander's erasure of established political boundaries. The spreading cult of the Anatolian mother goddess is perhaps the best example of this religious movement. Cybele's association with the untamed power of the wild attracted Greeks and, even more, Romans, in whose hands her cult was transformed into an immensely popular mystery religion focused on rites of fertility that resemble those of older Greek goddesses like Demeter.

Rome became involved in Anatolia by aiding Pergamum in repelling the Seleucids in the early second century B.C., and when the childless king of Pergamum bequeathed the kingdom to Rome, Pergamum became the core of the Roman province of Asia. Thereafter, the slow advance of Roman authority in Anatolia seemed irresistible, as one kingdom after another capitulated. The kings of the Black Sea coast, especially the great Mithridates Eupator, held out until subdued by Pompey in the middle of the first century B.C. Armenia was contested between Rome and the Parthian kingdom centered in Iran, with Rome working to keep it as a client state. The inscription of Augustus's Deeds in the temple of Cybele at Ankara publicly marked the Roman ascendancy in Anatolia.

CHRISTIAN ANATOLIA

Jesus was a Palestinian Jew, but it is apparent in the Acts of the Apostles that important growth of the early church took place on Anatolian soil. This was due to the work of Saul of Tarsus, the Cilician Jew who became St. Paul. The earliest Christian literature consists of the letters written by St. Paul from Anatolia to congregations of Christian converts whom he met on several missionary journeys. One ancient stream of Christian tradition has it, moreover, that the Virgin Mary traveled to Anatolia in the care of St. John, living out her life in Ephesus, the greatest Roman city in Anatolia. Anatolian Christians became thoroughly involved in the liturgical and theological discussions and debates that occupied the early church. Roman imperial control of western and central Anatolia provided the emperors, beginning with Constantine who converted to Christianity in the early fourth century, the economic and popular authority to direct the development of Christian doctrine and ecclesiastical organization. The church councils of Nicaea (A.D. 325), Ephesus (A.D. 431), and Chalcedon (A.D. 451), all held under Roman imperial authority in Anatolia, guided the formulation of orthodox expressions of basic Christian teachings. The Christianization of the Roman citizenry transformed the empire into the body of Christ, the physical representation of Christ in the world, and the Roman Emperor into Christ's living image.

Roman authority, however, as well as Roman orthodoxy, faced challenges east of the Kızıl Irmak, where the Armenian King Trdat the Great had converted to Christianity about the same time as Constantine. Constantine moved the imperial center to Anatolia and then built Constantinople, formerly called Byzantium, an old Eastern Greek colony at the Straits, as a new Roman capital. In the fourth and fifth centuries, the western provinces of the Roman Empire were lost to Germanic warlords.

In the east, a settlement was reached between Constantinople (Istanbul) and the new Persian Sassanian dynasty in 387, dividing Anatolia into spheres of interest. Armenia, which flourished when the imperial powers in the Aegean and in Iran were comparatively weak, resisted the imperial orthodoxy of the creeds honed in church councils in western Anatolia and adhered to the Monophysitism, which stressed the divine nature of Christ over the human.

The victory of the Byzantine Emperor Heraclius over Sassanian Persia in the early seventh century led to attempts to compromise over the creeds, but these negotiations became moot when Muslim Arab armies both defeated Byzantium and toppled the Sassanian dynasty a few years later. In 640, the Arabs invaded Armenia, taking Dvin. In return for tribute, Armenia retained considerable autonomy under Arab rule. Although Arab armies also invaded western Anatolia and besieged Constantinople in the eighth century, the Taurus Mountains became a fairly stable boundary between Christian Anatolia and Muslim Syria. In Anatolia itself, the tenth and early eleventh centuries saw the gradual encroachment of the Greek and Orthodox west upon the Armenian and Monophysite east, particularly during the reign of the Byzantine Emperor Basil II (976–1025), the high point of Byzantine power. It was in this context that the Greek term *Anatolia* began to be used to refer to the whole of the peninsula between the Black, Aegean, and Mediterranean Seas.

After the death of the great Bagratid Armenian ruler Gagik (990–1020), the Byzantine system of themes or provinces, developed earlier in the western seaboard and plateau, was extended to parts of Armenia. Under this system, rural estates were given to cavalry soldiers in return for the obligation of military service. In this way, Anatolia provided the Byzantine Empire with a deep reserve of manpower, and the population of Anatolia bore a heavy burden of taxation for the support of the imperial military.

By the end of the first Christian millennium, Anatolian Greeks were aware of the great antiquity of their land. They thought of themselves as Romans, heirs of the empire of Augustus in an unbroken continuity with the past. But at the end of the eleventh century, Anatolia entered another period of great upheaval. By the end of the twelfth century, European writers would begin to call the Anatolian plateau *Turchia*.

3

The Turkish Conquest of Anatolia, 1071–1517

The metamorphosis of Anatolia into Turkey happened not suddenly but gradually, over a period of several centuries. It began with Turkish raids in eastern Anatolia in the mid-eleventh century, before the great Turkish victory at the Battle of Manzikert in 1071, and continued through intermittent conflict and stability. After Manzikert, Turkish nomads migrated into Anatolia and settled, the Byzantine Empire weakened and receded in stages, and several Muslim Turkish states were established on the plateau. The Mongol invasions of the thirteenth century set in motion a second wave of Turkish migrations, and Turkish princes founded a number of new states in western Anatolia. The unification of Anatolia was completed through the campaigns of Sultan Selim I of the Turkish Ottoman dynasty in the early sixteenth century.

THE TURKS

The Turks, tribally organized groups of semi-nomadic peoples who spoke Turkic languages, had inhabited the central Eurasian steppes for centuries. The Turkish raids in eastern Anatolia in the eleventh century belonged to a larger migration of southern, or Oghuz, Turks that had begun in central Eurasia in the previous century. In the tenth century, tribes of Oghuz and other Turks began converting to Islam and migrating into Khurasan from the region east of the Caspian Sea. In 1055, armies of the powerful Turkish Seljuk tribe entered Baghdad, capital of the Abbasid Empire and seat of the caliphate, the office of political and religious leadership of the Islamic world. Though they kept a member of the Abbasid dynasty on the throne as caliph, Seljuk begs (*beg* is a Turkish term meaning prince or commander) dominated the caliphate in Baghdad for three generations—under Tughrul, the conqueror of 1055, his nephew Alp Arslan (1063–1072), and Alp Arslan's son Malik Shah (1072–1092). Becoming rapidly settled and taking on the imperial culture of this ancient center of Islamic civilization, the Seljuk rulers of Baghdad encouraged the more restive Turkish tribal groups, often referred to as Turkomans or Turkmens, to continue raiding the Armenian and Byzantine provinces of Anatolia.

THE BATTLE OF MANZIKERT AND TURKISH MIGRATION

After the death of the emperor Basil II in 1025, the Byzantine Empire was slowly consumed by a political struggle between the imperial administration and Greek nobility in the capital city, Constantinople, and the military governors of the Anatolian provinces. As raids by Turkoman tribes in the east continued, Byzantine generals summoned large numbers of their troops to the struggle in the west, leaving the interior of Anatolia only sparsely defended. The city of Ani in Armenia fell to the Turks in 1065. Caesaria (Kayseri) was sacked in 1067. On 19 August 1071, the Emperor Romanus IV Diogenes was captured and his armies annihilated by the Seljuk army of Alp Arslan in a pitched battle at Manzikert, east of Lake Van. Byzantine eastern defenses collapsed and the interior of the Anatolian plateau lay virtually defenseless before the Turkish bands.

Turkish armies swept across central Anatolia. After more than a century of resisting the slow Byzantine encroachment, the Armenian strongholds of the east and southeast now fell to the Turks and the mainstream of Armenian life was pushed southward. The Byzantines conceded central Anatolia to the Turks, deciding to try to hold the Aegean and Marmara coasts. In 1078, just seven years after Manzikert, the Turkish chieftain Süleyman entered Nicaea (İznik) unopposed, proclaiming the city as his capital. His effective authority reached the shores of the Bosphorus, where he began assessing dues on commercial traffic. The semi-nomadic warriors who were his troops began calling him the sultan of what had become, in effect, a Turkish state in western Anatolia.

The borders of this state were only vaguely defined, and in the east, the leaders of a rival warrior clan, the Danishmends, were more powerful. The Danishmends held the northerly fortified points on the two main commercial routes to Iran, via Ankara, Sivas, and Erzurum. An Armenian state briefly revived in Cilicia, which attempted to control the other main route in cooperation with the Danishmends and other Christian princes in the cities of the Euphrates region. In 1084, however, Süleyman marched across Anatolia and seized Cilicia and Antioch. Süleyman fell in battle against Malik Shah, the new Seljuk ruler in Baghdad, in 1086, while besieging Aleppo in northern Syria. After Malik Shah died in 1092, the situation remained quite fluid. While the Seljuk Empire in Iraq and Iran slowly disintegrated, the Seljuk tribes in Anatolia became independent. Meanwhile, the spiritual revival gripping Christian Western Europe culminated in the Crusades. Armies of Christian knights answered the call, first issued by Pope Urban II in 1095, to take up the Cross of Christ and liberate Jerusalem from Muslim rule.

On their way to Jerusalem in 1097–1098, armies of the First Crusade recaptured Nicaea and defeated a combined Seljuk and Danishmend force at Doryleum, pushing the Turks back onto the plateau. The crusaders established a kingdom at Edessa and took Antioch. In 1176, the Seljuk ruler Kılıç Arslan II ambushed the Byzantine armies at the pass of Myriokephalon and destroyed them, confirming Turkish control of the Anatolian plateau. Crusading armies used the main highway across Anatolia throughout the twelfth century, but the Seljuks remained in control of it. The greater impact of the crusades on Anatolia came with the blow to Byzantine power caused by the catastrophic sack of Constantinople and the seizure of the Byzantine throne by knights of the Fourth Crusade in 1204. For the next fifty-seven years, until 1261, Constantinople and the southern Balkans were ruled as a crusader kingdom.

THE SELJUK SULTANATE OF ANATOLIA

The first forty years of the thirteenth century were a period of relative prosperity in Anatolia. Equilibrium prevailed between the Seljuk kingdom of Konya, in control of most of the plateau, and the Byzantine kingdom of Nicaea. The Seljuk kingdom is usually called the Sultanate of the Seljuks of Rum, in order to distinguish it from the empire of the "Great"

Seljuks in Iraq and Iran. Anatolia was known as the land of Rum, or Rome, to the Turks. The Seljuk state reached its apogee under the legendary Alauddin Kaykubad (1219–1236). Eastern Anatolia was divided between the Danishmends and several other Turkish tribes, including the Mengüjeks, the Saltuks, and the Artuks.

The Seljuk ruler was called a sultan, a term meaning a ruler whose legitimate authority was granted by the caliph in Baghdad, the ultimate leader of the Islamic world empire. The structure of Seljuk government remained uncomplicated. The army was the fundamental institution of the Seljuk state. The ruler was above all a military commander, and the main state officials and his advisors were army officers. The Seljuk army consisted of the fighting men of established Turkish warrior families and clans who were given fiefs and paid out of the land tax on the agrarian cultivators. To these soldiers were added troops recruited from the subject population. In keeping with the practice of military slavery familiar to them from the larger Islamic world, the Seljuks recruited military slaves from the Christian peasant population of Anatolia and forcibly converted them to Islam. Turkish clans had themselves first made their mark in the Islamic world as military slaves of Muslim rulers.

Although the actual number of Turkish warriors and other migrants who entered Anatolia in the late eleventh century must have been rather small in comparison to the total population of Anatolia, their influence was paramount. Large numbers of people had been killed in warfare or had died as a result of disease and starvation that accompanied the warfare. Thousands more had been displaced, fleeing their homes for the safety of the mountains or, in western Anatolia, the coastal regions outside Turkish control. The repetition of violence, as towns, fortifications, and whole regions changed hands and back again over the course of the twelfth century, deepened the impact of these events. The majority of the population throughout Anatolia probably remained Christian. Along the Aegean and Marmara coasts and around Trebizond on the Black Sea, Greek and, in certain cities in the southeast, Armenian Christian rule still held sway. But most of the interior of Anatolia was now ruled by Muslim states. In some regions, the proportion of the Muslim population was large, and everywhere the Christian population began the slow process of integration into a new, Muslim, Anatolian society.

In addition to the defeat of Byzantine Greek and Armenian states, the Turkish conquest also meant the destruction of the authority of the Christian church and its institutions. As a millennium before, Christian churches had been built on the sites of pagan temples to demonstrate the victory of Christ over the idols, so now sounding the call to prayer from Armenian and Greek churches marked the subordination of Christianity to Islam. At the level of symbol and public rhetoric, the victory of Islam over Christianity in Anatolia was made unmistakable. The new Muslim states confiscated the land and property of churches, granting much of it to Islamic monastic orders of monks called dervishes or organizations of the Islamic learned hierarchy, ulema. At the same time, the Muslim and Christian communities of Anatolia did not live entirely separate existences. Interaction of Muslims and Christians—including intermarriage—at all levels of society, from the peasantry to the family of the sultans, was ongoing. The new Muslim rulers willingly aligned themselves with Christian states and intermarried with their rulers, and several Seljuk sultans had Christian mothers.

Urban life was slowly transformed by the presence of immigrants and the new Muslim craft and commercial guild associations they formed. The life of these associations revolved around the work and production of the craft, mystical religious devotional exercises and rituals of the members, overseen by masters called *akhis*, and the maintenance of simple public welfare facilities such as hospices. Mystical Islam had a far-reaching impact on Turkish life in Anatolia through these guild associations and through the related institution of the mystical orders and their lodges. Members of mystical orders became the main vehicles for the spread of popular Islam in Anatolia and the gradual conversion of its population.

Muslim artists and mystics, preachers and scholars, merchants and scribes flocked from neighboring lands to Konya, which Alauddin developed into a rich cultural center. Here was his palace, built of stone, and the largest stone mosque in the country, as well as several leading Islamic colleges, or medreses, and a major market. Spreading abroad from Konya, along the commercial highways that were its true source of wealth, were built fortifications, inns known as caravanserais and mosques in an increasingly identifiable Anatolian style.

THE MONGOLS AND AFTER

As before, the fragile political equilibrium of Anatolia was upset by events whose origins lay outside Anatolia. In central Eurasia, armies of semi-nomadic horsemen, this time led by the Mongols and their great chieftain and general Chinggis Khan, once more began campaigns of conquest. After plundering the old Muslim kingdoms of the Ferghana valley and the eastern Caspian region, Mongol armies invaded southern Russia in 1237, Hungary in 1241 and, in late 1242, eastern Anatolia. The Mongols utterly destroyed the Seljuk Turkish armies at Köse Dagh, east of Sivas, on 26 June 1243. Sivas and Kayseri were sacked and pillaged.

Anatolia was reduced to the status of a tributary province under the rule of Hülegü, the grandson of Chinggis Khan who sacked Baghdad in 1258 and put to death the last Abbasid caliph. Hülegü's dynasty, known as the Ilkhans, ruled Iraq and Iran, its effective power reaching to the upper Tigris and Euphrates regions of eastern Anatolia, until 1335. The Mongol depredations set in motion a second major phase of Turkish nomadic immigration into Anatolia, whose impact was as dramatic as the first a century and a half earlier. Thousands of Turkoman warriors and refugees poured westward into Anatolia from Central Asia, northern Iran, and the upper Tigris and Euphrates regions, spreading out in raids over the plateau and into regions beyond Seljuk control. This pressure, combined with the political vacuum resulting from Seljuk weakness, made the second half of the thirteenth century a period of renewed Turkish conquest. Several new Turkish principalities appeared in Cilicia, along the Mediterranean coast, and in the heavily populated, agrarian coastal regions of the Aegean and Marmara, the Byzantine heartland that had since the Crusades resisted Turkoman migration and settlement.

The new immigrants injected a fresh vitality into Anatolian Muslim society. They emphasized their Turkishness and the political and social traditions of the grassy steppes of Central Eurasia. Writers like Yunus Emre, in Kütahya in the early fourteenth century, began creating literature in Turkish. The lively epics of the Oghuz Turks—the *Oghuzname*, tales of the legendary ancestor Oghuz, and the collection of legends about the hero Dede Korkut—were committed to writing at this time.

More recently converted to Islam, the Turkomans were generally interested in an active, syncretistic piety that emphasized mystical experience and the sacred aura of holy men, relics, and shrines. Popular preachers drew followings, and dervish cells and lodges flourished. They used the idiom of ghaza, the sacred struggle against unbelief, to describe their relations with neighboring Christian states. Turkoman chieftains built claims of legitimacy upon a combination of military prowess—particularly as ghazis, warriors carrying on the sacred struggle in battle against the Christian Byzantines—and personal piety shown by close relationships with holy men and their dervish orders.

The Turkoman chieftain Karaman established the earliest of the new principalities that displaced a formerly Christian state, defeating the Armenian kingdom of Cilicia. After the collapse of the Mongol Ilkhanate in Iran and Iraq in 1335, the principality of Karaman made Konya its capital, staking a claim as the true successor of Seljuk greatness. The principality of Germiyan, founded in 1283 at Kütahya, controlled the Aegean coastal region. In the years around 1300, several more Aegean and Mediterranean principalities appeared, including Aydın in the Meander (Menderes) River valley, Menteshe around Mughla, and Hamid at Antalya.

THE OTTOMANS

When the famous Moroccan scholar and world traveler Ibn Battuta reached Anatolia in late 1330, he was conscious of being at the frontier of the great Muslim world. Landing at Alaiyye and coming inland at Antalya, he visited Konya and traveled across the plateau via Kayseri to Sivas, Erzincan and Erzurum, and back. Then he made a tour of the Aegean region, visiting successively the principalities of Menteshe, Aydın, Saruhan, Karasi, and Balıkesir, lodging in guild hospices, enjoying the hospitality of the *akhis*, meeting the local rulers—all of whom he referred to as sultans—and surveying local commercial and religious life.

Ibn Battuta arrived at Bursa, seat of the Ottoman principality, in November 1331. He described Sultan Orhan of Bursa as "the greatest of the kings of the Turkomans and the richest in wealth, lands and military forces." Orhan was the son of Osman Beg, the Turkoman chief of Söğüt in Bithynia, who had achieved fame by besieging İznik (Nicaea) and defeating the imperial Byzantine forces sent against him at Baphaeon in 1301. Orhan captured Bursa in 1327 and İznik in 1331, a few months before Ibn Battuta's arrival. In his published travelogue, Ibn Battuta reported, "Of fortresses he possesses nearly a hundred, and for most of his time he is continually engaged in making the round of them, staying in each fortress for some days to put it into good order and examine its condition. It is said that he has never stayed for a whole month in any one town. He also fights with the infidels continually and keeps them under siege" (in the translation of H. A. R. Gibb, *The Travels of Ibn Battuta A.D. 1325–1354*, vol. 2 [Cambridge, 1962], pp. 451–452).

The victories of Osman and Orhan against the neighboring Byzantine Empire, their successful projection of the ghazi image of sacred warfare for the expansion of Islamic rule, and the attractiveness of Bursa as a commercial center combined to draw frontier adventurers and warriors, fortune seekers, merchants, preachers and teachers to the Ottoman sultanate in the first half of the fourteenth century. It was said that Osman had dreamed a marvelous dream, in which the moon had risen from Shaykh Edebali's bosom and come to rest in his own, and from it a large tree grew. The shaykh, Osman's companion and advisor, had interpreted it as a prophesy of a kingdom grown from his and Osman's descendants and had married his daughter to the prince.

While absorbing small, neighboring Turkish principalities in north-western Asia Minor, Orhan inevitably became deeply involved in Byzantine politics. He cemented an alliance with the Byzantine usurper John Cantecuzenos in his struggle with the rival Byzantine dynasty, the Paleologi, by marrying John's daughter Theodora. The sultan of Saruhan, allied with the Empress Anne, raided in Bulgaria and Thrace and plundered the outskirts of Constantinople. After 1346, Orhan and his successors, his son Murad and Murad's son Bayezid, concentrated on the problem of the Byzantine succession while simultaneously contending with rival Turkish princes in western Anatolia, who were understandably troubled about the growing strength of the Ottoman state.

Intervening on behalf of Cantecuzenos, Orhan sent his son Süleyman across the Dardanelles to take Tzympe in 1352; two years later, he captured the fortress of Gallipoli. When the Serbian King Stefan Dushan died in 1355, no significant Balkan power remained to confront the Turkish advance. Just before Orhan's death in 1361, Murad took Adrianople (Edirne) in eastern Thrace, key to the great European highway, transferring his residence there. When Murad destroyed a combined Macedonian and Serbian army at the Maritsa River in 1371, the Emperor John V Paleologos was forced to pay tribute, thereby making the Byzantine Empire a vassal of the Ottoman sultan. The first Ottoman province, called Rumelia, was established in Thrace and southern Bulgaria.

In the 1380s and 1390s, the Ottomans conquered most of the Balkan Peninsula and central Anatolia in piecemeal fashion. Sofia in Bulgaria fell in 1385, Nish in Serbia in 1386, and Salonika on the Aegean in 1387. In 1388, Bulgaria north of the Balkan Mountains, as far as the Danube, was taken. In these years, Murad also fought in Anatolia, intervening in the region of Amasya and defeating an army from Karaman, but the systematic conquest of Anatolia waited until after 1389. In that year, Murad destroyed a coalition of Balkan princes at the Battle of Kosovo and then lost his life to an assassin in the aftermath. In the next five years, his son Bayezid subjugated the Muslim principalities of Aydın, Saruhan, Menteshe, Germiyan, Hamid, and Kastamonu, which were organized into the second Ottoman province, Anatolia. Building a fort on the shores of the Bosphorus, he began a blockade of Constantinople in 1394. The fate of the Byzantine city seemed sealed with Bayezid's crushing victory against a Crusader army at Nicopolis in 1396. With the defeat of the independent kingdom of Sivas in 1398, ruled by Sultan Burhaneddin, and the annexation of Karaman, Bayezid's realm extended from the Danube to the Euphrates.

The appearance of a grave new threat in eastern Anatolia, however, not only saved the city of Constantinople but abruptly ended the Ottomans' drive toward empire at the point where it seemed certain to succeed. Another charismatic military genius, Temür, or Tamerlane as he is known in Western literature, unified the Turkic nomad armies to create the last of the great steppe empires, stretching from central Asia to the Black Sea and claiming the Mongol mantle of the Ilkhans. Temür conquered Iran in 1387, entered Baghdad in 1393, and sacked Delhi in 1398. Bayezid met utter defeat at the hands of Temür's forces in the Battle of Ankara in 1402 and was himself taken prisoner. Resentment of Bayezid's moves toward centralization of authority, including raising a slave army and beginning the registration of both agricultural lands and nomadic herds, drove the Anatolian Turkish begs Bayezid had so recently defeated into the arms of the central Asian conqueror.

THE OTTOMAN RECOVERY AND THE UNIFICATION OF ANATOLIA

Temür returned to the Turkish begs their former principalities and divided the patrimony of Osman among the several sons of Bayezid. But remarkably, in a period of less than twenty years after the death of Temür, the Ottoman sultanate recovered from complete defeat and dismemberment to regain its position as the leading power of western Anatolia and the Balkans. In eastern Anatolia, two powerful Turkoman states, known as the White Sheep (Ak Koyunlu) and the Black Sheep (Kara Koyunlu), succeeded the Ilkhans.

Even before Temür's death, the sons of Bayezid began a civil war over the Ottoman domain. The European neighbors supported whoever appeared to be weakest at a given moment, while the rival Anatolian principalities worked to prevent a centralized Ottoman realm. For a time there existed the real possibility of a partition between the European and Anatolian halves of the kingdom, a conclusion that probably would have doomed both. By 1411, however, Bayezid's son Mehmed defeated his brothers, successfully reuniting the Ottoman domain. The kingdom Sultan Mehmed bequeathed to his son Murad II when he died in 1421 was not yet the same kingdom as Bayezid had lost to Temür nineteen years earlier, but the danger of its disappearance had receded.

Against the many forces favoring the breakup of the Ottoman realm during this interregnum, the sons of Bayezid could call on a reservoir of strengths that ultimately held it together. The prestigious reputation of the Ottoman dynasty was not completely ruined by Temür. Most important, perhaps, Murad I and Bayezid had created a powerful central army, including a standing force of slave soldiers and a reliable body of Turkoman cavalry whom they settled on lands controlled by the Ottoman sultanate. Another factor in the Ottoman recovery was the absence of a truly equal adversary. This Ottoman army was stronger than that fielded by any of the Anatolian begs and stronger than any conceivable configuration of forces in the Balkans, where the Ottomans had already decimated the traditional military nobility. The exception to this was Hungary, which led a series of wars with the Ottomans between 1421 and 1448, especially under the leadership of the great General Janos Hunyadi. All of these eventually failed, however.

Sultan Mehmed II completed the Ottoman recovery with the conquest of Constantinople (Istanbul). The Byzantine capital, which the sons of Bayezid had already twice besieged during the civil war, fell to the Ottoman guns on 29 May 1453. The city, which the Turks called Istanbul, was in any case no longer what it once had been, its population mostly having fled and its economic circumstances severely reduced by blockade. Mehmed the Conqueror set about vigorously repopulating and rebuilding the city. As the Ottoman center, it would once more be an imperial city. By the time Sultan Mehmed II took Istanbul, most of Anatolia had been under Muslim Turkish rule for more than four centuries. Even the still heavily Greek and Christian Aegean coastal regions had become accustomed to the authority of Muslim sultanates after more than 150 years.

The conquest of Istanbul strengthened the position of the Ottoman Turks in an emerging world war over control of the products and trade routes of the Indian Ocean and Mediterranean commercial nexus at the end of the fifteenth century. During the long reigns of Sultan Mehmed the Conqueror (1451–1481) and his son Bayezid II (1481–1512), and the short reign of his grandson Selim I (1512–1520), the Ottoman leadership formed and developed institutions of state that supported powerful military forces that eventually won this war.

For the Ottoman Empire, this war was really several wars, fought simultaneously. One aspect of this war involved a conflict with Venice in the Aegean and Mediterranean that led to the Ottoman conquest of the Peloponnesus (the Morea) and Euboia. This was related to a second aspect of the war in the central and eastern Balkans and the Black Sea. Several campaigns were fought here, a Muslim Turkish client state was created in the Crimea, and strenuous efforts were made to prevent Hungarian incursions into the Balkans south of the Danube-Sava line. A third aspect of the war involved competition with several Anatolian Turkish principalities for control of the routes leading across eastern Anatolia. This part of the conflict abated somewhat with the Ottoman defeat of Karaman in 1468 and the death of Uzun Hasan, the great sultan of the Akkoyunlu state of the Euphrates region, in 1478. There was a religious dimension of the war as well, involving a conflict between the two major Islamic denominations, Shiism and Sunnism, that paralleled in some ways the conflict that was to begin a few years later between Roman Catholics and Protestants in Europe. The Ottomans, like the Seljuks, were Sunnite Muslims. The population of eastern Anatolia, large numbers of whom belonged to the Shiite denomination of Islam, became sympathetic to a powerful new Shiite Turkish state that arose in Armenia and Azerbaijan under Shah Ismail in 1500. In perhaps the most dangerous aspect of the war for the Ottomans, Shah Ismail promoted and supported Shiite rebellions all over Anatolia, captured Baghdad in 1503, and invaded Anatolia in 1507. Sultan Selim I, forcing the aging Bayezid II to abdicate in 1512, suppressed rebellions of Shiite partisans of Shah Ismail in Tekke and elsewhere in Anatolia. Two years later, Selim launched a massive campaign into Azerbaijan, defeating Shah Ismail in the epic Battle of Çaldıran in August 1514.

The final aspect of this world war comprised a conflict with Venice and with Mamluk Egypt over the overland trade routes through Cilicia to Aleppo and Damascus, and the Mediterranean ports of western Syria. Selim I won this war by invading Syria after his victory at Çaldıran. He seized Cilicia from the Muslim Ramazanoğlu dynasty, thus fully unifying Anatolia under Ottoman rule, and took Aleppo in 1516. He went on to defeat the Mamluks at Marj Dabik in Palestine, took Cairo in January 1517, and completed his stunning victory over the centers of Islamic civilization later that year with the conquest of Mecca and Medina.

4

Anatolia and the Classical Ottoman System, 1517–1789

The conquests of Sultan Selim I transformed the Ottoman Empire into a world power straddling the ancient routes between the Mediterranean Sea and the Indian Ocean. The Ottoman sultan had acquired a large number of new Muslim subjects in southwestern Asia and northeastern Africa and now controlled the great shrines of Mecca, Medina, and Jerusalem and the most important pilgrimage routes. The balance of the empire's identity gradually shifted as the former regional sultanate of the Balkans and Anatolia came to terms with its position of leadership in the Islamic world.

The campaigns of Selim I brought all of Anatolia under Ottoman rule. During the next two and a half centuries, the Ottoman dynasty governed these regions through its provincial administrative structure and its relationships with notable persons and families in the provinces. In the sixteenth century, the central government of the Ottoman Empire extended its fiscal and military reach, both through the incorporation of the various regions of Anatolia into a unified imperial economy and through the extension of the Ottoman central bureaucratic apparatus. After a long period of warfare, during the later seventeenth century Anatolian notables succeeded in forcing a gradual revision of the Ottoman central government's approach to provincial administration, capitalizing on new situations and manipulating the instruments of Ottoman political and economic control to their own advantage.

The area which would later form the Republic of Turkey was divided in the classical Ottoman age into several provinces. Eastern Thrace, including the city of Edirne, was part of the oldest and most important Ottoman province, the province of Rumelia, stretching across the southern Balkan Peninsula. The Ottoman province of Anatolia was smaller than the area thought of as Anatolia today. It included the Aegean and Marmara coastal regions, the northern mountains bordering the western Black Sea, and the western and north central parts of the peninsula, reaching as far as the city of Ankara. The province of Anatolia was divided into several districts called sanjaks, many of which were formerly independent principalities, including Saruhan, Karasi, Aydın, Menteshe, Hamid, and Tekke.

As for the remainder of modern Anatolia, the area east of Ankara, with the cities of Sivas and Amasya, made up the province of Rum. The eastern Black Sea coast formed a province centered on the ancient city of Trabzon. Heavily Armenian and Kurdish eastern Anatolia was divided into the province of Kars in the northeast, the province of Erzurum, and the province of Rukka in the southeast. In south central Anatolia, two formerly independent principalities comprised the Ottoman provinces of Karaman and Dulkadir. Adana and the Cilician plain fell into the province of Aleppo. In Diyarbakir province, the Ottoman dynasty reached a special arrangement whereby the Kurdish tribal chieftains maintained autonomy in exchange for tribute and acted as an important Sunni bastion against the Shiite progaganda of the Safavids, the dynasty founded by Shah Ismail in 1500.

THE CLASSICAL OTTOMAN ADMINISTRATIVE SYSTEM

The nostalgic view that became popular among later Ottoman writers—that under Selim's successor Sultan Süleyman Kanuni I (1520–1566) the Ottoman Empire reached an apogee of power and success, a classical age, or golden age—was an idea championed by Süleyman already in his own lifetime. Believing that in his reign Ottoman society could epitomize the Islamic world order, Sultan Süleyman consciously projected a messianic public persona, emphasizing his role as a just and wise monarch who set out righteous statutes. Although in Western lore he came to be known as Sultan Süleyman the Magnificent, in Turkish he is known as *Kanunî*, Sultan Süleyman the Lawgiver. Under Süleyman's rule, jurists codified much earlier Ottoman legal material and worked to lay the legal foundation of important Ottoman political, military, social, and economic institutions. The corpus of decrees of the sultan, the *kanuns*, regulated the institutions of the empire and were the law of the land. Some of these laws concerned matters outside the explicit jurisdiction of Islamic sacred law, the sharia, but others synthesized Islamic law and imperial decrees and gave a place to custom too. Thus, secular law and sacred law coexisted with customary law in the classical Ottoman Empire, as in all Islamic states.

The classical Ottoman system of Sultan Süleyman was built upon centuries of development within several intersecting traditions: the Turkish heritage of the steppe empire, the Islamic theological tradition, the Persian and Byzantine imperial traditions, and the first two centuries of Ottoman law and experience in Anatolia and the Balkans. The Ottoman Empire was a dynastic state. In Ottoman political theory, the territory of the Ottoman Empire belonged to the state by right of conquest by the victorious ruling dynasty. The sultan governed the state as a trust from God, as the shepherd of the flock of God, through his family, his advisors, and his household servants. In a certain sense, the government of the empire was regarded as an extension of the sultan's own household.

The sultan's immediate palace household operated from a personal treasury, funded partially out of the sultan's share of the fruits of conquest. The categories of state service—the Inner Service or *Enderun*, the Outer Service or *Birun*, and the provincial administration—corresponded to the physical layout of the courtyards of the imperial palace of Topkapı at Istanbul. The servants of the sultan's household went out from the palace to become the state officials who staffed the highest levels of the Ottoman imperial military and administration. The soldiers of the various corps of the sultan's palace guard and militia comprised the most highly trained divisions of the Ottoman military. As the ruling class of the empire, the sultan's extended household of state servants paid no taxes, serving society and living off its revenues. These state servants were the sultan's slaves, his *kuls*.

The sultan's palace and the harem were closely regulated arenas where the delicate and crucial business of preserving the dynasty was managed, where the work of communicating its attributes and vision was undertaken, and where issues concerning the nature of that work were debated. The women of the dynasty played a significant role in these matters. Moving away from the pattern of fathering children by slave concubines, as earlier sultans had done, Süleyman married and remained faithful to one woman, Hurrem Sultan. Hurrem and Süleyman established a new model of the royal family, in which the sultan's favorite concubine exercised considerable political influence by residing in the palace, advising the sultan, and forming political alliances with important statesmen. In subsequent generations, the mothers of reigning sultans became the most powerful political personages in the royal household, managing not only the political and financial affairs of the palace officials but also the sexual dimension of dynastic politics.

In the classical Ottoman system, the sultan's servants were slaves, many of them children taken from Christian villages in the Balkans. In this, the Ottomans adapted to their own circumstances a traditional system of elite military slavery practiced in numerous Middle Eastern Islamic states, including the Seljuk sultanate, for centuries before them. The Ottoman version of the system, called the *devşirme*, was an extraordinary levy on the Christian peasants of the Balkans. The children taken became slaves, but slaves of the sultan and of the state who could not be resold. The system was intended to create an Ottoman ruling class whose loyalty was owed entirely to the state. Muslim peasant families were exempted, according to Ottoman writers, because their loyalty to the state might be compromised by their links to provincial family networks. The slave boys were sent to Anatolia where they converted to Islam and learned Turkish before being brought back to Istanbul. There they enrolled in the palace educational system and passed through a series of grades based on their ability. Many graduates of the system entered the Janissary corps, the famous infantry of the Ottoman military. The more able pupils stayed at the palace, receiving additional training before entering palace service or being transferred to administrative and military posts in the provinces.

The highest governing body in the empire was the imperial council or *divan*, a cabinet-like group of men appointed directly by the sultan. It directed the political, judicial, financial, and administrative functions of government, meeting regularly in a room in the palace. The council was headed by the Grand Vezir, a military commander with great administrative acumen. The rest of the council included the governors-general (*beglerbegis*) of the two greatest provinces, Rumelia and Anatolia, who held the rank of vezir; the two high military judges, the *kadıaskers* of the provinces of Rumelia and Anatolia; the empire's two highest financial officers, the head treasurers; the Commander of the Janissary Corps; the Admiral of the Fleet; and the Chancellor, who led the bureaucracy and whose responsibility it was to affix the sultan's signature to documents.

Rumelia and Anatolia, the provinces closest to Istanbul, were the provinces most fully integrated into the Ottoman administrative model. The empire stationed many of its central administrators here. The governor, a senior military commander appointed from Istanbul, who was a slave and a graduate of the palace educational system, ran the province through his personal household in coordination with the provincial council and its scribal personnel. The provincial bureaucracy existed mainly to administer the Ottoman provincial army, which provided more than one-third of the total Ottoman fighting strength. Made up of garrison forces and a provincial cavalry, this army formed the link between the Ottoman imperial system and the countryside. In many cases, it represented the physical survival of an older local Turkish military class. They gave their military service in exchange for the right to collect the tax revenues of rural estates called *timars*.

The revenue of each timar was determined by a periodic detailed cadastral survey of the land and its expected production, carried out by Ottoman chancery officials in coordination with local authorities. The results of the survey, and the names of the Christian and Muslim peasant cultivators and their tax assessments, were recorded in registers and filed in the provincial capital and in Istanbul. The states handled petitions and complaints from peasants, and disputes concerning claims on timar revenues, through written communication between central and provincial officials. In these affairs, the Ottoman central government displayed an attitude of flexibility and a willingness to negotiate within bounds defined by the practical requirements of its local military force.

THE CLASSICAL OTTOMAN ECONOMY

The theoretical principles undergirding the Ottoman administrative system, that the Ottoman realm was ruled by the sultan as a trust from God, that all land belonged to the state, and that the state functioned as an extension of the sultan's household, had direct relevance for the operation of the Ottoman economy. Economic activity increased the power and wealth of the state, which acted to distribute its benefits to all.

The classical Ottoman economic system aimed broadly to maximize imperial prosperity and wealth by military conquest and by efficient methods of revenue extraction. It stressed the benefit of imperial prosperity to all sectors of society and saw the state's role as winning control of revenue sources and organizing collection and redistribution. The state itself and its servants were exempted from taxation. In the Ottoman

Empire, imperial wealth was acquired through support of the agrarian economy, small scale urban industry and trade to ensure the supply of commodities for the local market.

Revenues of the agrarian economy supported the provincial cavalry force. In the manner of feudal lords but regulated by the state, the Ottoman timar holders collected the rural dues from Muslim and Christian peasant families along a graduated scale. The timar system also had the benefit, for the state, of decentralizing collection of a significant source of revenue, relieving the central treasury of the burden of collecting it, and preventing removal of currency from the local economy. The same was true of another important revenue source, the canonical poll tax levied on non-Muslims living in towns and cities. Collection of this tax was typically farmed out by auction to local investors; the bulk of it stayed in the province and was recycled into the local markets. A system of revenue contracting (*mukataa*) was commonly employed for certain revenue sources. In contrast to agricultural revenues, farmed revenues tended to be from urban sources, including the poll tax, customs duties, and the revenues of state monopolies like salt and metal mining.

At the heart of the Ottoman urban economy was a set of economic and social institutions established by charitable foundations with the support of the state. These urban centers, called *imarets*, typically grew up around a mosque and included markets and other public services such as roads, bridges, water works, and caravanserais, inns, and hostels for travelers. The Islamic charitable foundation (*vakıf*) provided the legal financial basis of these complexes. A vakıf was a registered foundation in which the profits from a source were earmarked to the support of a specified charitable purpose and thereby became tax exempt. A charter defined the purpose and conditions of the vakıf, spelled out its management structure, and appointed its trustees. The foundation charter also provided for the salaries of employees out of the income of the endowment, as well as day-to-day maintenance and supplies. Any citizen had the right to create a vakıf foundation out of personal income sources, and the state also granted state lands to officials for the purpose of establishing a foundation. Vakıf foundations supported not only the great public architecture visible in Ottoman cities—mosques, markets, mausoleums, bridges, baths, fountains, and the like—they also lay behind such establishments as soup kitchens, dervish lodges, hospitals, libraries, seminaries, scriptoria, gardens, and calligraphy and other works of art. Common persons too, women as well as men, endowed vakıfs, sometimes for purposes as simple as the fees of a professional chanter to recite the Qur'an over the founder's grave.

Urban industries were organized through guild associations. Guild activities reached far beyond the strictly economic or industrial. It purchased and ensured the supply of raw materials, set production levels and prices, and regulated quality control. It provided for the families of its members through systems of what we would call workmen's compensation and insurance, and functioned as a banking institution, taking deposits, extending credit, and investing in such projects as long-distance trade. It investigated infractions and negotiated disputes. The guild's connection to a religious order—its liturgy, places of worship, and leadership—infused the guild community with a deeply spiritual character. Guild organization characterized urban economic activity among Muslim and non-Muslim (Christian and Jewish) communities alike. These confessional communities tended to live within separate quarters in Ottoman cities, but the quarters were organized in a similar fashion, with churches, synagogues, or mosques as the center point. The communities came together in the markets and in other state institutions.

The Ottoman conquest unified the Anatolian commercial economy by integrating it with international markets across its great caravan trade routes. While Istanbul became the largest market and the focal point of commerce in the Ottoman Empire, Bursa remained the commercial center of Anatolia. Merchants usually reached Istanbul from Bursa by sea, via Mudanya on the Sea of Marmara. At Istanbul, the routes from Europe converged, the overland route by way of the great highway through Edirne, Sofia, Nish, Belgrade, and Buda, and the sea route by way of the Straits. Merchants could also reach the Aegean and Mediterranean from Bursa through a land route to the increasingly important port of İzmir.

A road leading through Eskişehir, and across the Anatolian plateau via Ankara, Tokat, Erzincan, and Erzurum, connected Bursa to Tabriz, Iran, central Eurasia, and the overland routes to east Asia. At Tokat, this road was joined by one from Istanbul via İzmit and Bolu. The main trunk of the other great route across Anatolia went by way of Kütahya, Akşehir, and Konya, taking merchants and travelers through the Cilician gates to Adana, İskenderun, and Aleppo. At Aleppo, this route then connected western and central Anatolia to the pilgrimage route via Damascus to Jerusalem, Medina and Mecca on the one hand and, by way of the upper Euphrates, to Baghdad, the Persian Gulf, and the Indian Ocean on the other. A southern route to Tabriz via Birecik and Diyarbakir also branched off from Aleppo.

The Ottoman trade strategy was to create regional customs zones around the main urban commercial centers and permit goods to cross only on the official trade highways, which passed through the customs centers. The state collected duties on all merchandise once, in the customs center of each customs zone. Duties were essentially value-added taxes on the value of the commodity itself, as estimated by state officials in the customs centers, and not on commercial transactions. In the crucial customs zones on the borders of the empire, therefore, the duties amounted to a tax on imports and exports. In this way, the Ottoman Empire could maximize its profits from international trade while not discouraging the movement of goods within regional market systems. This Ottoman trade strategy gave European merchants the incentive to seek alternate international routes for the Indian trade in the late fifteenth and early sixteenth centuries, when the Ottoman Empire effectively monopolized the traditional commercial routes between the Mediterranean and the Indian Ocean. The "Capitulations," Ottoman grants of commercial privileges to merchants of European states beginning with France in 1536, also need to be understood in the context of utter Ottoman domination of commerce between the Danube and the Persian Gulf and between the Nile and the Caucasus Mountains after 1517.

Besides Indian spices, the most significant merchandise carried on the Ottoman trade routes were raw silk from Iran and textiles from Europe, especially woolens from Florence. The most valued homegrown Ottoman commodities included silk cloth manufactured in Bursa, the center of the Ottoman silk industry, mohair from Ankara, fine cotton cloth, rugs, hides, furs, rhubarb, bees wax, and musk.

THE SYSTEM STRAINED

The Ottoman classical system underwent modification in a long period of almost continual warfare between 1578 and 1639. The wars brought heavy casualties and strained the resources of the state while bringing limited material rewards. The wars coincided with a serious dynastic crisis and an economic downturn. After a period of transition, a new internal political and economic equilibrium emerged that restored Ottoman prosperity.

The Ottomans renewed the conflict with Iran over control of the trade routes in Armenia, Azerbaijan, and the Transcaucasus in a war that lasted from 1578 to 1590. A "Long War" of indecisive sieges against the Habsburg Empire in Hungary and east central Europe followed between 1593 and 1606. A pattern of military rebellion by Anatolian notables was repeated over several decades in the seventeenth century. These Anatolian warlords, who controlled their own military forces, pointed out the tactical obsolescence of the provincially based timariot cavalry and the consequent need for a reassessment of the entire Ottoman approach to provincial government under new circumstances. Ottoman authorities alternately suppressed the rebellions by force and negotiated compromises with the leaders, gradually recognizing the need for adjustment of the empire's provincial structure.

The increased presence of imperial Janissary troops stationed in the provinces during the late sixteenth century played a role in the revolts of these provincial notables. More than their military presence, the financial power of the Janissaries disrupted established commercial relations in Anatolia as they began to invest heavily in state tax contracting, competing with and outbidding local interests. When Sultan Osman II attempted reforms that seemed to side with the provincial notables, a violent Janissary coup deposed him in 1622. While the underlying financial issues continued to fester, the political fallout of that episode did not completely settle until after mid-century.

The escalating social crisis climaxed in a bloody uprising in Istanbul in March 1656 and a Venetian victory over the Ottoman navy at the Dardanelles in June. In September 1656, desperate palace officials, led by the Queen Mother, handed the Grand Vezirate to the octogenarian Mehmed Köprülü, who immediately installed a military dictatorship and restored order, executing hundreds of rebels. Mehmed Köprülü established a dynasty of Grand Vezirs who effectively ruled the empire for the remainder of the seventeenth century. Despite the Ottoman defeat at the hands of the Austrian Habsburgs in the second siege of Vienna (1683) and the subsequent loss of Hungary and other territory in the famous Treaty of Karlowitz (1699), the Köprülü decades saw the gradual emergence of a new economic and political equilibrium in the empire, which held for most of the next century.

CONSOLIDATION OF A NEW OTTOMAN POLITICAL AND ECONOMIC MODEL

The financial roots of this new equilibrium lay in a system of lifetime contracts for the collection of state revenues that evolved during the seventeenth century out of the practice of tax farming. Expensive wars depleted the central treasury, but instability in the countryside discouraged investors in short-term revenue farming, which was in any case dominated by local Janissaries. According to historian Ariel Salzmann, the lifetime revenue contract, or *malikane* system, attracted leading provincial notables to reinvest in state finance by offering contractors the right to collect taxes at fixed rates for their lifetime. The contracts could be divided into shares and held jointly by several investors. Shares could be traded or publicly auctioned separately when the holder died. Winning bidders paid the central treasury an advance, registration fees, and annual remittances, receiving in return an exclusive government charter (Ariel Salzmann, "An Ancien Regime Revisited: 'Privatization' and Political Economy in the Eighteenth-Century Ottoman Empire," *Politics and Society* 21 [1993], pp. 393–423).

In this way, the Ottoman central authorities responded to pressure coming from state officials in the bureaucracy, military and Islamic ulema hierarchy, essentially agreeing to share power with these coalitions of elites, many of whom had or cultivated provincial connections. These elites distributed the profits and other benefits of their positions to their own personal retinues and clients. Although the central government remained closely involved with the bidding process, it faced obvious risks. Major imperial projects that required large financial outlays— such as wars—now required negotiation with powerful coalitions of interests whose cooperation was secured by offering incentives for their investment and participation. The system worked well but did not provide much room for the central government to maneuver in times of crisis. And the potential, at least, existed for regional elites to invest in military technology in order to pose a direct challenge to the Ottoman central authorities. During most of the eighteenth century, this did not happen because provincial leaders preferred to cooperate with the central government in return for armed protection, seeing greater probability of success in joint action. No regional leaders yet possessed the moral and spiritual authority to challenge the prestige of the Ottoman dynasty, now more than four hundred years old. But later in the century and in the next, powerful regional centers arose in Egypt, in Iraq, and in the Balkans, laying the seeds of local political and economic autonomy.

Salzmann has shown that in spite of risks, the state derived benefits from the new fiscal arrangement. The Ottoman central government built and renewed long-term ties of patronage and loyalty with local elites. Using local notables, the empire could more successfully invest in and compete for revenues associated with the important maritime commerce. And by solidifying relations and links of patronage with leading figures in the commercial and religious establishment, the dynasty acknowledge a firmer grounding in Ottoman society. Naturally, the revised political order brought the end of certain prominent Ottoman institutions, including the *devşirme* levy of children and the periodic fiscal surveys of the provinces, tools for the functioning of the former system.

The reorganized Ottoman army performed with mixed success in the first half of the eighteenth century. Russia posed the most serious threat to the late classical Ottoman order. The efforts of Tsar Peter the Great to consolidate Russian control of the steppe zone south of the Urals brought him into conflict with the Ottoman client state in the Crimea in the 1690s. This and an interest in competing for the wealth of the rapidly developing world economy of Atlantic, Mediterranean, and Indian Ocean commerce by way of the Black Sea motivated Peter to attack the Ottoman Empire in 1710. At Pruth the next year, the Ottomans handed him an embarrassing defeat. But the threat did not go away. Shrewd Ottoman diplomacy in another war with Russia and Austria in the Balkans between 1736 and 1739 brought a stable peace to the northern frontier for a generation, but when Catherine the Great (1762–1796) took the throne, she adopted an aggressive stance.

Alarmed by Russian actions in Poland in the 1760s, the Ottomans declared war in 1768 after a Russian incursion across the border in Moldavia. The war turned into a total catastrophe for the Ottoman Empire, as Russian troops occupied Bucharest and all of Romania in early 1770 and advanced toward Bulgaria. The Ottomans were forced to sign the Treaty of Küçük Kaynarca. By this agreement, the Ottomans ceded several forts on the Sea of Azov, giving Russia a landing on the Black Sea. The Crimean Turkish principality, an Ottoman client state for two centuries, became nominally independent, ending Ottoman monopolization of commerce on the Black Sea. Russian ships were permitted free access to the Black Sea, including passage through the Straits at Istanbul; and Catherine won vague rights of protection of Orthodox Christians in the Balkans.

The Ottoman logistical system proved incapable of supporting and supplying the large army needed for late eighteenth century European combat. Serious Ottoman statesmen began to recognize the limitations of the decentralized Ottoman fiscal system and to plan for its reform.

5

The Late Ottoman Empire, 1789–1908

In the nineteenth century, the Ottoman Empire survived when several European powers possessed clear military advantages over it. The empire's European rivals often supported independence movements of the Ottoman Empire's subject peoples while at the same time developing clear economic interests in maintaining the empire. The Ottoman Empire possessed active and creative statesmen who were fully aware of its strengths as well as its weaknesses, a vibrant and developing economy, and a cultural production attuned to the empire's place in the world and in history. The threat posed by Russia in the Balkan Peninsula and in the Caucasus and eastern Anatolia provided the incentive for a series of fiscal and administrative reforms intended to strengthen the Ottoman military. The repercussions of these measures were felt in every area of Ottoman life during the nineteenth century.

SULTAN SELIM III AND THE NEW ORDER

Catherine the Great completed the Russian conquest of the steppe zone with the Russian victory of 1774 and the Treaty of Küçük Kaynarca, eliminating the Crimean Khanate and bringing the Russian Empire to the shores of the Black Sea. These victories were confirmed by Russian victory in another war between 1787 and 1792. From this point on, the Ottoman relationship with Russia revolved around two closely related issues. The first was Russian strategic interest in the Straits as the naval and commercial route to the Aegean and Mediterranean. The second was Russian political interest in the future of the eastern Balkans, where it claimed a vague right to interfere on behalf of Orthodox Christians.

Russian military success against Ottoman armies in the last third of the eighteenth century piqued the interest of some Ottoman statesmen in the "Russian model" of military modernization. Beginning with Peter the Great (1682–1725) and continuing with Catherine the Great (1762–1796), the Russian state had increasingly adopted and manufactured European-style military technology, deployed it in newly organized central armies using European-style tactics, and financed it through a variety of new taxes. The new Sultan Selim III, who took the Ottoman throne in 1789, immediately began reforming the Ottoman army along these lines.

At first, these steps stressed the need for closer inspection of the existing army corps, including the Janissaries, for promotion through merit, for regular drill, and attention to discipline. Soon, however, Selim introduced a basic organizational distinction between the administrative and military aspects of command, appointing separate officers for each. He began efforts at expanding recruitment by demanding the service of sons of the corps. He built new barracks and made efforts to keep the provincial timar forces under arms throughout the year. The artillery and mining corps underwent more thorough reorganization. The old naval engineering school was expanded, and in 1795 a parallel school of army engineering was created. The imperial naval arsenal was expanded and provincial arsenals opened and began building a large number of modern ships. New army and navy medical schools trained doctors and surgeons for military medical service. The Ottoman Empire opened foreign embassies in the major European capitals of London, Paris, Vienna, and Berlin.

Yet these moves were insufficient to prepare the empire's military for the possibility of renewed conflict with Russia or another European adversary. In 1794, therefore, Selim III created two entirely new institutions, a new army corps called the "New Order" Army (*Nizam-ı cedid*) and a new treasury, called the "New Fund" Treasury (*İrad-ı cedid*) to finance it. Manned by Turkish peasant conscripts, the New Order Army was organized in the European manner, trained in European tactics, given European-style uniforms and weapons, and commanded by European experts, not only French but also British and German. Expansion to three corps brought the total strength to 22,685 men and 1,590 officers by the end of 1806.

The New Fund Treasury became the instrument of a fiscal transformation of the Ottoman central state. The foundation of the new treasury was the allocation to it of all lifetime tax franchises over 5,000 kurush in value at the death of their holders. These were taken over by the state, renegotiated, and bid out on a short-term basis to qualified applicants. Eventually, these retracted lifetime tax franchises constituted nearly half the funds of the New Fund Treasury.

The expansion of this new state financial strategy drew intense criticism from various sectors of Ottoman society, who saw in it a thinly disguised assault on the system of lifetime tax franchises used by the central treasury over the past century. Provincial elites as well as state officials, including the Janissaries in the capital, had used these lifetime tax franchises to build powerful financial portfolios and, as a class, significantly reformat the relations of power between the Ottoman central government and its provinces. Their opposition to the new force and the new treasury, though often expressed in a religious idiom—the uniforms of the New Order Army, for example, were attacked as being nontraditional Islamic garb—nevertheless were directed at the financial and political implications of the sultan's initiatives.

Napoleon Bonaparte's defeat of the Habsburgs and landing at the Nile delta in 1798 brought a new war. A hastily arranged triple alliance of Britain, Russia, and the Ottoman Empire succeeded in defeating Napoleon—who left his army and returned to France—and driving the French from Egypt in 1801. As a consequence of this war, powerful provincial notables took the opportunity to challenge Ottoman authority in their regions, including Muhammad Ali in Egypt, Ali Pasha of Janina in Albania and western Thrace, Pasvanoğlu Osman Pasha around Vidin, and Tirsinikli İsmail Agha in eastern Bulgaria and eastern Thrace. In 1804, a local Serbian Christian notable, Kara George, revolted against the regime of the Ottoman Janissaries in Belgrade.

Selim III faced dangerous circumstances in his efforts to field an army and finance another war with Russia, caused by Napoleon's conquests, in 1806. Debased currency and inflation contributed to a deteriorating situation, and in May 1807, a Janissary auxiliary force outside Istanbul assassinated a New Order Army officer and marched on the city. Reactionary Muslim leaders and aggrieved state officials leaped to the forefront of the rebellion. When conciliatory gestures failed on 29 May 1807, Selim III abdicated in favor of his cousin Mustafa IV. In July 1808, Balkan strongman Bayraktar Mustafa Pasha defeated the rebels and overthrew Mustafa IV in a coup d'état with the intention of returning Selim III to the throne. But Selim was murdered in the palace before his rescuers could save him, and instead Bayraktar Pasha brought to the throne the young prince Mahmud II, the brother of Mustafa IV and the lone surviving male member of the Ottoman dynasty.

SULTAN MAHMUD II AND THE END OF THE OLD ORDER

After the assassination of the coup leader Bayraktar Pasha in late 1808, Sultan Mahmud II reached a rapprochement with the leading provincial magnates and state officials, allowing them to preserve their privileged positions in the restored financial order. Between 1808 and 1812, the young sultan kept scrupulously to this agreement, assuring the loyalty of these powerful men. The war with Russia ended in 1812; Muhammad Ali, the strongman in Egypt, was accommodated; and the Serbian revolt won a degree of autonomy for a Serbian principality in the central Balkans in 1815.

Thereafter, Mahmud II, learning from the political mistakes of Selim III, spent several years carefully building alliances with lesser notables and state officials in the capital and in Anatolia whose interests lay in circumventing the monopolistic practices of the large tax franchise holders. He appointed personal allies to key positions in the ulema hierarchy, the imperial bureaucracy, and the military. Throughout the next decade, he staged a series of campaigns, first in western Anatolia and then in the Balkans, using force of arms to intimidate recalcitrant notables into submission. The Christian and Muslim notables of east and southeast Anatolia and of Cilicia, and the Kurdish chieftains resisted central government interference for nearly another half-century.

Mahmud carefully chose the moment to decisively crush the entrenched financial and political power of the old order. A Greek uprising broke out in 1821, arousing the sympathy of many Western Europeans, who imagined Greece as the birthplace of what they saw as peculiarly European ideals of human dignity, rationalism, and freedom, and Turkish authority as the archetypal tyranny. When the Ottoman military experienced difficulty against the Greeks, in 1825 Mahmud II called on Muhammad Ali of Egypt to extinguish the rebellion. The revolt seemed over with the Ottoman victory at Missolonghi in 1826.

Mahmud now revived the New Order Army of Selim III, though he was clever enough to name it instead the Trained Victorious Army of

Muhammad, aligning himself with the liberal Islamic scholars and leaders who saw no incompatibility between Islam and modern science and technology. Mahmud meticulously prepared for the predictable rebellion of the Janissaries, which came ten days later. He turned his heavy artillery on the Janissary mob that assembled before the palace, decimating their ranks and destroying their barracks. A decree issued the same day abolished the corps altogether, and a mopping up operation captured any who chanced to escape. The venerable Janissary corps was finished. The Bektashi order of dervishes and its network of houses, the spiritual and social sustenance of the Janissary community, was shut down. The diverse separate corps of the Ottoman military were unified into a single command under a *serasker*, a commander in chief.

At the same time, Mahmud II struck a blow at the power of the Ottoman ulema, a staunch support of the old order. The ulema organization was made a government department under the ultimate control of the Shaykhulislam, the top religious authority in the empire and an appointee of the sultan, and the far flung religious endowments (vakıf) were brought under the central control of a government directory and later a ministry. This was the first step in a century-long effort to tap this vast source of wealth, which as perpetual endowment was protected by law from taxation and formed the immediate financial and economic basis of religious and social life in the Islamic world.

The revival of the New Order Army was accompanied by a revival of the New Order Treasury, this time named the Treasury of the Victorious. A variety of new and reorganized revenues were earmarked for the new treasury, including a set of new duties named the Holy War Taxes (*Rüsumat-ı cihadiye*). Like Selim III, Mahmud was clearly motivated primarily by the need to equip and finance a modern army, but the changes went beyond the specifically military. In 1831, he ordered a census of the entire empire outside of Egypt and Arabia to identify the sources of manpower and revenue for the central treasury.

In the mid-1830s, Mahmud took some initial steps toward a rationalization of the central government bureaucracy, dividing the responsibilities of the office of the Grand Vezir into several departments, which became proto-cabinet ministries. Mahmud also restructured the palace service in such a way that in years to come it began to take on the look and function of a palace secretariat, directing the entire state apparatus under the sultan's immediate authority. In 1831, the Ottoman government began publishing an official gazette, *Takvim-i Vekayi* (Calendar of Events), the empire's first newspaper in Turkish, as an instrument of communication with state servants and the literate among its subjects, and three years later a regular postal service was established within the provinces.

THE ERA OF THE TANZIMAT AND ECONOMIC DEVELOPMENT

Two reforming decrees of the Ottoman central government, the Rose Garden Decree of 1839 and the Imperial Rescript of 1856, became landmarks of administrative, social, and economic policy in the empire. These decrees aimed to win continued Western European economic and political support, articulate principles for the conduct of administrative reform of the Ottoman government, and establish the ongoing commitment of the Ottoman government to economic and social development. The Rose Garden (*Gülhane*) Decree declared that the sultan guaranteed the life, property, and honor of all Ottoman subjects and the equality of all before the law, regardless of religious affiliation. It also announced a system of conscription for the Ottoman army and the abolition of tax farming and a system of rational taxation to replace it.

The period from the issuing of the Rose Garden Decree by Sultan Abdülmecid in 1839 to the suspension of the constitution by Sultan Abdülhamid II in 1878 is often referred to as the era of the Tanzimat, the "Reorganization." Political initiative for the changes in this era typically lay less with the sultans—Abdülmecid (1839–1861), Abdülaziz (1861–1876), Mustafa IV (1876) and Abdülhamid II (1876–1909)—than with the leading officials of the Ottoman civil bureaucracy, the "men of the Tanzimat." Hence the term *Sublime Porte* is often used as a synonym for the Ottoman government in this era. The term was a translation of *Bab-ı Âlî*, the name of the building where the offices of the Ottoman administration were housed, as contrasted with the palace, the residence, and offices of the sultan.

The ascendancy of the civil bureaucracy is evidence of the almost complete inability of the Islamic ulema to provide leadership for the empire during this time. In an age calling for visionary thinking to meet new and unprecedented challenges, their obsolete intellectual preparation seemed to leave the ulema paralyzed. Even more surprising was the eclipse, for the moment, of the military leadership in directing the reform movement. The weak performance of the Ottoman military in the 1820s and 1830s showed up inadequacies not only of military administration but also of officer training, which would take two generations to remediate. By 1876, Ottoman armies could defeat weaker Balkan states and, in the early stages of the Russian war in 1877, achieve moderate success against the Russian army. It was not until the turn of the twentieth century, however, that a vibrant officer corps reemerged in the Ottoman Empire.

Mustafa Reşid Pasha, a young career administrator who had served as ambassador to Paris, led the Council of Justice. A creation of Mahmud II, now revised, enlarged, and given consultative and quasi-legislative functions, the Council of Justice was led by the men of the Tanzimat who spearheaded the reform movement in its initial phase. Mustafa Reşid Pasha served as Grand Vezir six times before his death in 1858 and he or one of his protégés, Ali Pasha and Fuad Pasha, held the powerful post of foreign minister continuously until 1871, except for a brief period in the 1840s.

The Council of Justice began a reorganization of provincial government and revenue collection in 1840. Taxation was simplified. The main taxes, the tithe on Muslims, a poll tax on non-Muslims, and a group of other fees, were to be collected by government officials; tax-farming, contracting, and franchising were abolished. Meanwhile, a general conscription began, and the state sponsored the building of factories for the production of military supplies and clothing. Although direct taxation and conscription fell far short of expectations due to a shortage of trained officials, experimentation with ways of improving central control of the provinces—including a brief trial of a representative provincial council in 1845—continued until 1858.

Legal changes accompanied these efforts. A new penal code and a new commercial code were issued in the early 1840s. The commercial code, revised periodically throughout the 1850s and 1860s, was designed to accommodate the economic and commercial liberalism of the Tanzimat. Commercial tribunals composed of mixed boards of judges, Muslim and Christian, including European, administered it after 1847. The Ottoman Bank, founded in 1841, channeled European investment in the empire. In spite of its name, it was not Ottoman owned.

The second phase of the Tanzimat era began with the Imperial Rescript of 1856, which reiterated the principles of 1839 and added some new measures. After the death of Mustafa Reşid Pasha in 1858, the dominant figures were his pupils Ali Pasha and Fuad Pasha. The Council of Justice continued to evolve, being at first divided into two bureaus in 1856, one a specifically legal body and the other called the High Council of the Tanzimat, with Fuad Pasha as president. The two bureaus merged in

1860 and then were once again divided in 1868, one becoming a nascent Ministry of Justice under the important scholar and jurist Ahmed Cevdet Pasha, the other a State Council on which sat both Muslims and Christians. Cevdet Pasha became the principal author of a new civil code, usually called simply the *Mecelle*, promulgated between 1869 and 1876. Cevdet represented a slightly different strain of Tanzimat thinking, being less apt to distinguish imperial law from Islamic law than Reşid Pasha, who had once responded to a question about the relationship of his civil code to sharia, Islamic holy law, "this has nothing to do with sharia." Significantly, he had titled the 1840 penal code *kanun*, evoking the classical Ottoman ideology of the parallel authority of Islamic and sultanic law. Cevdet's interest was in exploring the integration of faith with various aspects of imperial life. Under his authorship, the *Mecelle* was essentially a codification and rationalization of Islamic law for imperial purposes. It lay the foundation of all subsequent Ottoman, Turkish, and Middle Eastern legal reform.

In pursuit of the aim of the equality under the law of all Ottoman citizens, the Imperial Rescript of 1856 abolished the poll tax on non-Muslims. Now non-Muslims were subject to military conscription, but they could pay an exemption fee, which became essentially the equivalent of the old poll tax. The status of non-Muslims in the empire had become increasingly ambiguous during the era of the Tanzimat for a number of reasons.

Non-Muslims in the Ottoman Empire had always lived under conditions of simultaneous official state toleration and official state discrimination. Community life among Jews and Christians evolved into a symbiotic relationship between community religious and commercial leaders and Ottoman state officials, much as it did among Muslim communities. Christian and Jewish peoples related to the Ottoman state and its officials through the semiautonomous institutions of their *millets*, their religio-national communities. There was freedom of worship; the sacred texts were copied, read, and studied; weddings, baptisms, and funerals were conducted; and the like. Christian and Jewish communities in the major cities operated their own schools and courts of law. These communities or millets were organized only very loosely at the empire-wide level, and Christian and Jewish communities in the far-flung corners of the empire evolved with a fair degree of independence and some regional variety, establishing their own set of traditional rules and relationships with local Ottoman officials and Muslim community leaders. In this way, the Christian and especially the Jewish communities of the

Ottoman Empire had flourished during the period of greatest Ottoman power.

In the nineteenth century, several factors brought a gradual change in the status of the Christian and Jewish populations of the empire. The Ottoman government and the non-Muslim religious leaders tended to cooperate in the gradual centralization of authority in officials of the religious hierarchy, each finding it to their advantage. Hence, the increasing tendency among both to think in terms of an imperial "millet system" during the era of the Tanzimat. The Imperial Rescript of 1856 sought to curb the authority of the often obscurantist high clerics of the Greek and Armenian Christian millets in particular and to bolster the power of lay leadership. This accorded well with the Tanzimat aim of encouraging a broadly Ottomanist loyalty among all subjects of the empire, Muslim and non-Muslim. It also pleased the Western European powers, whose Catholic and Protestant missionaries and whose merchants had difficulty penetrating the Christian communities of the empire because of the entrenched power of the Ottoman clerical hierarchies and their commercial clients.

Jews and urban Christian merchants were generally in the best position to take advantage of and benefit from the Ottoman Tanzimat policy of economic liberalization. These men possessed the greatest available assets to invest in foreign trade. They often had the best business contacts both in the empire and abroad and the best access to foreign capital. Some even succeeded in applying the Capitulations to themselves. The Capitulations were a set of agreements between the Ottoman government and foreign commercial communities reached at various times during the sixteenth and seventeenth centuries, granting privileges such as tax exemptions and low tariffs, and allowing them to fall under the legal jurisdiction of their own consuls rather than the Ottoman courts. During the Ottoman classical age, when the Ottomans were a dominant power, the foreign merchants few in number and the scope of their commercial activities limited, it caused little harm to make such arrangements. In the eighteenth and nineteenth centuries, however, the power relation shifted in favor of the European governments represented by the foreign merchants. The merchants and their consuls, backed by their home governments, manipulated and exploited the old agreements to their commercial and political advantage, using their rights of extraterritoriality to build powerful financial enterprises in Ottoman lands that stood wholly outside the Ottoman political reach.

Some Muslim communities in the cities and large towns gradually began to resent the relative prosperity of their Christian and Jewish neighbors, perceiving that official policy favored the non-Muslims. Demoralized by the poor performance and defeat of the "victorious armies of the Prophet" in wars with non-Muslim powers, many Ottoman Muslims began to emphasize the Islamic character of the empire. Finding nationalist ideas and literature everywhere the topic of discussion, and faced with the increasing hostility of the Muslim communities, Ottoman Christians became especially attracted to nationalism and, even in the majority Muslim regions of the empire, came to sympathize increasingly with the national aspirations of their coreligionists in the Balkans.

The Law of Provinces of 1864 extended the compromise of centralization and local control, thereby reorganizing the provinces hierarchically as *vilayets* under the full control of a *vali* or governor. Each vilayet contained several subordinate sanjaks or districts, each district contained a number of *kazas* or counties, each county was made up of several *nahiyes* or townships, and each township contained numerous villages. The governors were assisted by local general assemblies, composed of representatives, both Muslim and non-Muslim, from each sancak. Four vilayets piloted the new provincial order beginning in 1865, among them the reconfigured province of Erzurum in northeastern Anatolia.

Eastern Thrace and Anatolia, the territory which would later comprise the Republic of Turkey, was divided into about eighteen new provinces. The independent sanjak of İzmit bridged both sides of the Bosphorus, and Biga became another independent sanjak along the southern Marmara coast, while Thrace on both sides of the Maritsa, together with the Gallipoli Peninsula, comprised Edirne province. The Anatolian vilayets included Hüdavendigar, centered on the city of Bursa; Aydın in the Menderes Valley; Ankara, Kastamonu, Konya, and Sivas in central Anatolia; Trabzon along the eastern Black Sea coast; Erzurum, Van, Bitlis, and Diyarbakır in the east; and Adana in Cilicia. The towns of Maraş and Urfa were part of the vilayet of Aleppo. The great lords of southern and southeastern Anatolia, who had in cooperation with the Armenian clergy successfully held out against the imperial campaigns when Mahmud II defeated the lords of western and central Anatolia in the 1820s, were now brought to heel. Using a combination of intimidation backed by force, conciliation through the offer of imperial service, and imperially funded public works projects such as swamp drainage, Ottoman armies finally incorporated Cilicia and the southeastern steppes into the new provincial system between 1865 and 1876.

THE EASTERN QUESTION

In 1826, at the urging of the Russian tsar, the European powers inter-vened in the Greek rebellion, destroying the Ottoman fleet at Navarino Bay in October 1827. Russian armies took Edirne and advanced within forty miles of Istanbul. In the Treaty of Adrianople of 1829, the Ottomans were forced to cede territory to Russia in eastern Anatolia and at the mouth of the Danube. Russia won a protectorate over the Danubian prin-cipalities, and Greece gained recognition of its autonomy; it gained in-dependence the next year.

At the height of the crisis with Russia, in 1829, Muhammad Ali of Egypt turned on the Ottoman Empire, sending troops into Syria in late 1831 under the command of his son Ibrahim, to claim what Mahmud II had promised him in return for his aid in the Greek rebellion. In 1832, the Egyptian armies took all of western Syria and Cilicia and crossed the Taurus Mountains into the Anatolian plateau. At Konya in December 1832, they defeated the main Ottoman army and took the Grand Vezir prisoner. The road to Istanbul lay open before them. At this point, Russia came to the assistance of Mahmud II, forcing Muhammad Ali to with-draw across the Taurus and signing an alliance at Hünkiar İskelesi in July 1833 that gave Russia a privileged naval and commercial position regarding the Straits. The Straits Convention of 1841 closed the Straits to foreign warships when the Ottoman Empire was at peace, pleasing Rus-sia, but in effect made the regime of the Straits a matter of international importance. For the remainder of the century, British and French policy concerning the "Eastern Question," as it came to be known, aimed to prevent Russian domination of east central Europe. The Crimean War (1853–1856), ostensibly about control of the Christian shrines of Jerusa-lem, was really a war over the balance of power in Europe, in which a coalition of French, British, and Ottoman armies defeated Russia.

The unification of Italy (1860), the defeat of the Habsburg Empire by Prussia and its subsequent reorganization as the Austro-Hungarian Empire, and the unification of Germany under Prussian leadership (1871) put the issues of the Eastern Question into a slightly different context. Both Italy and Germany showed interest in influencing and investing in the Ottoman Empire. Russia and Austria began to cooperate with Ger-many, forming the conservative "Three Emperors' League" in the early 1870s. Habsburg policy, moreover, was affected by the creation of the Dual Monarchy and the new influence of the Hungarian parliament. Britain and France began to consider that there might be worse possibilities than those presented by a Russian domination of east central Europe. Domination of east central Europe by a united and powerful Germany had equally dangerous potential for European security. Thus, when a new crisis arose in the Balkans in 1875, it was keenly watched by the European powers.

The crisis of 1875 was precipitated by the crash of international stock markets in 1873 and the beginning of a world depression. In that year and the next, disastrous agricultural harvests in Anatolia produced widespread famine and urban migration of peasants. By 1875, the Ottoman government faced a desperate financial situation. Finding it impossible to reschedule payment of its loans with its European creditors, the Ottoman Empire defaulted on its foreign debt.

In July 1875, an insurrection of peasants in Bosnia and Hercegovina broke out. Ottoman authorities were unable to suppress the revolt, which was aided by sympathetic Serbian and Montenegrin volunteers. In April 1876, Ottoman officials discovered a conspiracy of Bulgarian nationalists, hatched in the Danubian principalities with aid by Serbia. The Bulgarian rebels, forced to act prematurely, slaughtered many Turks. Their revolt was violently suppressed by the Ottomans, who committed shocking atrocities, murdering several thousand Bulgarians. Popular opinion in Western Europe turned with revulsion against the Turks. On May 30, Sultan Abdülaziz was overthrown and replaced by the liberal Murad V. Weeks later, Serbia and Montenegro declared war on the Ottoman Empire. The Ottoman armies rather handily defeated them, opening the way to Belgrade by the fall. In August 1876, Murad V was deposed due to mental incompetence, and the comparatively unknown Sultan Abdülhamid II acceded to the Ottoman throne.

That fall, the Ottomans promulgated a constitution and rejected the peace settlement the European powers attempted to dictate. In March 1877, the war with Serbia and Montenegro was finally concluded, but Russia promptly declared war. At first encountering surprising difficulty, in the late fall and early winter, however, the Russians turned the tide, taking Edirne in February 1878. In Anatolia, Russian troops occupied Batum, Kars, and Ardahan. The Ottomans were forced to sue for peace.

The outstanding feature of the severe Treaty of San Stefano (1878), dictated by the Russians, was its creation of a Greater Bulgaria encompassing lands on both sides of the Balkan Mountains and Thrace and Macedonia. The treaty granted independence to Montenegro, almost tripling its size, and to Serbia, which gained Nish, and to the Romanian principalities, which gained the Danubian delta and Dobrudja but lost southern Bessarabia to Russian annexation. The Bulgarian state, likely to be the strongest in the Balkans, was to be occupied by Russian troops for two years and was to serve as an instrument of Russian control of the Balkans. The Balkan states other than Bulgaria and Montenegro found these terms unacceptable, as did Britain and Austria-Hungary. The European powers then forced Russia to renegotiate the treaty at an international congress called for Berlin in the summer of 1878.

The Treaty of Berlin redrew the map of southeastern Europe. The Greater Bulgaria of San Stefano was divided into three parts. Bulgaria became an autonomous tributary principality north of the Balkan Mountains, with Sofia as its capital. Russian troops would be withdrawn after nine months. South of the Balkan Mountains, Eastern Rumelia was created as a semiautonomous province with a Christian governor chosen by the Ottoman authorities with the approval of the European powers. Macedonia, Thrace, and Albania remained under Ottoman control. Montenegro, reduced in size somewhat, became independent, as did Serbia, with Nish, and Romania. Greece was largely unaffected and left to negotiate its precise border in western Thrace with the Ottoman government. Austria-Hungary occupied the Ottoman provinces of Bosnia and Hercegovina and won the right to administer the Sanjak of Novi Pazar, northeast of Montenegro. Russia kept the eastern Anatolian provinces of Batum, Kars, and Ardahan. In a separate agreement, the Ottoman Empire ceded the island of Cyprus to Great Britain.

The Treaty of Berlin dramatically changed the Ottoman Empire. The empire's territory in Europe had been significantly diminished through the creation of mostly hostile, expansionist states for whom anti-Turkishness became an element of national ideology and the continued existence of Turkish or Muslim minorities within the national boundaries a source of discomfort. Hundreds of thousands of Muslim refugees from the Balkan states flooded across the Ottoman border in Thrace or made their way to Istanbul. In Bulgaria especially, the war had produced a human disaster. Nearly half the 1.5 million Muslims, mainly Turks, living in prewar Bulgaria were gone by 1879. An estimated 200,000 had died and the rest became permanent refugees in Ottoman territory. Some of these were Crimean exiles driven from the Russian Empire in the previous generation. An estimated one-third of the Muslims of Bosnia and Hercegovina died or fled. Most of the much smaller Muslim populations of Serbia and Montenegro left those countries. With the loss of the Balkan territories and the influx of Muslim refugees, Muslims now constituted the great majority of the population of the Ottoman Empire—approximately 75 percent of the total. Geographically and demographically, the center of the Ottoman Empire had shifted to Anatolia.

THE REIGN OF SULTAN ABDÜLHAMID II

In the midst of the international crisis that was shortly to lead to war with Russia, in August 1876, the Ottoman liberals raised Abdülhamid II to the throne, after having received the prince's prior approval of a draft constitution. The Ottoman constitution of 1876 arose ultimately from ideas expressed by a small group of dissidents critical of the free trade liberalism, the bureaucratic authoritarianism, and the perceived inattention to Islamic tradition of the Tanzimat. These dissidents, called as a group the Young Ottomans, had organized in the mid-1860s against the Tanzimat regime of Ali Pasha and Fuad Pasha. Prominent among them was the journalist and poet Namık Kemal, who had read widely in French and English enlightenment literature. He brought together Islam and constitutionalism in a system of political philosophy that made use of the ancient notion of an ideal Islamic community governed by the *meşveret*, or "consultation," of the prophet and his closest followers in the interpretation of the word of God. To the Young Ottomans, constitutional liberty and Islamic holy law were not only compatible but mutually reinforcing.

The constitution guaranteed personal liberty and the rule of law. It provided for a bicameral parliament. Unfortunately, a number of clauses actually preserved the unrestricted authority of the sultan. The constitution became law only by his decree and did not deny his right to continue to rule by executive order. His ministers initiated bills to be considered by the parliament, and the sultan kept veto power over its acts. He could exile any person deemed a threat to the security of the empire, and he could dissolve the legislature without setting a date for new elections. Early in 1877, it became clear that Sultan Abdülhamid II had little intention of becoming a constitutional monarch. After the first elections were held in December 1876 through January 1877 and the new legislature called to session, Midhat Pasha, author of the constitution, was sent into exile. Within a year, Abdülhamid dismissed parliament and suspended the constitution indefinitely. Parliament did not meet for the remaining thirty years of his rule.

It might at first appear that Sultan Abdülhamid was opposed to modernization and reform, but this was not the case. The reign of Abdülhamid II represents the culmination of the Tanzimat by summing up the nineteenth century Ottoman effort at modernization through authoritarian reform from above. Abdülhamid continued the policies of bureaucratic centralization and administrative rationalization begun by the early Tanzimat reformers, but now the reigns of power became increasingly concentrated in the sultan's own hands. The palace secretariat achieved a dominant position over the Ministry of the Interior so that Abdülhamid personally ran the empire from his own household.

The most important areas of modernization during the reign of Abdülhamid then were, not surprisingly, in education and communications. There was no unified system of education in the Ottoman Empire at this time. Several overlapping systems existed, including public schools, a military academy system of schools, private schools run by the millets, the Islamic system of mosque schools and medrese seminaries, schools operated by foreign missionaries, and secondary technical schools such as an agricultural school, a veterinary school, a school of industrial arts, and the like. Abdülhamid's contribution came in the expansion of the public school network, particularly at the primary level which Ali Pasha had laid out on paper in 1869. And it was under Sultan Abdülhamid II that the first Ottoman university, the Darülfünûn in Istanbul, opened in 1900.

The miles of paved roads in the empire quadrupled between 1858 and 1904—although the total was still quite small. Distances covered by telegraph lines more than doubled between 1882 and 1904, and the volume of mail carried by the postal network more than doubled between 1888 and 1904. Telephone service and electricity were introduced, but the sultan's personal fears prevented its spread beyond small quarters of Istanbul. Railroads showed the biggest communications advance of all. Railroad building progressed very slowly after its start in the 1850s, and by 1888, there were only 1,780 kilometers of operational track laid in the empire. In Anatolia, these were limited to a line between İzmit and Haydarpaşa Station in Istanbul, between Bursa and Mudanya, and a line in the Menderes Valley to İzmir. But in 1888, the Ottoman government contracted with the Deutsche Bank for the extension of the Istanbul-İzmit line through Ankara, Adana, and Aleppo to Baghdad and the Persian Gulf. The railroading boom took off in the Ottoman Empire. By the end of Abdülhamid's reign, the total length of track laid in the empire had tripled. After 1888, the railroad industry became the most important sector of foreign investment in the Ottoman economy.

But Abdülhamid was a paranoiac. He built up a vast network of spies, whose reports he collected and read by the thousands. His secret police was notorious. In public, this aspect of Abdülhamid's personality was expressed in the regime's obsession with image. Historian Selim Deringil has shown that Abdülhamid perfected the use of imperial ceremonies and symbols and public representations and demonstrations as a means of communicating the power of the Ottoman state both to its citizens and to its international rivals, (Selim Deringil, *The Well-Protected Domains: Ideology and the Legitimation of Power in the Ottoman Empire 1876–1909* [London, 1998]). Ironically, his arming of the Hamidian Regiments, units of Kurdish irregulars who carried out brutal killings and massacres of thousands of Christian Armenians in eastern Anatolia in the 1890s, probably irreparably damaged his reputation abroad.

A main feature of the regime's construction and manipulation of its image consisted in emphasizing Sultan Abdülhamid II as caliph of the Muslims. The Ottoman sultans inherited the title when Sultan Selim I conquered Egypt in 1517. The sultans had occasionally made rhetorical use of the title, but for most of the Ottoman centuries it was more or less taken for granted that the Ottoman sultans held the caliphate. In a world increasingly overrun by powerful European Christian empires, possession of the caliphate allowed Abdülhamid to stake a claim for the rightful place of the Ottoman Empire as the legitimate representative of Islam on the world stage. And in an empire whose population now had a strongly Muslim majority, it had potential as a unifying imperial ideology.

THE OTTOMAN DEBT

During the reign of Sultan Abdülhamid II, the financial situation of the Ottoman Empire was dire as a result of its overwhelming level of foreign debt. The Ottoman Empire in the last quarter of the nineteenth century was obviously not a poor country. Once a slow recovery from the depression of 1873 began, in the last years of the nineteenth century and first years of the twentieth the Ottoman economy prospered as never before. The unfettered laissez-faire policies of the Tanzimat were reigned in through the imposition of moderate import duties and protective trade restrictions, under which both manufacturing and agriculture experienced a significant boom between 1881 and the beginning of the First World War in 1914. The Ottoman bankruptcy came as a consequence of overly ambitious loan policies followed by European banks and by the persistently inadequate Ottoman methods of revenue assessment and collection.

The Ottoman debt problem dated back to 1854, when the empire contracted its first loan with European creditors shortly after the beginning of the Crimean War. In the next twenty years, the Ottoman debt soared to 21 billion kurush. The main investors—the French and after them the British and then the Germans—channeled most of the capital through the Imperial Ottoman Bank, shares of which were held by European financial institutions. In the empire, the government used the money especially to modernize the army and the navy, which reached respectable standards by the time of the war with Russia in 1877–1878. The general staff was reorganized, conscription comprehensively enforced, and new equipment and weaponry purchased.

After a time, the majority of the money, however, went simply to service the debt itself. Interest on the debt consumed 1.4 billion kurush annually, more than half the entire 1876 Ottoman budget. Through negotiations during the next five years, Abdülhamid's government handed over to its European creditors a substantial percentage—about one-third—of the Ottoman economy. In 1881, the Ottoman Public Debt Administration (PDA) was created for the purpose of administering the empire's debt repayment. This European administrative bureau eventually employed about 5,000 people—more than the Ottoman Ministry of Finance. It collected and administered the revenues of whole provinces, certain state monopolies, and a host of other taxes and duties. After satisfying overhead costs, these revenues were assigned to the service of the Ottoman debt. The PDA operated more efficiently than did the Ottoman finance ministry and succeeded in improving the process of revenue collection. The PDA also served as the broker for additional foreign loans contracted by the Ottoman government.

By the beginning of the twentieth century, the Ottoman central government had largely succeeded in recovering control of administration of the provinces that remained to it, and it had used this control to direct a strong program of economic development. The purpose of arming, outfitting, and staffing a modernized military to defend itself had mostly proved successful. The Ottoman army defeated Greece in a brief war in 1897, and although it was not in the same league as the major military powers of Western Europe, it could confidently expect to perform well in a war against its most likely adversaries, the Balkan states and even Russia, if the war were of short duration. In the first years of the new century, however, its most ominous weaknesses stemmed from the domination of the economy by foreigners and non-Muslim minorities, and the tight control of the civil bureaucracy and the senior officer corps by an aging and eccentric sultan.

6

Revolution and War, 1908–1923

In July 1908, junior officers of the Ottoman Third Army, stationed in Macedonia, and Second Army in Edirne, mutinied, demanding restoration of the 1876 Ottoman constitution. The Young Turks who revolted were members of the Committee of Union and Progress (CUP). Their rebellion, and the revolution it began, completely altered the modern history of Turkey.

THE REVOLUTION OF THE YOUNG TURKS

The Committee of Union and Progress had been formed in Paris in 1889 by Ottoman émigrés opposed to Sultan Abdülhamid's regime. The group, known there as *Jeunes Turques* or "The Young Turks," was led by Ahmet Rıza, the son of a member of the first Ottoman parliament. In 1895, he began publishing a journal in both French and Ottoman called *Meşveret*, or Consultation, whose motto was "Order and Progress." Two major schools of thought emerged at the Young Turks congresses held in Paris in 1902 and 1907. One group supported Ahmet Rıza, who envisioned a secular nation of Turks pursuing the modern European ideals of scientific advancement and rational progress. They advocated nationalist economic policies and opposed European intervention on behalf of

Armenians in the empire. The other group supported Prince Sabahettin, a member of the Ottoman dynasty who had arrived in Paris in 1899 with his father and brother. Prince Sabahettin was an economic liberal and an Ottomanist, who wanted to create a unified, multinational and multireligious empire. Prince Sabahettin favored decentralization and free enterprise, and advocated the introduction of foreign capital into the empire as a means of economic development and cooperation with the European powers for protection of the rights of Armenians. Prince Sabahettin, moreover, expressed a greater sympathy for the role of Islam in a modernized Ottoman Empire.

Secret opposition cells also formed in the empire's major cities and particularly among army officers in Jaffa, Jerusalem, Damascus, and other places but with little contact or coordination among themselves or with Armenian opposition groups. In Salonika, a group called the Ottoman Freedom Society (*Osmanlı Hürriyet Cemiyeti*) was formed in 1906. The deft administrative leadership of Mehmet Talat, the chief telegraph clerk in the post office of Salonika, and the work of Major Enver, an officer in the Third Army there, brought greater coordination of small groups scattered throughout Macedonia. This group established contact with the Ahmet Rıza group of émigrés in Paris, adopted its name, and quickly became the center of the opposition within the empire.

In the summer of 1908, Tsar Nicholas II of Russia and King Edward VII of Britain met to settle the Macedonian question. The CUP members among the Ottoman officer corps in Macedonia, seeing in this meeting the potential for the dissolution of the empire, decided that the time for action had come. Majors Enver and Niyazi, refusing a summons to Istanbul, fled instead to the hills with their troops, demanding the restoration of the Ottoman constitution. Efforts to suppress the rebellion failed, the mutiny spread, and the Third Army threatened to march on Istanbul. The sultan capitulated to the rebels' demands.

In spite of their victory and the enthusiasm it generated, the Young Turks did not want to depose the sultan or overthrow the government directly but preferred to manipulate politics from behind the scenes. Acutely aware of their own weakness in numbers and organization, they also recognized the formidable reputation of Sultan Abdülhamid. The CUP, though well organized in the southern Balkans, was not especially strong elsewhere in the empire. Concentrating on its delicate relationships with members in the other provinces, as well as with other opposition groups, the CUP prepared for elections to the first parliament of the new era, to be held in December 1908. In these elections, the CUP faced the only one organized opposition party, the Ottoman Liberal Party of Prince Sabahettin.

The CUP won a sweeping victory, with the Ottoman Liberal Party winning only one of the 288 seats. Ahmet Rıza was elected speaker. But the CUP victory galvanized the conservative opposition. In February 1909, the Grand Vezir Kâmil Pasha challenged the committee by dismissing two of its cabinet ministers, of war and of the navy. The CUP engineered a parliamentary vote of no confidence, forcing the Grand Vezir's resignation. The anti-Unionist opposition groups then mounted a press campaign against the committee. The anti-Unionist discontent was diverse. There were Young Turk liberals who preferred the ideas of Prince Sabahettin, and there were religious conservatives, including many lower-ranking ulema and dervish order leaders who claimed that the revolution had overturned a sharia regime. Other opponents of the CUP included unemployed civil servants, who had found themselves the unfortunate victims of public sector budget cuts, and career soldiers, who resented the new emphasis on academy training and new tactics and technology. The anti-Unionists had almost nothing in common except their opposition to the CUP.

Demonstrations broke out at the funeral of Hasan Fehmi, a slain anti-Unionist editor. On the night of 12 April 1909, members of the Muhammadan Union, an extremist religious organization, provoked an armed uprising among troops of the First Army in its Istanbul garrison. Crowds of people joined the troops in the public square in front of parliament, demanding "restoration" of the sharia, and dismissal and banishment of unionist ministers and officers. Overly confident of their strength, the liberals had probably instigated the revolt but, seriously underestimating the intensity of religious resentment of the new order, found themselves unable to control or direct the unrest. Prominent Unionists went into hiding or fled. Demonstrations and violence broke out elsewhere in the empire; in Adana, thousands of Armenians were killed in a brutal anti-Christian pogrom.

In Macedonia, still the center of the CUP strength, the Unionists regrouped. Units of army regulars, led by the respected commander of the Third Army, Mahmud Şevket Paşa, advanced by rail to positions outside Istanbul. On 24 April 1909, Mahmud Şevket Paşa's "Action Army" occupied the capital. Three days later, parliament deposed Sultan Abdülhamid II, replacing him with his brother Mehmed V Reşad. In mid-May, public executions finished the attempted counterrevolution.

THE YOUNG TURKS AND OTTOMAN POLITICS, 1909–1913

Between the suppression of the counterrevolution in April 1909 and the final Ottoman defeat in World War One in October 1918, the Young Turks began a reform of the Ottoman regime. These years may be divided into two distinct periods, before and after January 1913. Before that date, the political position of the CUP was weak. In January 1913, the CUP staged a coup and took over control of the machinery of government. From this point forward, they attempted a thorough transformation of Ottoman society from the top down. Recently, historians such as Erik Jan Zürcher have stressed that many of the political, economic, and social measures initiated by the CUP during this period anticipated the reforms enacted later under the republican regime of Mustafa Kemal Atatürk (Eric Jan Zürcher, *The Unionist Factor: The Role of the Committee of Union and Progress in the Turkish National Movement* [Leiden, 1984]; see also the same author's *Turkey: A Modern History* [London and New York, 1993], pp. 97–183). The Young Turks were ultimately unsuccessful because they were handicapped by the enormous burden of the Ottoman debt and because they fought World War I on the losing side.

A series of measures consolidated the constitutional regime. The authority of the sultan was restricted to appointing the Grand Vezir and Shaykhulislam, and the palace budget was scaled back. Only a vote of no confidence could dissolve parliament, and that now had to be followed by timely elections. Parliament made laws and contracted treaties. Restrictive new laws on rights of assembly, organization, and the press were enacted.

In economic policy, the government initially followed a classic liberal approach in order to improve the position of the empire in the hopes of attracting additional foreign loans. Laws on ownership, association, and commerce were modernized, and tariffs and other barriers removed in favor of free trade. Agricultural policy favored the large landholders; modern machinery and infrastructure were available, inducements were offered for investment, and no efforts were made toward land redistribution. Measures to improve the efficiency of tax collection helped increase revenues, and budget cuts were achieved by eliminating many positions in the bureaucracy, including the army. Organized labor was discouraged. It therefore came as a disappointment when the British and French governments rejected looser loan arrangements sought by the Ottomans in 1910. The Young Turks turned to a more willing German government to contract the loan on better terms.

The international situation of the empire deteriorated steadily after 1908. The Young Turk government found itself in a perpetual state of crisis from the moment of the revolution in 1908. In October 1908, Austria-Hungary annexed the Balkan provinces of Bosnia and Herce-govina that it had occupied since 1878. At the same time King Ferdinand of Bulgaria declared independence from the empire. In the following years, the Young Turks dealt with the revolt of Imam Yahya in Yemen, with recurrent unrest among nationalist Albanians in Kosovo and Mon-tenegro, and with the Italian occupation of both Libya and the Dodeca-nese Islands in the Aegean Sea.

Disaffected by the general drift of the CUP policy, a group of deputies led by a Colonel Sadık Bey left the CUP to form a new party. Its platform declared support not only for democratic institutions but also for "pre-serving general religious and national ethics and morals," and the main-tenance of historic Ottoman traditions, specifically the "sacred rights of the Caliphate and Sultanate." A radical secularist group of the CUP re-sponded to this conservative declaration, forming the Progress Party. The local by-elections in December 1911 brought all of the latent anti-Unionist opposition out into the open, becoming serious contests in which true opposition candidates ran against and defeated mainstream CUP mem-bers. But the CUP leadership shrewdly dissolved parliament in January and called general elections for April 1912. The CUP rigged these elec-tions and won 269 of 275 seats.

A group of young officers headed by Colonel Sadık now conspired against the CUP. Calling themselves the "Savior Officers," they forced the cabinet to resign in July 1912. Their government, however, suc-cumbed to foreign policy difficulties. The ease with which Italy had im-posed its will on the Ottomans had not gone unnoticed in the Balkan states. Serbia and Bulgaria signed a defensive alliance in the spring of 1912, secretly agreeing to divide Macedonia. A Balkan coalition was con-structed, involving Serbia and Bulgaria, and Montenegro and Greece. On October 8, the First Balkan War commenced with a Montenegrin attack on the Ottoman Empire. Bulgarian troops quickly reached the outskirts of Istanbul. As the Bulgarian and Greek armies laid siege to Edirne, the Ottoman government floundered. On 8 November 1912, Salonika, home of the CUP and birthplace of the Young Turks revolution, fell to the advancing Greek army. By the beginning of December when an armistice was arranged by Britain, France, Germany and Russia, all that remained of the Ottoman Empire in Europe were four besieged cities: Istanbul, Edirne, Scutari, and Janina in Albania. This was the situation when on 23 January 1913, a group of the CUP officers led by Major Enver Bey burst into the room where the cabinet was believed (wrongly) to be discussing the surrender of Edirne, shot Nazım Pasha, the Minister of War, and forced the resignation of Kâmil Pasha at gunpoint.

THE CUP IN POWER

Having seized control of the empire, the CUP set itself to resolving the crisis and directing Ottoman government and society toward a modern transformation. They did so during the next several years while in an almost continual state of war. The officers turned once more to Mahmud Şevket Paşa, who became Grand Vezir and Minister of War and resumed the war. On March 26, Edirne fell to the Bulgarians, and the CUP was compelled to sue for peace. In the Treaty of London, signed on 10 June 1913 Istanbul and its immediate environs remained in Ottoman hands, but all the rest of the Balkan Peninsula was lost. Bulgaria kept the city of Edirne. A few days later, gunmen assassinated Mahmud Şevket Paşa in Istanbul.

The ink had hardly dried on the signatures of the peace treaty before the erstwhile allies fell to quarreling over the fruits of their conquest. In particular, the Macedonian issue resisted easy resolution and was further complicated by the problem of the independent Albania the peace conference had created. Seeking compensation, Greece and Serbia came to a mutual understanding and received Turkish help in forcing a revision. Bulgaria, rejecting the Serbian and Greek ultimatum and refusing a Russian offer of mediation, launched the Second Balkan War with a preemptive attack on Serbia at the end of June 1913. In this war, the Bulgarians, incapable of contending with Greece, Serbia, Romania, and the Ottoman Empire simultaneously, suffered a disastrous defeat. On July 20, the Ottoman army, led by Major Enver Bey, successfully reconquered Edirne and recovered eastern Thrace.

In Istanbul, where the recovery of Edirne was greeted with relief, the CUP faced the task of governing with a hardened attitude. The committee now came out into the open as a true political party. A powerful group of about fifty men, including certain cabinet ministers, provincial governors, and party operatives, directed important affairs. The Grand Vezir was Sait Halim Pasha. Talat, perhaps the most powerful man in the government, became Minister of the Interior. Major Enver Bey was promoted, made a pasha, and became Minister of War in the new cabinet. His army rival Cemal, the military governor of Istanbul, was also made a pasha. Enver Pasha made reorganization of the army a high priority, appointing the German General Bronsart von Schellendorf chief of staff and assigning numerous commands to other German officers.

In 1913, the CUP began a steady movement to reduce the legal reach of the Islamic sharia. A new civil code was enacted, and legislation pushed through in 1917 thoroughly reorganized religious affairs. The post of shaykhulislam was downgraded to subcabinet level, and three ministries took over responsibility for religious institutions: the Ministry of Justice gained control of the sharia courts, the Ministry of Education took over the religious colleges (*medreses*), and the Ministry of Religious Foundations was created to administer vakıfs. The legal reforms of the previous fifty years were codified.

The new CUP legislation attempted to improve the status of women generally. In the new family law, marriages must be conducted before a magistrate, the age of the bride must be eighteen and the groom twenty, and the capacity of women to initiate divorce was expanded. Compulsory primary school was extended to girls in 1913. Some courses at the Istanbul university were opened to women the following year. Women participated in the new nationalist clubs opening in many parts of Anatolia and the Balkans. Several new popular women's and family periodicals appeared regularly, such as *Kadmlar Dünyası* (Women's World) and *Çocuk Dünyası* (Children's World), both of which were first published in 1913. The first women's periodical in Turkish, *Hanmalra Mahsun Gazete* (Women's Own Journal), had been published since 1895.

The Balkan Wars seemed to many Young Turks to have shown the fruitlessness of Prince Sabahettin's ideal of a multinational empire. The Balkan peoples of the empire, even the Muslim Albanians, had clearly preferred nationalist solutions to their problems over anything offered in a multinational, multireligious Ottoman Empire. In the major cities of Anatolia, too, the non-Muslim businessmen and entrepreneurs had shown sympathy for the national aspirations of the Balkan peoples. The Young Turks regime after 1913, therefore, followed a more strongly nationalist economic policy in an effort both to free itself from the crippling restrictions imposed by foreign control of Ottoman finances and to protect and encourage the emergence of a genuinely national industry.

The Balkan wars gave added thrust to a nascent Turkish nationalism

among Turkish-speaking peoples in the Balkans and Anatolia, with official encouragement by the CUP. Under the influence of writers like Yusuf
Akçura, a Tatar immigrant to the Ottoman Empire from the Volga region, and Ziya Gökalp, a part-Kurd from Diyarbakır, who advocated
pan-Turkist ideals, this nationalism inevitably took on a broad, pan-
Turkist outlook, anticipating the unity of all Turks—in Anatolia, in
southeastern Europe, even in the Caucasus and in the central Eurasian
parts of the Russian Empire—in a single political entity. Enver Pasha
subscribed to this idea and spent the rest of his career working toward
this goal. A favorite project of Yusuf Akçura, the CUP-sponsored Turkish
Hearth movement of local civic cultural clubs also often expressed this
kind of feeling. It published a journal called *Türk Yurdu* (Turkish Homeland). It was not yet possible to think in terms of an Anatolian Turkish
nationalism because the Turks of Anatolia were not different from the
Turks still living throughout the Balkan Peninsula.

Turkish nationalism was not the only ideology enjoying wide popular
support among Turks on the eve of World War I, Islamic groups, liberal
as well as reactionary, actively published journals and organized both
nationally and locally. Other intellectuals and government officials advocated a wholesale westernization of the empire. Among these, the
writer and publicist Abdullah Cevdet should be mentioned for his rather
unusual atheism. "There is no second civilization," he had written in his
journal *İçtihad* in 1911. "Civilization means European civilization." This
exciting intellectual and cultural activity was not halted by the outbreak
of war in 1914 but continued right through the war and into the postwar
era.

THE OTTOMAN EMPIRE AND THE FIRST WORLD WAR

World War I began with the assassination of the Austrian heir, the
Archduke Franz Ferdinand, by a Bosnian Serb in Sarajevo on 28 June
1914. Serbia's rejection of an Austrian ultimatum activated a complex
system of military alliances among the European powers with the result
that by August 1914, much of Europe had gone to war. Austria-Hungary,
Germany, and Italy were linked in the Triple Alliance, while Russian
backing of Serbia invoked its alliance with France. Russia, France and
England formed the Entente powers. As the European diplomatic situation deteriorated and the states of the continent slid toward war, the
Young Turk government sought an alliance with one of the two power
blocs, its paramount concern being to avoid the kind of diplomatic iso-

lation that it had endured in the Balkan wars of 1912–1913. The CUP approached France and Britain but they rebuffed the Ottoman advances, having already determined that their best interests lay in maintaining their ties with Russia. The CUP inner circle turned to Germany, entering a secret alliance on August 2, but even this did not necessarily mean that the Ottoman Empire would join the conflict. Terms of the agreement called for German protection of the Ottoman Empire and for the continued role of the German military mission in the event a Russian attack brought Germany into the war. The Young Turks stayed out of the conflict until November, when Germany's, and Enver's, skillful manipulation of the celebrated incident of the *Goeben* and the *Breslau* ended the official Ottoman neutrality.

The *Goeben* and the *Breslau* were German warships sent to the Straits in August 1914 to compensate the Ottomans for the loss of two ships the Young Turks had ordered from Great Britain in 1911, which the English never delivered. The *Goeben* and *Breslau* arrived at the Dardanelles, dodging and outrunning the British and French navies across the length of the Mediterranean Sea. Enver Pasha permitted them entry and, when under the conditions of the Ottoman's neutrality the British demanded their return, purchased them for a nominal fee. Renamed the *Yavuz Sultan Selim*, the battleship *Goeben* attacked the Russian navy in the Black Sea in early November, provoking a Russian declaration of war and bringing the Ottoman Empire into the conflagration on the side of Germany. Sultan Mehmed V declared jihad, Holy War, on November 14.

Ottoman troops fought in World War I in four main theaters: in eastern Anatolia and the Caucasus, in Iraq, in Syria, and at the Straits. Russian troops attacked in the Caucasus before the end of November 1914. Repelling this thrust, Enver Pasha personally led a counterattack. The Ottoman advance stalled and was halted in a devastating defeat at Sarıkamış, where 86 percent of an Ottoman force of 100,000 troops were lost in January 1915. The following year, the Russians penetrated deep into Anatolia, taking Trabzon on the Black Sea, as well as Van and Erzurum. Even after the Russian revolution, the Russians did not evacuate these positions before the spring of 1918, when the treaty of Brest-Litovsk had been signed. During the summer of 1918, the Ottomans launched a new offensive in eastern Anatolia. In this campaign, Ottoman troops occupied Azerbaijan, including the city of Baku on the Caspian Sea, before they were forced to withdraw with the war's end.

Cemal Pasha was turned back at the Suez Canal in February 1915. Returning to Syria, these troops saw little action until 1916. In Syria,

Cemal Pasha's harsh administration alienated the Arabs from Ottoman rule. A second attempt to seize the Suez Canal failed in the late summer of 1916, and in June of that year Arab irregulars under the leadership of Husayn, the Sharif of Mecca, and his sons, attacked the Ottoman garrison at Medina. Thus began the famous Arab revolt, in which T. E. Lawrence—Lawrence of Arabia—figured prominently. The Arab troops succeeded in cutting the Ottoman supply line to the Hejaz and capturing the port of Aqaba. In the last year of the war, the Arab troops linked up with the British who, pushing out of Egypt, advanced north and took Jerusalem in December 1917.

In the spring of 1915, the British navy attempted to force its way into the Straits, launching a full-scale invasion of the Dardanelles at the end of April. Not expecting the Ottoman defenses to hold, the Young Turk government drew up contingency plans for an evacuation of the capital and flight to Anatolia. To the surprise of all, however, the British offensive withered after they had gained a beachhead. The British were forced to abandon the project and withdraw by the spring of 1916. At the same time, the British expeditionary force invading Mesopotamia stalled at Kut al-Imara in July 1916.

Performing well in most engagements until about 1917, the Ottoman armies significantly affected the outcome of the war by obliging the Entente powers to commit thousands of troops to theaters of war in the Ottoman Empire. By the end of 1917, however, the position of the Ottoman armies had declined. The Ottomans suffered heavy casualties in the campaigns of the first three years of the war, especially in eastern Anatolia. When Russia quit the war in late 1917, leaving Great Britain as the main Ottoman adversary, Ottoman troops were not as successful. After the Russian exit, the Ottomans fought on, hopeful that the Central Powers would eventually win the war. The complex and sometimes contradictory structure of diplomatic agreements the British had built with their allies, nearly all of which assumed the division of the Ottoman Empire, made them, too, spurn a negotiated peace.

Nowhere was the situation more grave than in eastern Anatolia, where an unparalleled human disaster had begun with the Russian invasion of late fall 1914. The Ottoman armies spent the winter in Erzurum after the Ottoman counteroffensive collapsed in early 1915, and when spring arrived, Russia resumed its advance. Hoping that Russia would support an independent Armenia after the war, thousands of Armenian nationalists fought in the Russian army against the Ottomans, deserted from the Ottoman army to the Russian army, or participated in guerrilla actions behind Ottoman lines. In response, the Ottoman authorities demobilized Armenians and then began killing them. Beginning in April 1915, efforts by Armenian communities around Lake Van to defend themselves were used as the justification for a policy of mass deportation of the Armenian population of Anatolia to the province of Diyarbakır that turned into a program of mass killing. Hundreds of thousands of Armenian men, women, and children were murdered or died of disease or starvation. The exact number of those who died is a matter of dispute, but most historians agree it was around 800,000 to 1,000,000 people.

In the aftermath of World War I and the Turkish War of Independence that immediately followed it, Turkish statesmen typically refused to acknowledge responsibility for the killings. Indisputable evidence that the Ottoman government ordered the extermination of the Armenians has never been found, and some of what has been purported to be evidence has been forged. But it is also true that the records of the Ottoman Special Organization (*Teşkilat-ı Mahsusa*), a shadowy unit controlled by the inner circle of the CUP leaders, were destroyed. It was the Special Organization that, through local provincial party bosses, directed the deportations and thus must be held ultimately responsible for the mass slaughter of Armenians.

Several factors—the policy of mass deportation itself, the scale of the killings, the arrest of Armenian members of parliament—make it difficult to escape the conclusion that at some level the atrocities perpetrated against the Ottoman Armenians in 1915–1916 were carried out and coordinated by Ottoman authorities. Mass deportation of Armenians, from not only the war zone but from all over the empire, seems a disproportionate and inhumane response to the problem of Armenian guerrilla activity and terrorism. And the death of close to a million people over the course of a year seems unlikely to have resulted merely from spontaneous outbursts of intercommunal violence, even given the level of tension between Christians and Muslims in Anatolia.

But according to historian Ronald Suny, the Armenian genocide was probably not planned in advance by the Ottoman government. Above all, there never was any Young Turks ideology of racial or religious superiority to Armenian Christians. It seems likely that the Ottoman policy carried out by the Special Organization was one of a harsh suppression and that with the removal of legal and social constraints against persecution, the policy turned into a drive of ethnic cleansing, to rid Anatolia of Armenians.

Since the foundation of the republic, Turkish officials have persisted in a denial of these massacres. The republican state was ethically compromised by having materially benefited from the confiscated land and property of Armenians. The republican leadership shared the goals and the nationalist ideology of the Young Turks, and feared that an admission of culpability for the genocide would jeopardize the project of nation building.

MUSTAFA KEMAL AND THE TURKISH NATIONALIST MOVEMENT

The First World War ended for the Ottoman Empire in the armistice of Mudros on 31 October 1918. All Ottoman troops were to be disarmed and demobilized except for a small policing force, Entente prisoners of war were to be freed, and German and Austrian-Hungarian military personnel were given two months to leave the empire. The victorious powers occupied the Straits, seized control of all rail and telegraph lines, and claimed the right to intervene to protect the Armenians in eastern Anatolia.

In November 1918, Sultan Mehmed VI, who had succeeded to the throne in July, dissolved parliament, determined to crush the Young Turks whom he held responsible for the defeat of the empire. On 1 January 1919, he opened court martial proceedings against Enver, Talat, and other leading Young Turk officials. He appointed his brother-in-law, Damad Ferid Pasha, Grand Vezir, a position he was to hold for much of the next two years in several different cabinets, and adopted a stance of cooperation with the conditions of the armistice in order to gain a reasonable peace settlement.

Nearly two years passed before the Entente statesmen finally concluded a peace treaty, the Treaty of Sèvres, for the Ottoman Empire. Preoccupied by the problem of the peace terms with Germany and believing the Ottomans must at any rate accept a dictated peace, the allies put off as long as possible the difficulties of sorting out their contradictory promises to one another about the postwar disposal of the Ottoman lands. They hoped, moreover, that under the aegis of the League of Nations, the United States would accept a mandate over Istanbul and the Straits and over the six provinces of the empire in which the heaviest concentrations of Armenians lived. But U.S. President Woodrow Wilson was in the end unable to deliver American support to the League of Nations or to take responsibility for a mandate in former Ottoman territory.

In contrast to the attitude of the sultan's government, most of Anatolia resisted domination by the Entente authorities from the beginning. Already in the winter and spring of 1919, an embryonic resistance movement formed in Anatolia, consisting of local councils and partisan fighting units. These were helped by last-minute efforts of Enver and Talat to ship out supplies and armaments before they fled the country, and by the existence of plans laid earlier during the Dardanelles campaign. A national guard called Karakol, founded by the CUP leadership just prior to the end of the war, supervised guerilla activities and the foundation of local "Societies for the Defense of Rights," and helped smuggle Unionist operatives out of Istanbul. But the movement was without strong leadership. In a decision that was to be momentous for Turkish history, the heads of the Karakol group contacted Mustafa Kemal Pasha. In Mustafa Kemal Pasha, later known as Atatürk, the Turkish nationalist resistance found a leader of extraordinary gifts.

Born in Salonika in 1881, Mustafa Kemal graduated from the War College in Istanbul in 1904. While in Damascus in 1906, he founded a secret opposition group. Transferred to the Third Army in Macedonia in 1907, he joined the CUP and took part in the army revolt that produced the Young Turk revolution, as well as the "Action Army" of Mahmud Şevket Pasha. He served in Libya in 1911 and in the Balkan Wars, after which he was posted to Sofia. Thought to belong to the party of Cemal Pasha, his relations with Enver Pasha were strained, and he was not brought into the government after the January 1913 CUP coup. During the First World War, he gained distinction for his valor at Gallipoli and was promoted to brigadier and pasha. In the last months of the war, as commander on the Syrian front, he supervised the Ottoman retreat from Syria. Karakol approached him because of his unassailable integrity, his commitment to the CUP, and because he had no personal links to the wartime policies of Enver and Talat Pashas.

At the same time, the sultan's government requested that he go to Anatolia to enforce the disarmament of the Ottoman troops there, in accordance with the conditions laid down in the Mudros armistice. He was assigned to eastern Anatolia with the title Inspector of the Third Army and given broad authority. While he prepared for this mission, in May 1919, the Entente powers permitted the Greek army to land at İzmir to enforce the armistice in western Anatolia. Greek troops seized the opportunity to begin an invasion of western Anatolia.

Landing in the Black Sea port of Samsun on 19 May 1919, Mustafa Kemal Pasha went to Amasya and immediately contacted the leaders of the local nationalist groups in eastern Anatolia by telegraph. In particular, he established a good working relationship with Brigadier Kâzim Pasha, commander of the Ninth Army based in Erzurum. In collaboration with Kâzim Pasha, Mustafa Kemal, and two staff officers, Hüseyin Rauf Bey and Refet Bey, composed and distributed a memorandum to the nationalist groups in eastern Anatolia. Dated 21 June 1919, this "Amasya Declaration" emphasized the peril of the nation, denounced the capacity of the sultan's government to defend it, and called on the nation to come to its own defense. A national congress was summoned to meet in Erzurum in July. Before that meeting took place, on July 5 the sultan's government, suspicious of his activities, recalled Mustafa Kemal to Istanbul. On July 8, alarmed at the lack of a response, the sultan relieved him of his command. Without an official command, the basis of Mustafa Kemal's authority evaporated, but Kâzim Pasha's unflagging support assured him his position.

At the Erzurum congress, which opened on July 23 and continued in session until 17 August 1919, the delegates drafted the first version of a document that came to be known as the National Pact. A short document of six articles, it declared that the nation would be independent, without foreign mandate or protectorate. It renounced claims over former Ottoman territories except where Turks predominated. Within these boundaries, foreign powers and citizens would not hold extraterritorial rights, and minorities would not receive special privileges. The nation would accept assistance from any power not having imperialistic designs.

A second national congress convened in Sivas three weeks later, between 4 and 11 September 1919. Here the delegates, endorsing and expanding the Erzurum declaration, absolved the sultan of blame for the current national crisis and blamed the sultan's advisors, and especially the Grand Vezir Damad Ferid Pasha instead. Sounding a more revolutionary tone, the delegates threatened armed resistance to the Entente plans. Already in control of telegraph communications in Anatolia, the nationalists moved to master the print media, publishing a newspaper called *İrade-i Milliye*, "The National Will."

Meanwhile in Istanbul, where details of the peace terms had leaked out and where it was obvious these would be unacceptable to the Turkish population, a British occupation was anticipated. At public rallies and meetings of literary and patriotic clubs, there was ongoing agitation against foreign influence and the Greek invasion and in support of the nationalists. Nationalist orators, among them the novelist Halide Edib Adıvar, addressed a mass rally in Sultan Ahmet Square in early June.

Karakol actively recruited and worked at sending assistance to the nationalists. The city was swollen with hundreds of thousands of refugees from Anatolia and from the Balkans, where new national states were forcing out Muslim populations. Relief workers began to contend with the seemingly inextricable confusion, reuniting families, making determinations about custody of minor orphans, transporting demobilized soldiers, attending disabled war veterans, and the like.

In the elections held for the first postwar Ottoman parliament, sympathizers with the nationalist movement won a majority of the seats, among them Hüseyin Rauf and Dr. Adnan Adıvar. Moving the headquarters of the nationalist resistance to the Anatolian town of Ankara in December, Mustafa Kemal urged the new parliament to convene there, but a majority of the deputies disagreed. They wanted to stay in Istanbul, the legitimately elected government of the nation, until the Entente powers forced them to close down.

Parliament opened in January 1920 in Istanbul. In mid-February it adopted the National Pact. On 16 March 1920, the British army occupied the city. Numerous nationalists were arrested, while others went into hiding or made their way to Anatolia to join the nationalists. Parliament prorogued itself on April 2. Damad Ferid Pasha denounced the nationalists as "false representatives of the nation," and the Shaykhulislam pronounced them enemies of the faith, making their death a duty of Muslims. In April, a small army was raised to fight the nationalists, and in May Mustafa Kemal was convicted of treason in absentia by a court martial and sentenced to death.

Over the course of these weeks, meanwhile, ninety-two members of the elected Ottoman parliament fled to Ankara, where they joined the thirty-two regional representatives of the Societies for the Defense of the National Rights, constituting the first nationalist parliament (*Büyük Millet Meclisi*, Great Assembly of the Nation, or Grand National Assembly).

THE WAR OF INDEPENDENCE

On 10 August 1920, the government of Sultan Mehmed VI signed the Treaty of Sèvres, whose provisions had been anticipated for months. The Ottoman Empire became a small principality in northwestern Asia Minor with the city of Istanbul as its capital. All the Arab lands were lost. The city of Mosul in the eastern Jazira plain fell into the British mandate of Iraq, and the port of İskenderun (Alexandretta) and its environs, into the French mandate of Syria. Anatolia was divided into several new states and spheres of influence under the control of the Entente powers. Italy was awarded southwestern Anatolia, and France, Cilicia and the city of Adana. Greece won most of western and northwestern Anatolia and all of Thrace. The Straits were internationalized. The treaty made Kurdistan an autonomous province under Ottoman suzerainty, with the possibility of petitioning the League of Nations for independence after one year. The six eastern Anatolian provinces, where the main part of the Armenian population had lived, were added to independent Armenia, which had first emerged as one of three successor states to the short-lived Transcaucasian Republic in spring 1918, when Russian control of the region had collapsed. The Ottoman advance during that last summer of the war had briefly interrupted its independence, but it quickly reappeared when the Ottomans withdrew.

Not only was the treaty completely unacceptable to the nationalists, but by the time it was signed, even some of the parties to its provisions realized it would be impossible and undesirable to enforce. After negotiations with the Bolshevik government in Russia broke down, Turkish nationalist armies under Kâzim Pasha advanced from Erzurum to Sarıkamış at the end of September 1920. This advance, and the Bolshevik coup against the Armenian government in Yerevan, finished the possibility of an independent Armenia in eastern Anatolia. France and Italy had already begun seeking an understanding with the nationalists. British public opinion refused to consider military action against the nationalists in order to impose the peace terms. The exception, it quickly became apparent, were the Greeks, whose Prime Minister Venizelos persuaded the British to allow them to enforce the treaty.

Twice in the first four months of 1921, Greek armies advanced toward the critically important railroad juncture of Eskişehir, on the direct route to Ankara in northwest Anatolia. On the first occasion, on January 10, nationalist armies led by İsmet Bey defeated the Greeks and halted their offensive at İnönü, just west of Eskişehir. During these four months, the international situation shifted slightly in favor of the nationalists. Venizelos lost an election in Athens and fell from power, and Damad Ferid Pasha was forced to resign. A conference called by the British in London to begin revising the peace treaty quickly broke up without much progress when the Greeks refused to cede territory in Anatolia. The Greeks renewed hostilities, but on April 7 were stopped once again at İnönü by İsmet Bey. Both the French and the Italians, however, concluded separate arrangements with the nationalists, agreeing within a few days of each other in March 1921 to withdraw from their designated spheres of influence in Anatolia in return for future economic concessions. The negotiations with Russia bore fruit at length in a treaty of friendship with the Bolsheviks.

These successes bought precious time for the nationalists, who also were engaged in critical discussions of the nature of their regime. The Ankara parliament passed, after considerable debate and disagreement, a Law on Fundamental Organizations in January 1921, the first article of which declared, "sovereignty belongs without reservation or condition to the nation." The rebel regime, it asserted, "rests on the principle that the people personally and effectively directs its own destinies." And the assembly took full legislative and executive authority in its own hands, declaring itself the national parliament, "the only true representative of the people."

The Turkish people now faced a defining moment, if they were in fact as well as in word to direct their own destiny. The Greek army mounted another offensive in the summer of 1921. This time, the Greeks succeeded in capturing the important towns of Afyon-Karahisar and Kütahya, and finally Eskişehir. As the Ankara government prepared to flee, it granted extraordinary authority to Mustafa Kemal, who assumed personal command of the army, for three months. In a bloody two-week long battle fought in August and September 1921 on the Sakarya River fifty miles southwest of Ankara, the nationalist forces led by Mustafa Kemal won the war. Greek forces continued to occupy western Anatolia, including Eskişehir, for another year, until they were defeated by Mustafa Kemal at Afyon-Karahisar on 22 August 1922 and again outside İzmir a week later. As the Greek armies withdrew from İzmir, much of the city burned. An armistice was signed on 11 October 1922 at Mudanya, on the southern coast of the Sea of Marmara.

A month later, the peace conference met at Lausanne, Switzerland. İsmet Bey, the hero of İnönü, led the Turkish delegation and proved to be an effective spokesmen for the nationalists, stubbornly insisting on the full ramifications of their victory. The Lausanne treaty, finally concluded in July 1923, affirmed the Turkish nationalist military victory. The Straits remained demilitarized and internationalized, under the jurisdiction of an international Straits Commission, but the Turkish nationalists regained eastern Thrace and all of Anatolia. The treaty provided for a compulsory exchange of populations between Greece and Turkey. Although Turkey agreed to accept about two-thirds of the Ottoman debt, the Capitulations were gone forever, and of the defeated forces of the First World War, Turkey alone paid no war reparations.

Although they had lost the First World War, their organization and the loyalty they had built for the concept of the nation enabled the Young Turks in the end to reverse the verdict of the war and the peace settlement of Sèvres. Under the leadership of Mustafa Kemal Pasha, the Turks won Turkish sovereignty over Turkish territory.

7

The Early Turkish Republic, 1923–1945

After the victory in the War of Independence and the signing of the Treaty of Lausanne, Mustafa Kemal Pasha enjoyed tremendous prestige as the national hero, the victor, the Ghazi. But the new nation faced enormous human problems of refugees and displaced people, of an economy crippled by war, and the breakdown of political institutions. It also faced profound disagreements about how to proceed under the circumstances.

In *The Turkish Ordeal*, her memoir of the War of Independence, novelist Halide Edib remembered a dinner meeting with Mustafa Kemal in the days after the victory outside of İzmir, in late August 1922. As Mustafa Kemal greeted her, she felt in his voice and in the shake of his hand "his excitement—the man with the will-power which is like a self-fed machine of perpetual motion." She urged him to rest, now that the war had been won, but he spoke darkly of those who had opposed him. Halide Edib replied, "Well, it was natural in a National Assembly." But he answered, "Rest; what rest? . . . No, we will not rest, we will kill each other" (Halide Edib [Adıvar], *The Turkish Ordeal* [New York and London, 1928], pp. 354–356).

A member of Mustafa Kemal's inner circle of advisors, Halide Edib had been active in the Young Turks movement since 1908. She and her husband, the prominent scholar Dr. Abdülhak Adnan Adıvar, a member of the postwar Ottoman parliament of 1920, had escaped to Anatolia to join the nationalists. Her popular novel of the independence war, *Ateşten Gömlek* (Shirt of Fire), was serialized in newspapers during the last months of the struggle and subsequently published as a book. In her attitude toward the role of Islam in public life as well as in other matters, she differed with many in the nationalist movement. She and her husband left Turkey in 1925, and other than one brief visit, returned only after the death of Mustafa Kemal.

FOUNDATION OF THE REPUBLIC

When the delegates took their seats in parliament on 23 August 1923, the first major action they took was to ratify the Treaty of Lausanne. Then they fell to fighting each other, as Mustafa Kemal had foreseen.

The first clash came almost immediately over the issue of what manner of state the new nation would be. Throughout 1920–1922, the Ankara parliament debated extensively two questions: the political orientation of the movement and the nature of its future regime. Two broad groups coalesced. The "Westernists" wanted to accept foreign assistance and even a mandate. They wanted to retain the sultanate and caliphate in a democratic Islamic order. The "Easternists" took a more radical approach, advocating the complete autonomy of the nation and the sovereignty of the people in a secular "people's democracy." Eventually this group became the core of what Mustafa Kemal called the "People's Party." The Westernists established what was at the time usually referred to simply as "the second group."

These debates brought to a head the question of the position of the sultan and caliph. To do away with the House of Osman after more than 600 years of continuous rule, to abandon completely the political tradition of the Ottoman Empire, was unthinkable for many in the nationalist movement. The idea of a republic was associated in their minds with revolution, radicalism, and godless, secularized Western culture. Mustafa Kemal tirelessly emphasized that sovereignty belonged to the people. By signing the Treaty of Sèvres, the sultan, he said, had betrayed the nation, agreeing to forfeit its sovereignty to foreigners. Now the people had risen up and, under the direction of their elected national representatives, won sovereignty for themselves through suffering and arduous struggle.

As the discussion in parliament dragged on, Mustafa Kemal showed he was not above using intimidation. Interrupting a lengthy disquisition about the origins of the caliphate, he stood on a desk and declared, "Gentlemen, sovereignty has never been given to any nation by scholarly disputation. It is always taken by force and with coercion." He threatened that heads might roll, but that national sovereignty would be won. Parliament voted to abolish the sultanate the same day. The sultan did Mustafa Kemal the favor of fleeing under British protection in November 1922. Parliament then deposed him and raised his cousin Abdülmecid to the throne, but as caliph only, with the understanding that the office would have no political authority. The parliament saw the caliphate as analogous to the papacy, an office of spiritual leadership of world Muslims. With the sultanate gone, however, many in parliament tried to vest the caliphate with political power, aiming to make the new nation an Islamic state by this means. The delegates came to an impasse over formation of the cabinet.

Mustafa Kemal Pasha found an opportune moment to suddenly propose that, to solve the problem of the caliph's political authority, a fairly simple amendment of parliament's Law of Fundamental Organizations would suffice—"Turkey is a state governed by a republican form of government." The delegates were taken by surprise, and many important figures of the War of Independence who would probably have opposed the move as premature, were not even in Ankara at the time. The oldest member of the assembly, Abdurrahman Şeref, who was the last holder of the office of historian of the Ottoman Empire and first president of the Ottoman Historical Society, rose to address the delegates. "One hundred years of the Turkish transformation is giving birth to a child," he announced. "Are we afraid to spell his name? Let us face it: it is Republic!" Parliament declared the Republic of Turkey on 29 October 1923.

The next spring, parliament, at Mustafa Kemal's urging, abolished the caliphate and at the same time abolished the Ministry of Religious Endowments and the office of Shaykhulislam, giving their responsibilities to the newly created Directorate of Religious Affairs and General Directorate of Religious Foundations. It closed the sharia courts, unifying the system of public justice, and shut down the mosque colleges, the medreses, unifying the system of public education. The Law on the Unification of Education placed religious secondary education under the Ministry of Education in Ankara, which organized a relatively small number of schools for mosque liturgists and prayer leaders. As for religious higher education, the medrese at the Süleymaniye Mosque in Istanbul was reorganized as a new Faculty of Divinity at the Istanbul Darülfünûnu.

Parliament ratified all these changes in the Republican constitution it passed on 20 April 1924. In response, however, thirty-two deputies broke with the People's Party caucus in parliament, forming the first opposition party. These deputies included well-known heroes of the War of Independence, led by Hüseyin Rauf and Kâzim Pasha. They called the new party the Progressive Republican Party, prompting the People's Party to change its name to the Republican People's Party.

Mustafa Kemal Pasha and his allies in parliament had effectively crushed the Islamic ulema, by removing the financial basis of their power and eliminating the institutions through which they worked. The significance of this victory can hardly be overemphasized for the subsequent history of the Turkish Republic. The single most important potential challenger to the legitimacy of the Republican regime, the potential of an Islamic state based on an interpretation of the sharia, had been crippled. In addition, parliament had accepted the reality that Turkey was no longer a world power. Many found this ruinously demoralizing. They had clung to the caliphate as a way of maintaining a position for Turkish Islam in the world that salved the defeat of the Ottoman Empire in World War I. But Mustafa Kemal and his allies faced the difficult reality squarely. They would have no delusions about a great empire of the Turkic world, as Enver Pasha had dreamed of, in the end hoping to lead an army into Anatolia with Soviet assistance. He had failed. The frontiers of Turkey were to be at the limits of the Turkish speaking population of Anatolia and eastern Thrace. Nor would parliament entertain fantasies of world leadership in the religious realm. In Mustafa Kemal's conception of the nation, no institution, no idea, would be permitted to compete with the sovereignty of the people.

This kind of Anatolian Turkish nationalism was an almost entirely new phenomenon, arising, in 1919 at the earliest, with the Greek invasion and the threat of the partition of Anatolia. Until that time, the Turks of Anatolia and eastern Thrace could not have thought in terms of an Anatolian Turkish nationalism because they were not different from the hundreds of thousands of Turks living in the Balkan Peninsula and northern Syria. But beginning in 1919, when so many of those Turks found themselves refugees in Anatolia or eastern Thrace and when a permanent division was drawn between the Bolshevik state in eastern Anatolia and the British and French mandates of Iraq and Syria, respectively, on the one hand, and the state partitioned at Sèvres on the other, and when the independence of the Turks of Anatolia was threatened by foreign invasion, only then did the conditions arise in which a peculiarly Anatolian Turkish nationalism could flourish.

This raised the question of the Kurds, about 20 percent of the population of the country in 1923, who had for the most part supported the nationalists. Mustafa Kemal himself had made statements promising some measure of autonomy for the regions in the southeast where large Kurdish populations lived, but these had fallen by the wayside in the months since the victory over the foreign invaders had been won. The abolition of the sultanate and the caliphate drove a wedge between the Turkish nationalists and the mostly conservative Sunni Muslim Kurds, and the laws passed by parliament in 1924 forbidding publications in Kurdish made the chasm between the two groups yawn even wider. A Kurdish revolt erupted in February 1925, led by an influential shaykh of the Nakshibendi dervish order, Shaykh Said. The rebellion was expressed in a powerful religious idiom, calling for restoration of the caliphate and rule by the sharia. The Shiite Alevis of Anatolia, suspicious of the Islamic state envisioned by the Sunnis, tended to support the more radical Turkish nationalists' conception of a secular republic, anticipating that it would provide a measure of protection against the religious prejudices of the Sunni majority, whether Turkish or Kurdish.

In parliament, Prime Minister İsmet quickly pushed through a Law on the Maintenance of Order giving the government extraordinary authority for a period of two years. The opposition group argued that the law would allow the banning of any group or publication deemed a threat to national security. Their worries turned out to be well-founded. Under cover of the law, the government established "Independence Tribunals," one in Ankara and one in the east where the rebellion was strongest. Through the arrest of 7,500 people and the execution of 660, the Independence Tribunals played a significant role in the suppression of the rebellion. The rebellion was ended fairly quickly with the capture and arrest of Shaykh Said on 27 April. He was convicted by the Independence Tribunal and executed in June 1925.

The Independence Tribunals also snared the most important Islamic thinker of the Republican era, Said Nursi (1873–1960), called Bediüzzaman, "Wonder of the Age." An ethnic Kurd and Islamic modernist, in his writings Said Nursi mapped out an accommodation between the ideas of constitutional democracy and individual liberty and religious devotion. Nursi had developed good relationships with the Young Turks, and during the war years he spoke out against modern Islamic authoritarianism and economic and political backwardness. He developed ideas of a modern Islamic consciousness that insisted on the necessity of a significant role for religious belief in public life while it rejected obscurantism and embraced scientific and technological development. He was disappointed by the general trend toward secularism in the constitutional discussions and legislation since the declaration of the Republic. Although it possessed no irrefutable proof of his involvement in the Shaykh Said rebellion, and Nursi denied it, the Independence Tribunals sentenced him to exile in western Anatolia.

After a conspiracy to assassinate Mustafa Kemal was uncovered before his visit to İzmir in the spring of 1926, the government turned the Independence Tribunals on all its enemies during the next two years, using them to suppress even the loyal opposition. All major national newspapers except *Cumhuriyet* (Istanbul) and the official Ankara daily *Hakimiyet-i Milliye* were closed and their staff arrested for publishing stories that compromised national security. The Progressive Republican Party was closed and all of its leaders, accused of collaborating in the conspiracy, were arrested for treason. Several of the most prominent heroes of the War of Independence—Kâzim Pasha, Ali Fuad, Refet—were released under public pressure, but other men who had worked closely with Mustafa Kemal were executed. Hüseyin Rauf and Adnan Adıvar escaped only because they were out of the country at the time.

THE GREAT REFORMS, PHASE ONE: SECULARIZATION

The Republican People's Party now moved swiftly to consolidate its hold on the nationalist enterprise. In two phases, in the 1920s and the 1930s, Mustafa Kemal and his allies brought massive changes to Turkish life. Renewing the Law on the Maintenance of Order, in the three years between the summer of 1925 and the fall of 1928, they enacted a series of measures to secularize Turkish public life. This intense legislative activity was furthered by the election in September 1927 of a strongly Kemalist parliament. The great reforms were the work of what had become essentially a one-party state.

The canonical tithe tax, crucial to the power of the local notables who collected it, was abolished. Soon, the dervish houses were permanently closed, their ceremonies and liturgy banned, and their distinctive dress outlawed. Mustafa Kemal also attacked two other important symbols of politicized Islam: the fez and the veil. The campaign against these articles of clothing had the effect of permanently politicizing dress in the Republic of Turkey.

The fez, a red felt cap, had a history of only about 100 years in the Ottoman Empire. In that relatively short time, it had become a tenacious symbol of conservative, religious-minded people. The veil, and by extension the long black outer shawl called a *çarşaf* with which conservative women covered themselves in public, had come to symbolize the subordinate status of women in the ideology of reactionary Islamic politics. Touring Anatolia during the summer of 1925 and wearing a western-type billed cap, Mustafa Kemal ridiculed the fez as the headwear of a barbarous, backward people. He publicly denounced the veil, pointing out that it was a foreign innovation and that Turkish peasant women had traditionally worn a scarf wrapped around their hair but no veil. In these speeches, Mustafa Kemal repeatedly insisted on the need of the nation to make use of all its human potential, including women, stating that the nation consisted of "two kinds of human beings, called men and women." In order to progress, the nation needed the involvement of both. Mustafa Kemal's own wife, Latife, to whom he was briefly married between 1923 and 1925, became an outstanding public example of a modern woman. In November 1925, parliament passed a law requiring men to wear hats and outlawing the wearing of the fez, but they stopped short of banning the veil. The veil never was completely outlawed in Turkey, but its use in public buildings and events was prohibited by parliament at a later time.

In 1926, parliament adopted a new civil code explicitly repealing Islamic Holy Law, a new penal code based on the Italian code and a commercial code based on the German code. This affected family relations and especially improved the legal status of women. It lowered the legal age of marriage to eighteen for males and seventeen for females, and required that all marriages be performed by a magistrate. Polygamy and divorce by renunciation of the wife were both outlawed. Of course, the actual practice of Turkish families changed only slowly, and, for example, in eastern and central Anatolia, polygamous marriages were contracted for many years after this. But the impact of the new code should not be underestimated. The author of the new civil code, Mahmud Esad, wrote that a modern society was an organized, rational society, and the modern nation was based on a rational social order. Mustafa Kemal believed that world history told the story of the progressive advance of human civilization. In the twentieth century, European civilization led that advance. If Turkey desired to become a civilized country, it must leave its past behind and follow the example of human progress set by Europe. The capstone of this transition was laid when on 5 April 1928 parliament deleted the phrase "the religion of the Turkish state is Islam" from the constitution. The constitution did not yet state that Turkey was a secular state—that was to come in 1937—but the intent of these reforms was clearly to secularize the social order of the new state.

Two more great changes completed the first phase of the great reforms. These brought transformations of time and of history. On 26 December 1925, the day after Christmas, parliament adopted the international 24-hour clock and the Gregorian calendar. Time itself would be measured according to the standard accepted by the advanced nations of the world. The Western calendar, based on the Christian era of the Incarnation of Jesus Christ, had replaced the Islamic calendar, based on the foundation of the Muslim community with the Prophet Muhammad's migration from Mecca to Medina.

And finally, perhaps the most radical change of all: In the last two months of 1928, the Arabic script was abandoned in favor of the Roman. The new Turkish alphabet contained twenty-nine letters and was entirely phonetic. During the late summer and early fall, the indefatigable Mustafa Kemal went on the road, introducing and ceaselessly promoting the script, beginning on an August evening at Gülhane Park in Istanbul, where he demonstrated the new letters to his audience on a blackboard set up on an easel. He and the commission offered two main arguments for the new script. The Arabic script, they asserted, was ill-suited to the Turkish language. This was of course true: The orthography of Arabic, a Semitic language, relied on consonants arranged in groups and offered only three symbols for writing vowels. Many of its phonemes were foreign to Turkish and thus the written symbols for them had no relevance. These difficulties were not unusual—most world languages only more or less fit the scripts used to write them.

Another argument for the alphabet change was that a phonetic alphabet would aid in raising literacy among the Turkish population. This probably was true also, but the low level of literacy in Turkey could hardly be blamed on the use of the Arabic script. The Arabic script had adequately served written Turkish for about a thousand years. For most of these centuries, few people anywhere in the world, including in Europe, had believed it necessary or good to educate common people. Low levels of literacy were more especially the result of the absence of a system of national public education and the belief that such a system was unnecessary.

The advantage in script reform was historical and cultural. Use of the Arabic script had identified the ancient Turkish tribes migrating in southwestern Asia as belonging to the Islamic civilization, the greatest civilization of that age. In the twentieth century, adoption of the Roman script would identify the modern Turkish nation as belonging to the Western European civilization, the greatest civilization of this age. By this one break, the modern Turkish nation totally renounced its past and embraced its revolution. Not learning the Arabic script, its children would not learn the Islamic tradition, indeed, would be unable to read its greatest literary monuments. The children of the Turkish revolution would also be unable to read the documents produced by the Ottoman Empire only a few years before.

THE NATIONAL ECONOMY

Turkey required a fundamental economic reconfiguration, as Mustafa Kemal himself recognized in an economic congress held at İzmir in February 1923. At the outset, the economic circumstances of the country were grim.

Demographic historians estimate that 20 percent of the Muslim population of Anatolia, about 2.5 million people, died during the period between 1912 and 1923. In the eastern Anatolian combat zones, in the provinces of Van, Bitlis, and Erzurum, 40 percent of the Muslim population died. The deaths of Anatolian Armenians, something on the order of 800,000 to 1,000,000 people, and Anatolian Greeks, about 300,000, must be added to the numbers of Muslims.

Besides these deaths, the population of Anatolia was transformed by refugees. Refugees from the Balkans first arrived in Anatolia after the 1877–1878 Russo-Turkish war. According to statistics of the Turkish Ministry of the Interior, more than 400,000 new Muslim refugees came to Anatolia between 1912 and 1920. During the same time, hundreds of thousands of Armenians and Greeks left Anatolia. Greek refugee statistics of 1928 list more than 900,000 Greeks who fled Anatolia between 1912 and 1923. In the brutal compulsory exchange of populations agreed to in the Treaty of Lausanne, another 190,000 Greek Orthodox residents of western Anatolia—virtually the entire remaining Greek population of the region—were uprooted from their homes and forcibly moved to Greece, while about 355,000 Turkish residents of Greece—virtually all the Turks of Greece outside of western Thrace—were uprooted from their homes and forcibly moved to Turkey.

The result of all this left Turkey with about 30 percent fewer people than it had had before the Balkan wars, and it was a far less ethnically diverse country than it had been. There remained only two major population groups: Turks, forming about 80 percent of the total population, and Kurds, who made up most of the rest. Only in the major cities like Istanbul did sizable populations of Jews and Christian Greeks and Armenians continue to live. The Republic of Turkey was about 98 percent Muslim, two-third to three-fourths of whom were Sunnites and the rest Alevi Shiites.

The economic meaning of the catastrophe was unambiguous. Turkey contained an even more rural population than before the war, and its productive industry was devastated by the exodus of the Armenian and Greek population. Compared with a 1912 population of about 17.5 million, the first Republican census (1927) counted 13,648,000 persons, and only fifty-two towns and five cities—Istanbul, Ankara, İzmir, Adana, and Bursa—with a population of more than 10,000. An Ottoman industrial survey of 1915 had listed 284 industrial establishments employing more than five workers, about half of which were in Istanbul and all the rest in İzmir or western Anatolia. Eighty-five percent of the capital behind these establishments had been Jewish, Greek, Armenian, or foreign. The Young Turks had not been unaware of this situation. They had abolished the capitulations immediately on their entry into the First World War in 1914, and they had taken measures during the war years to encourage the development of a Muslim industrial and business class. This class, especially among large landowners in Anatolia, also received an unintended boost from the circumstances of war—shortages of and speculation on key commodities, and legal and illegal manipulation of personal relations with government officials who ran the railroads and other communication lines. But the numbers of people in this group of Anatolian Muslim entrepreneurs was exceedingly small in 1923.

After 1923, the economic policy of Turkey unfolded into two chronological periods. During the first period, from 1923 until about 1930, the state followed a policy of actively supporting private enterprise in an open economy. Beginning in 1930, in response to the depression, the state gradually shifted to a policy of protectionism and etatism, which hardened as the decade of the 1930s wore on.

During the 1920s, the aim of economic policy was to create conditions in which an indigenous entrepreneurial and business class could develop. The Turkish Lira, made equivalent to 100 kurush, was established as the national currency. Tariffs were kept low and investment by foreign capital was encouraged, especially in partnership with Turkish firms. About one-third of the firms established in Turkey in the decade of the 1920s were partnerships between Turkish merchants and foreign investors. In 1927, the Law for the Encouragement of Industry allowed the transfer of state land to private citizens for the purpose of building or expanding an industrial establishment; these industries received numerous tax exemptions, state subsidies, and a discount on rates for transportation by sea and rail. State monopolies were awarded to firms involved in the development of new industries. Monopolies were established for the production, import, or export of sugar, tobacco, oil, alcohol, matches, explosives, and other commodities.

Policymakers reconsidered these approaches in the 1930s. The effects of the Great Depression in the 1930s deepened the effect of problems rooted in the peculiarly Turkish situation. The first payment on the Ottoman debt—the bulk of which was shouldered by Turkey—in 1929 had a rippling effect in a monetary crisis. After delivery of another installment in 1930, the government suspended payment on the Ottoman debt. During 1929–1930, the Turkish state took measures to shift to a policy of protectionism and import substitution in trade policy.

The collapse of agricultural prices during the depression caused peasants to go dangerously into debt, and industrial wages stagnated. Government economic policy suffered fierce criticism, which occasionally became violent. Hoping to release some of the political pressure in a constructive manner, Mustafa Kemal permitted an opposition political party. Fethi Bey, exiled to the Turkish Embassy in Paris in 1925, returned in September 1930 to create the Free Republican Party with Mustafa Kemal's blessing. But Mustafa Kemal was evidently unprepared for the massive popular support the new party received. Thousands attended political rallies as Fethi Bey toured Anatolia, and some industrial workers went out on strike. The opposition party was hastily shut down in November. In December, in the Aegean town of Menemen, a Nakshibendi dervish shaykh named Mehmed proclaimed himself the Messiah and provoked an uprising, demanding restoration of the caliphate and rule by the sharia. When the local gendarme commander went to arrest him, Dervish Mehmed attacked and killed him, and the crowds paraded the severed head through the streets on the end of a pole.

Taken aback by the violence, once again Mustafa Kemal went on the road with his advisors, traveling extensively in Anatolia in the fall and winter of 1930 and 1931 and viewing firsthand the economic damage and the plight of the masses of peasants and workers. Out of their discussion of this experience and observation of the apparent weaknesses of the Western capitalist economies and the comparative strength of the Soviet economy of the time, there emerged a new economic strategy of massive state investment in industrialization, or etatism. They did not attack or discourage private enterprise. The state intervention and centralized economic planning of the 1930s were intended to supplement the struggling private sector in the development of national industrial capacity, not replace it.

Turkish etatism developed out of several new or existing investment banks, which were organized as joint stock companies with specific industrial or economic objectives. The Agricultural Bank, a central government institution since 1888, had already been reorganized in this way in 1923, shares being proportionately distributed to its district offices. Its purpose after 1926 was to provide agricultural credit at the village level. It was taken over again by the state in 1937 and assigned the revenues of a fixed percentage of the land tax and of .5 percent of the national budget. The Ottoman Bank, owned by British and French interests, was closed in 1931 and nationalized as the Central Bank of Turkey (Türkiye Merkez Bankası). The Business Bank (İş Bankası) was formed in 1924 as a semi-public savings bank and given the mission of developing the Zonguldak coal mines. The Turkish Industry and Mining Bank was reorganized as Sümer Bank, with the same objective of financing industrial expansion. One more such institution, the Eti Bank, was established in 1935 for the purpose of developing the mining and power industries. An important feature of these enterprises was their location all over the country: The Turkish state hoped to avoid the social problems of rapid migration of villagers to a few industrial centers by decentralizing industrial production. These state economic enterprises, and the government monopolies on communications—telephone, telegraph, post, railroads and, beginning in 1933, the state airlines—were directed by government planners who prepared the first five-year plan for adoption by parliament in 1934. Two more five-year plans followed, 1937–1942 and 1946–1950.

Over time, these state-owned enterprises came to dominate the Turkish economy, but this was probably not the intention of economic planners. Through political patronage, the government officials and former military officers who staffed the bureaucracy of the new republic, seeing the opportunity to create and build state-sponsored personal fiefdoms, seized control of the state economic enterprises. Taking advantage of the tax exemptions, state subsidies, and low-interest capital, and the priority in scarce resources, foreign exchange, and trained personnel they enjoyed, these officials and officers turned the SEEs increasingly against private sector competition. Private enterprise survived, not least because of the built-in inefficiencies of the heavily bureaucratized state economic enterprises.

THE GREAT REFORMS, PHASE TWO: TOWARD A NATIONAL CULTURE

Establishment of the Turkish nation produced a period of intense reflection on the meaning of the Republican revolution—and hence, the meaning of history—and the place of the individual in society. The nation, it seemed, had to rediscover itself, as all nations do, as an ancient people reborn. The diverse parts of Anatolia and eastern Thrace now united in the Republic of Turkey had not heretofore considered themselves part of a single community and had paid little attention to what they held in common. The history of Çukurova differed markedly from the history of the Menderes Valley, for example, and the history of the Menderes Valley appeared little like the history of Kars or the eastern Black Sea coast. Now the nation needed to uncover its heritage as a nation, identify its common heroes, and determine its common values. Directed increasingly through the apparatus of the one-party state and, by the vision of Mustafa Kemal, these issues dominated the scientific, literary, and artistic activity of the later 1920s and 1930s. Between the Republican People's Party congress of May 1931 and the end of 1935, Mustafa Kemal and his allies took a series of steps that deepened the reach of the revolution.

Like all new nations birthed through revolution and war, early Republican Turkey was selective in its remembrance or appropriation of the past. Fascinated with the new findings on Anatolian antiquity and keen to the prospects of linking it to the emerging national identity, Mustafa Kemal founded the Turkish History Research Society to ensure that ongoing research furthered the needs of the Republic. At a historical congress held in Ankara in 1932, he set out the agenda of the new society. Anatolia, homeland of the new Turkish nation, had been a Turkish land since antiquity, he theorized. It had been first settled by the Sumerians and the Hittites, whom he claimed as Turkic peoples that had migrated from the central Eurasian steppes, carrying with them the fundamental characteristics of Western civilization. Scholarly research, according to Mustafa Kemal, should focus on these and related topics and should aim to fully describe the antiquity of Turkish history. In linguistics, for example, the new theory asserted that Turkish was the primeval human tongue from which all others were derived. In anthropology, craniological studies were carried out to demonstrate that Turks belonged to the Caucasian race. The society, renamed the Turkish Historical Society in 1935, published the results of research based on these ideas.

The theories were largely abandoned by scholars after the death of their champion, but they made a deep and lasting impression on Turkish life. Generations of Turkish school children grew up reading them in textbooks. In addition, the teaching also communicated to these pupils and citizens a sense of pride in a Turkish identity, a suspiciousness about the recent Ottoman past, and an antidote to persistent Western stereotypes and prejudices about Turks and Turkey. Gradually the scientific research generated by the nationalist theory also disproved its major tenets, establishing along the way a genuinely Turkish scholarly tradition in disciplines such as biology, anthropology, historical linguistics, archaeology, and the like.

A Turkish Language Society was also created in 1932, alongside the historical society, by order of Mustafa Kemal. The expressed task given the language society was that of cleansing the Turkish language of the accumulated encrustations from the Arabic and Persian languages and from the conceptual categories of the Islamic intellectual tradition. Its officials expended a concerted effort in the following decades to identify and eliminate foreign words and grammatical constructions in Turkish and find substitutes, either by combing the vocabulary of Turkic languages, past and present, for suitable models or by creating neologisms. As a consequence of their success in this ongoing task, literary works produced even in the early Republican era—the constitution, for example, or the speeches of Mustafa Kemal—are unintelligible to the current generation of native Turkish speakers and must be translated into contemporary Turkish.

Another important, though not explicit, dimension of the work of the language society was the task of creating a national language. Publication in languages other than Turkish was forbidden. The dialects of Turkish spoken in the different regions of Turkey would be melded into a national idiom. In this great labor, the power of the mass media was effectively harnessed by Mustafa Kemal. In his speech opening parliament in 1935, he specifically referred to the importance of radio broadcasting (begun in 1927 in Istanbul) in the dissemination of a national culture. In 1936, the authority to broadcast was monopolized by the government post, telegraph, and telephone agency. Inevitably, the literary and intellectual elite of Istanbul dominated the development of the national language, and the Istanbul dialect overwhelmed the regional Anatolian speech patterns to become the national idiom.

Turkish reformers calling for a true Turkish religious renewal had advocated the use of Turkish in Islamic liturgy and texts for decades. Mustafa Kemal had failed to convince the poet Mehmed Âkif, author of the national anthem, to undertake the translation of the Qur'an into Turkish, for which parliament established a translation fund. Now, however, he encouraged the use of Turkish for mosque prayers and Friday sermons and, amid much controversy, for the call to prayer. The mosque liturgy remained in Arabic, but the call to prayer began to be done in Turkish, and was made compulsory in 1941.

Mustafa Kemal had plainly become interested in laying the intellectual foundations of the new nation. In May 1933, parliament passed a law reorganizing the Darülfünûn at Istanbul into Istanbul University, the first university in the Republic. The faculty of the former institution was purged to resemble a body more sympathetic with Mustafa Kemal's notion of the role of an institution of higher learning in national life. It was to remain the only university in Turkey until the founding of Istanbul Technical University in 1944 from the School of Advanced Engineering, and of Ankara University—combining several institutes and faculties of higher education in the capital—in 1946.

The decision to grant female suffrage and to adopt family names belongs to this phase of the reforming movement. In women's suffrage, Mustafa Kemal fulfilled the commitment, made in his speeches of ten years before, to employ all the human resources of the nation. He pushed through parliament a bill granting women the right to vote and to hold office, and in the 1935 elections, seventeen women won seats in parliament. All Turkish citizens twenty-two years of age and older now had the right to vote.

In 1934, the Turkish state required that all citizens adopt and register family names. Until this time, Turkish families followed traditional Muslim naming practices, bestowing only a single name at birth. This personal name might be supplemented later in life by a second name, which might be suggested by the child's father's name, by the place of birth, by a distinctive personal characteristic, or the like. Of course, a number of potentially useful administrative advantages might be imagined from a system of family names that could be readily alphabetized, but the change fit other important national purposes as well. Requiring that the names be authentically Turkish—names derived from Arabic or Persian roots were not permitted—the state reinforced the national and even ethnic identity of the community as opposed to its religious identity. By means of this very potent and at the same time very intimate symbol, the state effectively linked the personal destiny of its citizens with that of the nation. In 1935, the Turkish parliament bestowed on Mustafa Kemal the family name Atatürk, "Father Turk." İsmet Pasha became İsmet İnönü in honor of the two victories won there during the War of Independence. Kâzim Pasha became Kâzim Karabekir.

In both literature and music, early Republican artists followed three important trends. Some created works in genres originating in modern Europe—the novel, surrealist poetry, symphonic orchestral compositions, and the like. Others explored the potential of ancient and medieval Turkish artistic forms, including the poetry of the fourteenth century mystic Yunus Emre, and the pre-Islamic heroic epic of Dede Korkut. Still others began publicizing the popular genres of the Anatolian folk tradition, such as the ribald and anti-ulema humor in the stories of the folk wit Nasreddin Hoca, the coarse vulgarity of the shadow theater character Karagöz, the repertoire and instruments of Anatolian folk music, and the tradition of the dueling minstrels like the blind and illiterate genius Âşık Veysel. Again, in both literature and music the genres of the Ottoman court—divan poetry, art, music, Qur'an recitation, and so forth—were decidedly out of fashion. Certain genres of the immediate Ottoman past did survive. Popular singers still performed in the cabarets of Istanbul, somewhat neglected now as attention shifted to activities in Ankara. Not a few women singers attracted a following, thanks partly to the emerging recording industry in Istanbul, including Safiye Ayla, who became the most famous singer of her generation.

The nationalist objectives, to define and shape a national identity and character, were expressed in two other major Turkish institutions in the 1930s, the *Halkevleri*, or People's Houses, and the Village Institutes. The People's Houses were a weakly concealed Republican People's Party replacement for the old Turkish Hearths founded by the Young Turks in 1911. These were local clubs where literature, political ideas, manufacturing development, agricultural improvements, and other issues could be discussed by those attending the meetings. They played an important role in the development of popular democratic loyalties during the Young Turks era but were closed in 1930 because they functioned perhaps too well as a forum for debating the political and economic program of the regime. Less than a year later, the People's Houses opened to great fanfare. By 1940, more than 4,000 People's Houses were operating. Through their activities, the People's Houses, and their village-level counterparts, the People's Rooms, worked to communicate to the citizens the mission and values of the nation as advanced by the regime.

The Village Institutes grew out of the literacy drive that began with the introduction of the new script in 1929. In 1935, Mustafa Kemal gave the German-trained educationist İsmail Hakkı Tonguç permission to develop a new strategy for education in the Anatolian countryside. The program went nationwide in 1940. The Village Institutes provided rural Anatolian boys and girls a five-year secondary educational program in a boarding school, where they received a complete education and learned a skill, such as carpentry or midwifery. The graduates were expected to go out to villages where they would become schoolteachers of other village youth, emphasizing modern techniques of agriculture and home industry, and seeking to inculcate the fundamental ideology of the Republic.

Much of the population resented the Village Institutes and they, like the People's Houses, became a casualty of the political liberalization of the late 1940s and 1950s. Tonguç was accused of being a leftist and a communist. In fact, leftists also denounced Tonguç and the Village Institutes as agents of the single-party state. The Village Institutes may have failed because the Turkish state underestimated the depth of animosity toward the regime or did not adequately understand its sources. Much of the Anatolian peasantry mistrusted the Republic for its secularization, which it interpreted as irreligious and Godless. And the Republic had disappointed peasants by its failure to consistently follow through on what they really wanted, which was land redistribution and relief from the power of landlords. In addition, implementation of the Village Institutes was accomplished by Atatürk's successor İsmet İnönü, whose wartime administration incurred a reputation for inflexibility and heavy-handedness.

THE DEATH OF ATATÜRK

After an illness diagnosed as cirrhosis of the liver, Mustafa Kemal Atatürk died on 10 November 1938. It is impossible to overstate his profound legacy to the Turkish Republic. The political system of the Republic is often summarized by the term *Atatürkçülük*, or "Kemalism." A definition of Kemalism might begin with the ideological statement of six "fundamental and unchanging principles" Mustafa Kemal outlined in the Republican People's Party (RPP) platform of 1931. It stated that the RPP is "republican, nationalist, populist, etatist, secularist and revolutionary." These Six Arrows guided the party in the second phase of the great reforms and in 1937 were incorporated into the constitution of the Republic to define the basic principles of the Turkish state.

The first three principles did not generate much controversy. "Republicanism" meant that the people exercised sovereignty through elected representatives in parliament, the national assembly, to which no power in the state was superior. "Nationalism" meant the principle of the existence of the Turkish people forming the Turkish Republic on Turkish soil, united by a common Turkish national culture. "Populism" referred to government based on the faith of the Turkish people. The state belonged to all the people, regardless of sex, religion, education, and the like.

The last three terms were more contentious than the first three. "Etatism" meant the economic policy of state investment adopted by the RPP in the 1930s. It was not universally accepted as a basic principle of Turkish nationhood. "Secularism" has been interpreted variously by those at different points on the Turkish political spectrum. The principle referred to the administrative control of religious institutions by the state and the removal of official religious expressions from public life. The principle also implied freedom of religious practice and conscience within these bounds. "Revolutionism" gives the sense of an ongoing openness and commitment to change in the interests of the nation. More conservative people understand the Turkish İnkilapçılık to convey something closer to "reformism."

But ideology only partially describes a political movement. Kemalism was also an attitude and a way of life and has sometimes been called the state religion of the Republic. It was perhaps especially an attitude toward history, which emphasized the virtues of the new as opposed to the old. This attitude is a basic intuition of modernity, growing out of the revolutionary soil that nurtured the modern ages, and is a feature of all revolutions. In Turkey it manifested itself in a typically modern confidence or faith in the progress of the Turkish nation and the role of the Turkish state, its army, and its officials in guiding that progress, and a certain historical forgetfulness.

Kemalism also meant a devotion to Atatürk that sometimes resembled elements of a personality cult. This is perhaps best exemplified in the cultic status of Atatürk's image and of his sayings, especially his Address to Turkish Youth of 1935 and his famous six-day speech delivered to the Republican People's Party congress in October 1927. The speech purported to be a history of the Turkish revolution to that point, and for generations of Turkish citizens and historians both in Turkey and outside Turkey, it has been accepted as a kind of sacred text. The speech emphasizes the leading role in the events of the speaker, Mustafa Kemal himself, and downplays the contributions of others.

In Turkey, Kemalism may finally be seen as a perspective on the Turkish nation from the point of view of the new city of Ankara. Mustafa Kemal carried an antagonistic attitude toward the Ottoman past and an ambivalence toward the old city of Istanbul. He left Istanbul for Samsun and the revolution in May 1919 and did not return to Istanbul until July 1927, eight years later. He preferred the austerity of Ankara. Ankara had little to offer in the way of entertainment or culture to compare with the coffee shops, cabarets, concerts, and night life of Istanbul. But for Mustafa Kemal, Ankara also was without the ponderously orthodox piety, the elitist snobbery, and the pretensions to world influence of Istanbul. During his presidency, he occasionally made symbolic use of Istanbul. He introduced the alphabet in Gülhane Park. He called the meetings of the newly founded historical society and language society in Istanbul in 1932. He had a bronze sculpture of himself placed on Saray Point in 1926, the first statue of a Turk erected anywhere in the country, and he supervised the development of Taksim Square in the Beyoğlu commercial quarter, with an imposing monument to the Republic in its center (1928), as a modern, secular rival to the ancient Hippodrome, which is surrounded by Ottoman imperial mosques and palaces. Ironically, Atatürk died in the Dolmabahçe Palace in Istanbul where he had lain ill. His body was returned to Ankara, where it temporarily was placed in the Ethnographical Museum until its final resting place could be prepared.

İSMET İNÖNÜ AND THE SECOND WORLD WAR

When Atatürk died, İsmet İnönü overcame a brief struggle with other advisors to succeed him as the second president of the Republic. İnönü's presidency was crucial to completing the work of the reforms and consolidating the secular order. At an extraordinary party congress in December 1938, the Republican People's Party made İnönü party chairman and bestowed on him the title "National Chief," enhancing his authority in anticipation of possible challenges to the Republican regime. His term as president was largely taken up with issues surrounding the Second World War, which began less than a year after he took office. İnönü's management of the domestic political circumstances prevented a repetition of the national disaster that had resulted from involvement in the First World War, his shrewd use of the crisis forcefully ensured the maintenance of the Kemalist structure, and his adroit diplomacy kept Turkish troops out of combat for the entire duration of the war. None of these successes was fully appreciated at the time.

The priority of Turkish foreign policy after 1923 had been to consolidate the national independence won on the battlefield and to free the nation from the financial constraints within which the late empire had functioned. In 1939, all recognized that Turkey was in no position to fight another war. As the international atmosphere appeared more threatening toward the end of the 1930s, Turkey's statesmen approached the situation in Europe alert to the possibility of enhancing the Republic's international position but determined to keep out of the coming conflict. Although aware of the potential threat from the Soviet Union, Turkey maintained good relations with the Soviets, with whom a formal treaty had been signed in December 1925 and renewed in 1935. Additionally, Turkey entered two alliance systems. A Balkan conference brought a reconciliation with Greece and the announcement of the Balkan Pact in 1934 between Greece, Yugoslavia, Romania, and Turkey. Following this, Turkey concluded the Sadabad Pact in 1937, joining Iraq, Iran, and Afghanistan in a nonaggression agreement.

Turkey's relationship with Britain and France, by contrast, was weaker. The Treaty of Lausanne had left several issues still outstanding. In 1925, the League of Nations sided with the British that the district of Mosul should remain in the Mandate of Iraq, in spite of the fact that the majority of the population was not Arab but Kurdish, that a sizable minority of Turks lived there, and that the British had occupied the area only after the signing of the armistice in late 1918. Turkey thus lost the oil revenues from the province and faced the very real possibility that further Kurdish nationalist activity in northern Iraq would act as a magnet for Kurds within the borders of Turkey.

Turkey's chief foreign danger in these years, however, was thought to come from Italy. Italy had taken an aggressive position against the Young Turks regime, seizing Libya, advocating the creation of an independent Albania it could dominate across the Adriatic, and gaining the Dodecanese Islands. After the Treaty of Sèvres, Italy participated in the partition of Anatolia. Although it had withdrawn when it became clear the Turkish nationalists would force a revision of those terms, Italy still possessed and heavily fortified the Dodecanese and, in 1939, occupied Albania. Concern about Italy's intentions led Turkey to request a revision of the protocol governing the Straits at Istanbul. At the Montreux Convention of 1936, Turkey regained almost full sovereignty over the Straits, and its relationship with Britain and France began to improve. The convention abolished the international commission that had governed passage of ships through the Straits since 1923 and permitted Turkish refortification of the Straits. Passage of commercial traffic through the Straits remained free to countries not at war with Turkey. Restrictions were placed on the passage of warships; when Turkey felt itself faced with "imminent danger of war," it could close the Straits to warships of all nations, subject to a veto by a two-thirds vote of the League of Nations council.

At that time, the Turkish army at peacetime strength consisted of 174,000 soldiers and 20,000 officers. It was ill-equipped with mostly World War I era weapons. As war loomed in 1939, however, Britain and France hoped that Turkey might relieve pressure on a western front by compelling Germany to fight a war in the Balkans. President İnönü and Foreign Minister Şükrü Saraçoğlu wanted to avoid this, but they used it to make gains for Turkey. Through careful negotiation, they brought the region of İskenderun, which Lausanne had given to French Syria, back under Turkish control. In elections in 1937, the Turkish majority in the region's new parliament voted to unite with Turkey. In 1939, the region became the Turkish province of Hatay. Two months after the announcement of the Nazi-Soviet pact, on 17 October 1939, Turkey signed a formal alliance with Britain and France.

Knowing they could not fight Germany, İnönü and Saraçoğlu, and later Numan Menemencioğlu, the foreign ministers, throughout the war resisted intense pressure to draw them into the conflict. By the summer of 1941, the Nazis occupied much of the Balkans and held a prevailing influence in Bulgaria and Greece, on Turkey's border. İnönü believed that an engagement with the German army would lead to certain defeat. In July 1941, he concluded a nonaggression pact with Germany. He made gestures to the Germans, such as including Turkish pan-Turkists in his cabinet. These pan-Turkists were vehemently anti-Soviet Turkish fascists. İnönü also stalled the allies, begging for additional assistance and training. In December 1941, Turkey gained American lend-lease assistance. But İnönü aimed at all costs to avoid putting Turkey in a position where failure in combat against a superior foe might compromise the sovereignty and independence of the Republic.

In the first years of the war, İnönü also did not have many supporters in Turkey. The midwar years were difficult for Turkey. There were shortages of basic goods, inflation, and the government, cash starved, resorted to an extraordinary levy called the Capital Tax (*Varlık Vergisi*) to raise funds. In November 1942, the parliament announced it would levy property owners, big farmers, and businessmen who "amassed inflated profits by exploiting the difficult economic situation but do not pay commensurate taxes." They would be forced to pay an amount "commensurate with their profits and capacity." Indeed, two groups of people had profited enormously from the war: the mostly Muslim owners of large rural estates and the mostly non-Muslim urban merchants involved in the importing of scarce commodities. The tax lists, prepared without formal income data but rather according to the personal estimation of local bureaucrats, divided taxpayers according to religion: M for Muslim, G for Non-Muslim (*Gayrimüslim*) and later E for Foreigners (*Ecnebi*), and D for Sabbateans (*Dönme*, literally "converts"). It did not take long to figure out that this tax fell overwhelmingly on the non-Muslims. Many were financially ruined.

Although no appeals were permitted, and the Revenue Department rejected almost all of more than 10,000 petitions, taxpayers exercised their constitutional right of petition. Those who resisted were arrested and deported or sentenced to hard labor. By the time collection of the capital tax was finally completed in June 1943, the financial world of Istanbul and western Anatolia was severely shaken. İnönü admitted that almost 40 percent of what had been so far collected had been paid by minorities and foreigners but denied that it was any injustice, since, he said, they owned most of the wealth. Deportees were permitted to return—without paying!—in December, on the eve of a Cairo meeting between İnönü and Churchill and Roosevelt. In March 1944, all remaining outstanding obligations were canceled and defaults forgiven. Reparations, however, were not made. Many historians have noted that the conclusion of the capital tax fiasco coincided with the defeat of Nazi Germany. Fascist student demonstrations in May 1944 gave İnönü the opportunity he sought to suppress the pan-Turkist movement, whose prominent members were arrested on charges of plotting to overthrow the government and to bring Turkey into the war on Germany's side.

At the same time, Turkish villagers had grown resentful of Kemalist objectives in the countryside. The Village Institutes received strong government support. Villagers were forced to build school buildings and roads for schoolmasters who often turned out to be aloof and unsympathetic mouthpieces of the hated secularist order. Local law and order police violently suppressed dissent. In the towns, exasperation focused on the abysmal economic conditions, on censorship of the press, and similar restrictions on personal freedom. There was little to suggest that the unpopular and authoritarian İnönü regime would permit the formation of opposition parties and, eventually, free elections.

In his speech at the opening of the new session of parliament on 1 November 1944, President İnönü announced his intention to open the regime, stating that the main problem of the state in Turkey was the lack of a true loyal opposition. With the Second World War plainly in its final months, Turkey entered the conflict on the side of the allies in February 1945 in order to qualify for admittance to the United Nations. Combat involving Turkish troops having been successfully avoided, the delicate middle way between powerful allies having been carefully negotiated, and the grave danger of the nation's survival having passed, İnönü could turn his considerable political skills to the task of building Turkish democracy.

8

Multiparty Democracy, 1945–1960

Like the characters in Yaşar Kemal's novel *Memed, My Hawk*, the ordinary people of Turkey's 40,000 villages experienced the revolutionary changes of the 1920s and 1930s indirectly at first, by way of the traditional institutions and relationships of their village. Published in 1955 and translated into dozens of languages in the years following, *Memed, My Hawk* tells the story of Slim Memed, a young boy who rebels against the cruelty of the village chief, Abdi Agha. After wounding Abdi Agha and killing his nephew in a violent confrontation, Memed flees to the hills to become a bandit.

Yaşar Kemal used archetypal characters, a common human moral sense, and symbolic imagery in *Memed, My Hawk* to create a story of epic reach. The horizons of his characters' world, however, did not extend much beyond the fields and pastures surrounding their home village, located in a small plateau in the Çukurova plain. When on Memed's first visit to a nearby town he meets an old man who describes Maraş to him and who has seen Istanbul, Memed thinks it a fantastic thing. The world is big, Memed realizes, and his village seems suddenly to be "but a spot in his mind's eye," and Abdi Agha "just an ant." Excited by this vision, Memed seeks both personal revenge against Abdi Agha and an uncomplicated social justice, symbolized by the burning of the thistles that choke the village land.

Villagers were not ignorant of national politics, but Yaşar Kemal's novel is a reminder not to exaggerate the impact of the great Republican reforms and economic and social development on largely rural Turkey. The continued strength of the traditional rural order, as described by Yaşar Kemal, was partly a consequence of compromises made in forging the alliance of state officials, professionals, businessmen, and rural magnates who had successfully resisted the dismemberment of the country after World War I. Poor economic conditions and the growing power of the state threw the divergent interests of these groups into sharp relief in the 1940s, and the alliance threatened to break apart.

TRANSITION TO DEMOCRACY, 1945–1950

At the end of World War II, President İnönü faced pressure to liberalize the regime. The repressive authoritarianism of the Republican People's Party under İnönü had made people at all levels of Turkish society desire a more open political environment. Turkey had, after all, signed the United Nations Charter, which sought international cooperation in "promoting and encouraging respect for human rights and for fundamental freedoms for all." In Turkey, martial law continued for more than a year after the end of the war, press censorship remained heavy, and labor organizations were almost nonexistent.

Besides this, Turkey was still an underdeveloped country. Although heavy industrial development during the 1930s brought more than 2,000 miles of new railroads, in the whole country there fewer than 2,000 tractors and only about 300 miles of paved roads. Only a handful of villages were electrified. Villagers resented the increased state control brought by the Kemalist revolution, especially as it was felt in increased taxation and the symbols of government imposed secularization.

As significant as the complaints of the numerous but comparatively weak villagers was the bitterness of the rural landholding class. Inattention to the agricultural sector meant that production remained limited and aimed mostly at local markets and that only a fraction of the potential wealth of the nation's agricultural industry had been realized. At the same time, wartime price controls destroyed their profits, while taxation on agriculture hurt them. Those few who, especially in the rich regions of the Aegean river valleys and the Çukurova plain, had made a lot of money during the war in cash crops such as cotton found their new wealth taxed heavily.

Antigovernment sentiment also grew among two other groups in Turkish society during and immediately after the war. State civil servants who had suffered heavily from inflation, and businessmen, both Muslim and Christian, who had carried the greatest burden of the hated capital tax, united in opposition to the regime. Many businessmen had opposed the etatism of the 1930s and still held strong opinions in favor of a free market approach to economic policy.

Parliamentary debate over the land redistribution law of January 1945 grew acrimonious. Dissidents within the RPP sought ways of opening up the political system. Four party members, Celal Bayar, Refik Koraltan, Fuad Köprülü, and Adnan Menderes, formally requested that the constitutional guarantees of democracy be implemented. Köprülü and Menderes published articles in the press critical of the RPP including in the Istanbul daily *Vatan*, whose editor, Ahmed Emin Yalman, opened the pages of his paper to the dissidents. Köprülü, Menderes, and Koraltan were expelled from the RPP; Bayar resigned his party membership. But in a speech opening the session of parliament on 1 November 1945, İnönü affirmed his intention to gradually introduce real democracy, and in January 1946, the four dissidents formed the Democrat Party (DP). The personalities and social positions of these men helped ensure that their party would become a powerful national political force. Bayar, a banker by profession, and Koraltan, an attorney, had been CUP members and joined the nationalist resistance. Bayar had served as prime minister from 1937 to 1939, and Koraltan had been a member of parliament and then provincial governor. Köprülü, a deputy from Kars, was a respected academic, the leading historian of his generation. Menderes was an attorney and cotton grower from Aydın who, as a member of parliament, led the criticism of the land law.

The depth of the opposition expressed through the DP came as a surprise to İnönü. Many within the RPP leadership accepted that the economy needed to be opened to market forces, and society to liberalization, and hence İnönü emphasized that there was not much difference between his RPP and what the DP was advocating. There was more than a little truth to this, but the DP acted as an umbrella under which all who mistrusted or opposed the current government sought refuge. It served as a way for people to voice resentments that had been building during the war years. And DP rhetoric provided an attractive description of the road to salvation for Turkey, by way of unfettered capitalism—at the time the United States, victorious in the war and possessing the most powerful economy in the world, held enormous prestige in the underdeveloped world.

In the face of a potentially overwhelming opposition, the RPP decided in an extraordinary party congress in May 1946 to call early elections— municipal balloting for May and national polls for July 1946—hoping to catch the Democrats before they had time to fully organize. The Democrats, yelling foul, boycotted the municipal elections but knew they must contest the general elections if they were to remain viable. The Republicans won a resounding victory, taking 403 of the 465 seats in parliament. But the DP, barely six months old, had made a strong showing.

The next year was critical to the future of democracy in Turkey. The victorious RPP nearly split in a battle between orthodox, single-party etatists (led by the new party leader and prime minister, Recep Peker), and a faction of reform-minded members who favored an open society and a looser definition of etatism that would permit private enterprise. İnönü, abandoning the title National Chief that he had taken in 1938, and promising to become a truly nonpartisan president, intervened in favor of the reformers in a statement that came to be known as the "12 July Declaration," emphatically defending the right of the DP to stand in opposition. Peker, forced to resign, was replaced by Foreign Minister Hasan Saka, who had led the Turkish delegation to the UN conference in San Francisco. It may be that İnönü was also influenced in this by the embryonic Turkish relationship with the United States. In March 1947, President Harry Truman had announced the beginning of aid to Greece and Turkey in what became known as the "Truman Doctrine," and negotiations soon were underway for assistance through the Marshall Plan.

Those within the RPP who wanted to revive the nation's economy through market reforms now took the upper hand. The party abandoned the five-year plan of 1946 for a new Turkish Development Plan embracing a market orientation. The Turkish lira was devalued to increase imports, especially of heavy machinery like tractors, and to develop agriculture, and Turkey became a member of the International Monetary Fund. Implementation of the land law proceeded very slowly. In the transportation sector, investment went into an ambitious road-building program rather than railroads. Workers were permitted to organize trade unions beginning in 1947 (although their political activity, and strikes, were forbidden at first), and 239 trade unions were formed by 1952. An independent businessmen's organization was formed.

In other ways, too, in the timeworn fashion of party politics, the RPP moved to cut the legs out from under the opposition by adopting important elements of its program. İsmail Hakkı Tonguç, the hated director general of grade school education who had developed the Village Institutes, was relieved of his duties in the fall of 1946. The Department of Education ruled that religion could be taught in public schools, and in the fall of 1949, a Faculty of Divinity opened at Ankara University. These policies essentially stole the Democrats' thunder but required that the RPP mute its emphasis on etatism and reformism and relax its attitude toward popular Islam.

In the first half of 1948, the economy continued to perform sluggishly. The RPP watched as the DP benefited simply by virtue of not being the party in power; gradually the situation began to improve. The DP fell to quarreling, one group warming to cooperation with the RPP, while the radicals, particularly those sympathetic to politicized Islam, accused the DP leadership of collusion with the Republicans and of selling out true democracy. The radicals bolted, forming the Nation Party in 1948. The relaxation of press censorship led to the founding of new newspapers, including *Hürriyet* (1948) and *Milliyet* (1950). With Yalman's now well-established *Vatan* (1940), the newspapers published a variety of critical perspectives.

Having split the opposition and coopted its program, the RPP felt confident of victory as the May 1950 elections approached. But the Turkish voters turned out in huge numbers to give the DP a stunning victory. With an absolute majority (53.5 percent) of the popular vote, the Democrats took 408 parliamentary seats to the RPP's 69. The Nation Party won only one seat. Ordinary Turks still linked İnönü to the autocratic repression of the war years.

POLITICS AND THE ECONOMY IN THE DEMOCRAT ERA, 1950–1960

The elections filled parliament with younger men from a broader range of social classes and backgrounds—the old Ottoman order was being eclipsed. Kâzim Karabekir, speaker of parliament since 1938, had recently passed away, and now İnönü had been defeated. In Turkey in 1950, a single-party dictatorship peacefully handed over the reins of authority to an elected democratic government. Herein lies the greater part of the legacy of İsmet İnönü. When the top army brass offered to stage a coup d'état, to suppress the elections and keep him in power, İnönü declined. He would take it upon himself during the next decade to demonstrate the meaning of "loyal opposition." The country received the Democrat victory with a sense of euphoria, as if national independence had been won all over again. Parliament elected Celal Bayar president of the Republic, Adnan Menderes became prime minister, Refik Koraltan became speaker of the parliament, and Fuad Köprülü was appointed foreign minister.

During the years 1948 to 1953, the economy grew at an average annual rate of well over 12 percent and per capita real income rose at 3 percent per year. The greatest expansion occurred in the agricultural sector. Credit was available through the Agricultural Bank, and the state continued to subsidize grain production. In May 1949, the first consignment of Marshall Plan tractors had arrived; by 1953, more than 30,000 tractors had been imported, which farmers could purchase or finance through the Agricultural Bank. The amount of land under cultivation increased by more than 50 percent during the next decade, and total yields swelled. The miles of paved highways quadrupled, linking the major cities of the country in a national highway system for the first time. Improved unpaved feeder roads made it easier to get the farm produce to market. Thousands of newly imported trucks carried the goods.

Overall economic growth slowed in 1954 but was still strong enough to return the Democrats to parliament with an even stronger majority. The RPP found itself in nearly complete disarray, without an alternative economic plan, still identified in the voters' memories with the repressive wartime policies of İnönü.

The boom could not last forever. The expansion had been financed with borrowed money and fueled by splendid harvests. When the harvests returned to normal after 1953, Turkey's economic problems began to accumulate. Loosened import restrictions had brought Turkey much needed machinery, equipment, and consumer goods, but with low levels of hard currency, the country was left with huge foreign trade and balance of payments deficits. The decision to cover the deficits with Central Bank loans spurred inflation. Sugar had to be rationed in Istanbul in December 1954, coffee a few months later. Import restrictions returned in 1955. The government's aversion to central planning of any kind made Turkey's economic growth appear haphazard, even reckless, to foreign investors. The United States turned down a request for new loans in June 1955, giving only $30 million as emergency assistance to work out the immediate difficulties.

While agriculture became increasingly mechanized, especially in the advanced regions of the Çukurova plain and the Aegean, industrial development proceeded more slowly, revealing some of the underlying weaknesses of the economy. The privatization program never really got off the ground. Few Turkish citizens had amassed private savings, so there was very little indigenous private capital. Those few who had it tended to invest not in local industry but in import-export commerce, which yielded quicker and higher profits. Although the number of new corporations registered rose from only 6 in 1950 to 56 in 1954, and the number of factory units doubled in the same period to nearly 5,000, these were still very small numbers. Exceptions could be found, but the entrepreneurial spirit, aimed at long-term development, was weak in Turkish industry. Most investment by far still came from the state; indeed, the first half of the 1950s saw unprecedented levels of public investment, in spite of the Democrats' espousal of an antietatist ideology. By far the largest firms in Turkey were still the state economic enterprises, Sümer Bank, Eti Bank, İş (Business) Bank and the Agricultural Bank.

Perhaps the government's goal of catching up to the level of the advanced European economies within fifty years was unrealistic—perhaps trying to build cement plants, dams, highways all at the same time was too much. The national education system, moreover, did not as yet have the capacity to fully service the needs of a complex industrial economy. General literacy had improved, but in the whole country there were only about 7,500 engineers and 900 architects. As criticism of the economic failures mounted, the Menderes government passed a repressive press law under which reporters and editors faced fines and prison terms for publishing articles that "could be harmful to the political or financial prestige of the state" or which were "an invasion of private life."

When negotiations between Great Britain, Turkey, and Greece over the future of Cyprus broke down in September 1955, Greek nationalist clamoring for union of the island with Greece reached a fever pitch. Riots broke out in Istanbul and İzmir, ostensibly in protest of Greek actions. Evidence suggests that the Menderes government may have instigated them, manipulating latent popular resentments in order to divert pressure from domestic problems. The event turned ugly. Mobs attacked Greek merchants who were accused of hoarding. Menderes hastily declared martial law. *Ulus* and *Hürriyet*, two prominent Istanbul dailies, were closed for printing articles about the riots. When ten Democrat parliamentarians protested, they were expelled from the party.

It became increasingly apparent that the rapid growth of the first half of the decade had had social costs that the government, in its enthusiasm for the economic boom, had ignored. Yaşar Kemal first achieved prominence as a journalist for *Cumhuriyet* writing sensitive analyses of the mixed impact of mechanized agriculture. Most Turkish farmers held small plots on which the economies of scale possible through mechanization could not be realized. Many could not afford the equipment anyway, even through available credit. Circumstances encouraged these small farmers to sell to larger agricultural magnates. Sharecroppers, too, and landless agricultural laborers found themselves priced out of the market. This was particularly a trend in cotton-growing areas like the Çukurova plain in the south and the area around İzmir and Aydın in the west. Some of what were to become Turkey's largest industrial conglomerates, like the Sabancı group of Adana and the Koç group of the Aegean area, had their start during this era. Haci Ömer Sabancı began in the cotton industry in Adana in 1947, while Vehbi Koç, already established in the import-export business, founded several manufacturing firms during the late 1940s and 1950s.

In earlier decades, the Turkish state had envisioned no permanent exodus from the village as industrialization got underway. The state had wanted to avoid the creation of concentrated industrial metropolises, deliberately locating new industries all over Anatolia. Hence the percentage of the Turkish population living in urban areas remained fairly stable between 1927 (24.2 percent) and 1950 (25.2 percent). Now, however, many of the surplus agrarian laborers created by mechanization moved to the cities in search of work, marking the beginnings of the *gecekondu* phenomenon that was to be characteristic of urban growth especially in the 1960s and 1970s. The word, meaning, literally, "built in the night," refers to the makeshift shelters on the outskirts of the major Turkish cities where people lived in squalid conditions without basic communications or sanitary services. Though intended to be temporary, these quarters became permanent neighborhoods around Istanbul, Ankara, İzmir, Adana, and other large cities.

Uneven commercialization and industrialization also had social consequences, as a few successful urban traders and businessmen accumulated tremendous wealth, bought expensive imported consumer goods, and clamored for political power commensurate with their new economic standing. Democrat Party rhetoric, more strongly identified with free enterprise and free expression of religious sentiment, attracted many of these new men. Formation in 1952 of the Confederated Trade Unions of Turkey, called Türk-İş for short, expressed a similar desire for greater political participation by urban laborers. This did not yet take an anti-capitalist form. The lifestyle differences between these successful entrepreneurs and the migrant peasants became evident where they came together in the large urban areas but, in fact, the groups had much in common, particularly conservative Islam.

More ominous was the growing resentment between the new rich and the urban poor, on the one hand, and the traditional Republican bureaucratic, military, and intellectual elites, on the other, whose secularist and etatist assumptions about national life were challenged by democratic policies and whose state salaries did not keep up with inflation. Inexperienced at governing, suspicious of the loyalties of Republican bureaucrats and state servants, forced to appease the sometimes mutually incompatible demands of its constituent groups, and led by a charismatic but intolerant prime minister, the Democrats made crucial political errors. A purge of the army general staff had been carried out in 1950 in an effort to discharge the top brass with ties to İnönü, but fear of İnönü—the "Pasha Factor"—still haunted the Democrat leadership. The Democrats squandered the goodwill and potential neutrality of the university faculties toward the new regime, which intellectuals had hoped would bring a more liberal approach to free thought and expression. For example, a 1953 law prohibiting university faculty from political activity, and a 1954 law making faculty over age 60 or having 25 years of experience subject to retirement, enabled a purge of suspected leftist faculty. The law also applied to the judiciary and was used to force out RPP judges. Some of these measures were aimed to balance the continued support of the RPP among state employees and to reward the Democrats' own clients with politically influential positions, but they compounded the tendency of politicization in the bureaucracy.

The party took pains to declare its support of constitutional secularism but felt pressure from its constituency to find ways of giving public support to the personal religious devotion of most Turks. Within weeks of their election in 1950, the Democrats ended the 27-year ban on religious broadcasting, instituting daily readings of the Qur'an on state radio. Regular teaching of Islam in public schools began. More *İmam-Hatip* schools—for the training of preachers and Qur'an teachers—were opened, and the call to prayer was made in Arabic again. Defaming Atatürk became a criminal offense after religious iconoclasts smashed busts of the great leader. The courts dissolved the Nation Party, finding it guilty of using religion for political purposes. The Democrats closed the Peoples' Houses and shut down the Village Institutes.

From the beginning, the DP had consisted of a loose coalition of groups united only by common hatred of the RPP. More than the party's concessions to traditional secularism and etatism, the economic downturn strained this coalition. Forced into a tactical retreat from their laissez-faire economic policy, the Democrats lost the support of some disgruntled businessmen. Intellectuals and professionals became increasingly unhappy with the autocratic management style of Menderes.

After the riots of September 1955, Menderes introduced draconian restrictions on the press. Journalists now would face prosecution for publishing news that could "curtail the supply of consumer goods or raise prices or cause loss of respect and confidence toward authorities." Foreign journalists, too, could be jailed for exaggerating bad news. Dissident DP members formed the Freedom Party. The respected foreign minister, Fuad Köprülü, one of the founders of the DP, resigned his cabinet post and then his party membership in mid-1956. Opposition grew in other quarters as well. In the fall of 1956, the dean of Ankara University was dismissed for delivering a "political lecture." Three hundred students protested and a number of academics resigned. And from late 1955 on, junior officers in the armed forces began to conspire against the regime.

Discontent in the military stemmed from complicated social roots as shown in a study by historian Feroz Ahmad (in *The Turkish Experiment in Democracy, 1950–1975* [Boulder, Colo., 1977], pp. 147–176). Since the end of World War II, the prestige of the military career in Turkey had declined slowly. Democratization marginalized men who were accustomed to playing a leading role in Turkish development. Menderes, wary of the officers' influence and almost paranoid about İnönü, made a military reformer his first minister of defense, but opponents among the top military brass managed to get him fired. After that, Menderes ingratiated himself with the generals but failed to stay informed of the circumstances of the junior officers. Already frustrated by the rigid hierarchy of the officer corps, these men watched their standard of living steadily decline after 1953 as their salaries lost purchasing power. These very same young officers found themselves at the forefront of rapid military change when Turkey joined NATO in 1952. They received the technical training in engineering and the sciences critical to the operation of a modern, mechanized military force, as they were most interested in the new tactics relevant to the nuclear age. Travel to Europe and the United States, and after 1955 the basing of Americans and NATO officials in Turkey, gave these officers increased contact with their American and European counterparts, and their own situations did not stand up well in the comparison that such contact inevitably brought.

The chastened Democrats won early general elections in October 1957. In the countryside, the Democrats were still seen as the party that supported religion, and the memory of repression at the hands of the İnönü and the police during the 1940s was still strong. But the Democrats lost their majority, winning only 47.3 percent of the vote. The RPP, rejuvenated by a new program emphasizing political liberties and constitutional reform, seemed finally to be back on its feet. Finding new support among intellectuals and businessmen defecting from the Democrats, the RPP made a robust showing, winning more than 40 percent of the popular vote and 178 of the now 600 seats in the parliament to the Democrats 424. Two months later, in December, nine junior army officers were arrested for plotting a coup.

Throughout 1958 and 1959, the Menderes government struggled to regain control of the economy. Guidelines suggested by international lenders since the mid-1950s provided the basis for their efforts, including devaluing the Turkish lira, lifting restrictions on imports and exports, and ending price supports and subsidies. Prices on the government monopolies of tea, sugar, cigarettes, and liquor were raised in late 1958. In return for these measures, Turkey was permitted to reschedule its debt and received a further loan of $359 million from the United States, the Organization for European Economic Cooperation and the International Monetary Fund. In September 1959, Turkey applied for associate membership in the European Economic Community. A partial recovery began.

Discontent among state servants, intellectuals, and others did not diminish, however. Istanbul University law professor Hüseyin Naili Kubalı was suspended in 1958 for denouncing press regulations. In 1959, four Istanbul dailies printed blank front pages to protest the state of the press. The RPP, sensing its strength returning, went on the offensive. Menderes foolishly ordered troops to interrupt a speaking tour by İnönü in the spring of 1960, but when İnönü called their bluff, the embarrassed troops backed down. Police opened fire during student protests on April 28, killing five and injuring forty; two days later, martial law was declared after riots in Istanbul. Eight newspapers were closed. On May 14, the tenth anniversary of the free elections of 1950, large crowds protested in the streets. A fight broke out in parliament on May 25, leaving fifteen members injured in the fisticuffs and flying desks. At 3:00 A.M. on 27 May 1960, Colonel Alparslan Türkeş announced over the radio that the armed forces had taken over the state in order to "prevent fratricide" and "extricate the parties from the irreconcilable situation into which they had fallen."

REALISM IN TURKISH CULTURE

The most important currents in Turkish literature, film, and music during this period sprang from the conviction that a Turkish national literature ought to describe the life of the whole country, village life as well as city life, and that the purpose of national literature was to assist in the development of the nation. While the cities had advanced toward ideals of modernity, the villages had not on the whole made much progress. Many writers of this period turned their attention, therefore, to the wretched conditions of the majority of the population who lived in villages.

Mahmut Makal, author of the celebrated exposé of village life *Bizim Köy* (Our Village, 1950, published in English as *A Village in Anatolia*), was a young Village Institute graduate who returned to teach in the village. Schooled in the modern assumptions of the Republic, Makal described with frustration the ongoing vitality of traditional norms in rural Turkey. This work and the early novels of Yakup Kadri Karaosmanoğlu, especially *Yaban* (The Stranger, 1932), about an intellectual's alienation from the peasants of an Anatolian village, exerted a strong influence on the development of realism in Turkish fiction during the 1950s. Beginning as a journalist before turning to novels, Yaşar Kemal, himself born in a village in the Çukurova plain, wrote sympathetically of the social dislocations brought by economic changes of the early 1950s. In *Memed, My Hawk* and in several other novels and in collections of short stories, Yashar Kemal delved into the lives of characters in the remote villages of the Çukurova plain and the foothills of the Taurus Mountains. Orhan Kemal, one of the most important novelists of the Republican era, also set his works, like *Cemile* (1952) and *Bereketli Topraklar Üzerinde* (On Fertile Lands, 1964) in his native Çukurova, typically exploring the circumstances of the impoverished factory workers of Adana and the former villagers who had moved to the city looking for work. Sait Faik Abasiyanık, who published mostly short stories, wrote about the lives of the urban underclass—fishermen, panhandlers, coffee shop patrons, the unemployed. Aziz Nesin, one of Turkey's best known writers in the West, was a satirist and humorist whose characters often were simple town or city dwellers haplessly facing petty bureaucrats, police officers, landlords, and others out to take advantage of them.

A similar interest in the life of common people can be seen in some of the poetry of the period, in film, and in the expanding popularity of folk music among urbanized Turks and intellectuals. The 1950 collection by poet Fazıl Hüsnü Dağlarca, *Toprak Ana* (Earth Mother), comes closest to the concerns of the realist novelists. Poets of this generation adopted a more colloquial Turkish, the Turkish of the countryside. Varlık Press remained prominent in publishing this literature (it had published Mahmut Makal's *Bizim Köy*) and was rivaled now by Yeditepe, which like Varlık also published its own journal.

In film, the late 1940s saw a marked shift from earlier times. This was partly connected to government subsidies of the Turkish film industry. From an average of less than one and a half films per year, the national film industry grew to producing an average of more than fifty films a year by the end of the 1950s, and audiences grew too. A landmark in the realist movement was Lütfi Ö. Akad's *Vurun Kahpeye* (Strike the Whore, 1949), based on the Halide Edip Adıvar novel. Akad signed with Kemal Film in the 1950s. Kemal Film, a company founded in 1922, had produced the early silent works of Muhsin Ertuğrul, a pioneer of Turkish theater who was the only Turkish film director until 1939. The studio's new owner, Osman Seden, a screenplay writer, also moved into directing. With Kemal Film, Akad directed his masterpiece *Kanun Namına* (In the Name of the Law, 1952). One of the most popular films of the decade was Memduh Ün's *Üç Arkadaş* (1958), about a romance between two common people.

When it comes to music, the far-reaching influence of the Village Institutes and People's Houses must once again be reckoned with. The curriculum of the Village Institutes had included an introduction to peasant music. At first, this music was interpreted to urbanites through simplified rhythms and a polyphonized scale, on radio programs like "Airs of the Country" (on Istanbul radio), and "We Are Learning a Folksong" (Ankara), but by the end of the 1950s, there was greater interest in appreciating the original instruments and manner of performance.

THE RELATIONSHIP WITH AMERICA

By the late 1950s, it was becoming clear that Turkey's growing relationship with the United States had not only permanently reoriented Turkish foreign policy, but also had an impact on domestic politics as well. Turkey's membership in the OEEC and the Council of Europe, both dating to 1949, fit the traditional alignments of the Kemalist Republic.

The enhanced American relationship grew out of the relative weakness of Europe after the war, the gradual withdrawal of Great Britain from imperial involvement, and the acceptance by the United States of the implications of its position of world military and economic leadership. The relationship was shaped throughout its history by the conditions of the Cold War, conditions which Atatürk could not have foreseen a decade earlier.

At the end of World War II, the Soviet Union exerted pressure on Turkey through demands for territorial concessions along the Bulgarian border in Thrace, a revision of the Montreux Convention governing the passage of shipping in the Straits, and occupation of military bases along the Bosphorus and Dardanelles. The İnönü government rejected these and turned to the United States for help, fearing a Soviet attack. In response, President Harry Truman proposed the Truman Doctrine, assistance to Turkey and to Greece in a speech to the U.S. Congress on 12 March 1947. The basic idea behind the Truman Doctrine was that without American intervention, both Turkey and Greece would succumb to Soviet domination, leading to Soviet influence throughout the Middle East.

In May 1947, the U.S. Congress appropriated $100 million for aid to Turkey, and by the end of summer 1947, established the Joint American Military Mission for Aid to Turkey (JAMMAT) under the authority of the American Ambassador in Ankara. Through JAMMAT, the U.S. Air Force provided aircraft and training to the Turkish air force and assisted in the construction and improvement of several Turkish air bases, which had been contracted to American industrial firms. This military assistance was supplemented by economic assistance through the Marshall Plan, announced in April 1948. By mid-1949, Marshall Plan tractors began arriving in Turkey.

The İnönü government expressed immediate interest in joining the North Atlantic Treaty Organization (NATO) when it was formed in April 1949. The Menderes government made formal application for membership in 1950. The Turkish army contributed a brigade of 4,500 troops to the United Nations war effort in Korea. The impressive performance of Turkish soldiers in combat—they suffered the heaviest casualties of any participant country—generated support for Turkey's NATO membership. In February 1952, Turkey and Greece entered NATO at the same time.

Turkey's membership in NATO required that the Turkish government approve the Status of Forces Agreement and the Military Facilities

Agreement. When the Menderes government ratified these in 1954, the way was opened for NATO staff and American military personnel to be stationed in Turkey. In February 1955, the United States established at Ankara the headquarters of the United States Logistics Group, the unit coordinating support of American military forces in Turkey. The size of the NATO and American military forces grew rapidly. By the end of the 1950s, several thousand American military personnel and their families lived in Turkey under four different command structures. Two related facilities opened with the Ankara headquarters: an air station near Diyarbakır and a base at the recently completed Adana Air Field. A NATO support squadron was activated at İzmir later in the same year. The Adana Air Base, built and used jointly by the Turkish and U.S. air forces and in 1958 renamed the İncirlik Air Base after the village where it was located a few miles east of Adana, became especially significant in American military planning. It housed a squadron of B-47 bombers armed with Jupiter nuclear missiles and hosted rotations of F-100 fighter squadrons. By 1957, this base had become the main staging location for high altitude U-2 reconnaissance flights over the Soviet Union. Soviet anti-aircraft missiles shot down one of these planes in May 1960, during the last days of the Menderes government, and captured its pilot, Francis Gary Powers, alive, igniting an international crisis. Powers's plane had actually taken off that day from a base in Pakistan, but a diversionary flight along the Soviet border was flown from İncirlik. İncirlik was also used by American fighters deployed during the intervention in Lebanon in 1958.

It was probably inevitable that Turkey would be drawn into the Cold War, in view of Turkey's border with the USSR in the Transcaucasus and Russia's interest in access to the Mediterranean via the Black Sea. The conditions of American assistance, and the rationale of the Truman Doctrine specifically, deepened Turkish involvement. The American alliance was not the only element of Turkish foreign policy in the 1950s. Turkey maintained close relations with Great Britain, joining Britain and Greece as international guarantors of the independence of Cyprus in negotiations that were finally concluded in 1959. Turkey also pursued bilateral relations with Italy and entered relations with Greece and Yugoslavia. Yet the American alliance heavily influenced Turkey's regional diplomatic position. Encouraged by the United States, the Menderes government signed a diplomatic agreement with Pakistan in 1954 and a mutual defense pact with Iraq in 1955. These agreements became the centerpiece of an interlocking set of agreements between Turkey, Iraq,

Iran, Pakistan, and Great Britain called the Baghdad Pact. After the 1958 revolution in Iraq, this alliance system was reorganized into the Central Treaty Organization (CENTO) under American leadership. The announcement in 1957 of the Eisenhower Doctrine, offering economic and military assistance to countries that fought communism and promising American protection to any Middle Eastern country attacked by a communist state, solidified Turkey's position.

The American alliance subtly affected the climate of political debate in Turkey in the late 1940s and 1950s. Sensitivity to ideas and attitudes associated with communism in Turkey certainly predated American aid, but American aid exacerbated these tensions. There were occasional demonstrations against communist influence, and journalists, academics, and intellectuals accused of being communists were given prominent trials and sometimes became targets of violence. The poet Nazım Hikmet spent the period 1938 to 1950 in prison for his views, after which he escaped abroad and never returned to Turkey. Another famous incident occurred at the end of December 1947 at Ankara University. Charges of communism against three professors, Niyazi Berkes, Behice Boran, and Pertev Naili Boratav, had been dropped after a two-year investigation for lack of evidence, but student demonstrators demanded their resignation. A mob broke into the offices of the university president, Şevket Aziz Kansu, who was the brother-in-law of İsmail Hakkı Tonguç, the recently sacked director of the Village Institutes. Kansu escaped under police escort and resigned. Berkes, a sociologist, and Boratav, a folklorist, emigrated to Canada and France, respectively, where they completed long and influential academic careers. Boran, also a sociologist, went on to head the Turkish Workers' Party in the late 1960s, spent time in prison, and died in exile in Brussels. But in the 1950s, the state, which had persecuted communists and Islamists equally under Atatürk and İnönü, tolerated Islamists to an unprecedented degree, while maintaining the pressure on leftists.

Another important dimension of the Turkish-American relationship was the growing cultural and intellectual exchange. In June 1947, Pan American Airlines began regular service to Istanbul on its west-to-east route, facilitating unofficial American business and cultural connections with Turkey. Representatives from the American Federation of Labor (AFL) provided advice and assistance in the establishment of Türk-İş in the early 1950s. In 1949, funds became available through the Fulbright exchange program, and assistance from the American Council of Learned Societies and government agencies like the United States Agency for International Development (USAID) enabled American scholars and students to live and study in Turkey. Some of these exchanges led to research that benefited Turkey directly, including studies of Turkish communications infrastructure and business climate in the late 1940s and early 1950s.

The full impact of American aid on Turkish life was complex. The prestige that the United States, the main world economic power, enjoyed in Turkey bolstered the expectations of economic liberals. In a speech in 1957, President Celal Bayar said that he hoped Turkey would become a "Little America." By 1960, the United States had provided approximately $3 billion of aid to Turkey. This gave valuable assistance to the Turkish economy, especially to the mechanization of agriculture, and permitted a thorough modernization and reorganization of the Turkish armed forces. Except for the United States, Turkey's active-duty military of half a million men was the largest in NATO; it was well equipped and had received modern training. Historian John Vander Lippe has shown that this contributed to the continued militarization of Turkish society. By the late 1950s some Turks charged that the American relationship with Turkey was essentially neocolonial. They wondered whether, ironically, American financial aid by its sheer scale may have allowed Turkish politicians to avoid or delay some of the vital economic reforms that it was its mission to encourage.

9

Military Intervention and the Second Republic, 1960–1980

In several volumes of short stories published in a lengthy career that spanned the period from the late 1940s until the late 1980s, Aziz Nesin turned his devastating wit on Turkish society and culture. The naïveté of his heroes is matched only by the bigotry and condescension of their tormentors, who despite their ignorance jealously guard the puny authority they hold. In the first volume of his memoirs, he relates a story of interaction between "mansion kids," who live in a house with a high garden wall and have scrubbed, clean faces, and dirty "street kids," who play in the alley outside the wall and pick the fruit from the branches of a tree that overhangs it from the garden. Even children could not overcome the class differences that separated them (Aziz Nesin, *Istanbul Boy* [Austin, Tex., 1977], pp. 112–115).

Aziz Nesin's career, during which he was arrested a number of times for a variety of offenses, serves as an example of the extraordinary—and tragic—politicization of differences in Turkish society of the 1950s through 1970s. He was arrested in a sweep of leftists in December 1946 and condemned by military courts. Despite occasional arrests and jail terms, he continued to publish short stories, novels, and plays, and eventually his memoirs, *Böyle Gelmiş Böyle Gitmez*, beginning in the late 1960s. The title inverts the Turkish saying "It's the way it's always been, it's the way it's always going to be," making it come out "It's the way it's always been, but it's not the way it's always going to be."

THE MILITARY COUP OF 1960

The military coup d'état on 27 May 1960 was welcomed enthusiastically in Istanbul and Ankara but accepted with sullen disappointment in much of the Anatolian countryside, where it was widely regarded as an intervention against the Menderes government on behalf of the RPP. In spite of their declared nonpartisan objectives—to establish an administration transcending party politics, to hold free elections, and to return political power to the winners—the actions of the officers over the next few months strengthened the perception. The officers appointed a Constitutional Commission, chaired by Sıddık Sami Onar of the law faculty of Istanbul University. Another member, Hüseyin Naili Kubalı, had already achieved notoriety as a critic of the Democrat Party. The Constitutional Commission issued a statement justifying the coup on the grounds that the Democrat Party had become an instrument of class interests in Turkish society and had aligned itself with forces opposed to the secularist principles of Atatürk's revolution. All DP parliamentarians were arrested, and the party was closed down.

The young officers, calling themselves the National Unity Committee (NUC), exercised sovereignty on behalf of the nation until a new constitution could be written, elections could be held and parliament could resume its role. General Cemal Gürsel, the nominal leader of the junta and chairman of the NUC, simultaneously filled the offices of president, prime minister and commander in chief of the armed forces, giving him more power on paper than even Atatürk himself had ever held. President Gürsel appointed a cabinet, subject to the approval of the NUC. Feroz Ahmad's study, cited above, showed that the NUC, an unwieldy group of thirty-eight officers, contained three main factions who from the beginning disagreed about common aims and principles. The most powerful figure of the group was the charismatic Colonel Alparslan Türkeş. Like many of the new generation of officers, Colonel Türkeş had spent time in Germany and the United States, and had served at the NATO command in Ankara. General Gürsel had been chosen by the junior officers plotting the coup as a sympathetic figure who could get along with everybody, who was positioned in the military hierarchy so as to assist their aims. One faction, called the "pashas," consisted of old-school generals who saw the purpose of the military intervention as restoring civil order. They viewed politics as a gentleman's profession and favored a swift return to civilian rule. The second faction differed only slightly from the first. They were interested in how democracy could aid social and economic development. They supported a planned economy, led by state economic enterprises, and the development of a welfare state. Some wanted to simply hand power to İnönü and the Republicans, but some were not hostile to the Democrats. The third faction were radicals, junior officers who advocated fundamental political and social change and favored maintaining military rule indefinitely in order to direct it from above. They were conscious of the social and economic inequities introduced in Turkey as a consequence of the boom of the 1950s. Some of them, like Colonel Türkeş, were communitarian radicals who envisioned a nonparty nationalist populism in the mold of Nasser's Egypt.

A struggle for power between these factions continued for about six months. In November, the pashas struck against the radicals, dissolved the NUC and formed a new, smaller NUC. The fourteen junior officers expelled in this move were exiled to Turkish embassies abroad. Türkeş was assigned to India. The pashas knew, however, that the radicals had expressed views widespread among the junior officer corps. With the purge, groups of conspirators once again formed, plotting to seize control of the state and to bring about a complete overhaul of the Turkish political and social system. Aware of the continued danger of rebellion from junior officers, and wanting to prevent their economic marginalization, senior officers formed two new institutions, the Army Mutual Assistance Association (better known by its Turkish acronym, OYAK), and the Armed Forces Union (AFU). OYAK was a pension fund for retired officers, financed by obligatory salary contributions. It swiftly developed into a powerful conglomerate with vast holdings in the Turkish economy. The AFU, open to all officers, provided a forum for identifying and discussing issues of common concern, under the supervision of the top brass. The AFU acted as a control on the NUC and as a safety valve for discontent from below, allowing generals to gradually gain control over the junior officer corps. They wanted to make certain that there would never be another military rebellion that they themselves did not lead and direct.

THE CONSTITUTION OF THE SECOND REPUBLIC

The Constitutional Commission became deadlocked between those who favored full democratic liberties and those who favored a return to single-party directed development. After a purge, the commission eventually produced a document. Meanwhile, a rival group of professors from the Faculty of Law at Ankara University submitted a separate draft and convinced the NUC to appoint a Constituent Assembly. The Constituent Assembly, made up of the NUC and some politicians, asked two neutral academics, Professors Enver Ziya Karal and Turhan Feyzioğlu, to form a Constitutional Committee and reconcile the two documents. This committee completed its work during the spring, and the new constitution passed in a deeply divided national referendum on 9 July 1961.

The constitution of the Second Republic introduced important structural changes to Turkish society and government. It established a bicameral legislature. The upper chamber, or Senate, was directly elected for terms of six years, but members of the NUC and former presidents of the Republic became lifetime senators, and fifteen others were appointed by the president. The lower chamber was popularly elected by a system of proportional representation. Laws were required to pass both chambers, but the lower chamber alone had power to initiate legislation. The lower chamber could override the Senate's decisions by a two-thirds vote. The national budget was reviewed by a joint commission of the two chambers, but the lower chamber had the final approval. Votes of no confidence were held in the lower chamber. Another major innovation was the establishment of a Constitutional Court of fifteen members drawn from the judiciary, parliament, university law faculties, and presidential appointments. The Constitutional Court reviewed laws and orders of parliament at the request of specific persons or groups, including political parties. The president of the Republic would now be elected by parliament, from among its members, for a single term of seven years. He was to be a neutral political figure, to "represent the Turkish Republic and the integrity of the Turkish Nation," and his office maintained a certain independence from the legislature. The president appointed the prime minister, who chose the other cabinet ministers.

The new constitution also enshrined certain rights and liberties and principles not expressly provided for in the 1924 constitution. The constitution guaranteed freedom of thought, expression, association, and publication. The judiciary was made independent of the legislature. Universities, not the Ministry of Education, would have the right to hire and fire faculty members. Freedom of the press was limited only by the need to "safeguard national security and public morality." The rights to unionize, to collective bargaining, and to strike were explicitly protected, and workers had the right to social security and welfare.

The right to own and inherit private property was recognized, but the state obliged itself to provide land for landless farmers. The constitution granted the state power "to plan economic development so as to achieve social justice." The constitution stated that economic, social, and cultural development would be based on and carried out in accordance with a plan. The State Planning Organization functioned as an advisory body under the authority of the prime minister. The prime minister chaired the High Planning Council, the executive body of the SPO, on which also sat three cabinet ministers.

Another new institution, the National Security Council, was formed by law in March 1962. Chaired by the president of the Republic, the NSC was made up of the chief of the general staff, heads of the service branches, the prime minister, and ministers of relevant cabinet ministries. Its role was to advise the government on matters of national security, both domestic and foreign. Through its general secretariat and various departments, the NSC was to gradually develop into a political force of sometimes decisive magnitude, as greater and greater portions of national political, social, and economic life became defined as matters of national security.

Many of the democratic innovations of the new constitution were welcomed by all sectors of Turkish society, but certain contentious provisions were vigorously opposed by the old Democrat Party constituency, especially the clauses explicitly providing for a centrally planned economy. Some also resented the liberal approach to workers' rights, and to the new climate of open political debate permitted by the freedom of the press and association.

PARTY POLITICS, 1961–1970

The trial of hundreds of DP members and the execution of the Democrat leaders during the national elections of 1961 poisoned the political atmosphere of the Second Republic from the outset. The NUC commuted the death sentences of eleven of the fifteen sentenced to capital punishment, and former President Celal Bayar was spared on account of his advanced age and ill health. But the former DP Foreign Minister and Finance Minister were executed on September 16, and former Prime Minister Adnan Menderes the next day, despite efforts by İsmet İnönü and others to intervene.

İnönü's RPP won closely fought elections a month after the executions, but the returns were troubling. The RPP took 36.7 percent of the popular vote and 173 seats in the lower chamber. But between the second place Justice Party (JP), subscribed to by most former Democrats, with 34.8 percent and 158 seats, and the New Turkey Party, a close relative of the breakaway Democrats' Freedom Party of the mid-1950s, which polled 13.7 percent and 65 seats, the old DP element had taken 48.5 percent of the popular vote and was only three seats shy of a majority in the lower chamber. The rightist Republican Peasants' Nation Party took the remaining 54 seats. General Gürsel was elected president. It was not too far-fetched to read the election results as a repudiation of the constitution and the new regime. Prospects that the Second Republic would make any significant headway against the country's social and economic problems seemed dim.

Political instability marked the next several years, as a series of short-lived coalition governments headed by İnönü, with the support of the army, tried to implement the constitution and oversee economic development in the face of stubborn opposition. In the wake of elections that had seemed to vindicate the loyal DP supporters, there was little incentive for the JP to cooperate with the government. Even before the first cabinet could be formed, in late 1961, workers began demonstrating in the streets, demanding action on the constitution's guarantee of the right to strike. Angry junior officers, resolutely determined to prevent a neo-Democrat takeover, plotted a coup. Colonel Talat Aydemir, a key conspirator in the 1950s who had been unable to participate in the coup due to his posting in Korea, was arrested for attempting to take over the government in February 1962. This episode brought the JP to a brief rapprochement with the RPP, but their coalition lasted only until May of that year. When it collapsed, İnönü formed a second coalition, this time with the other two parties. Concessions to the right helped ensure that this second coalition lasted about a year and a half, during which time Colonel Aydemir was executed after a second coup attempt was thwarted in May 1963.

Local elections in November 1963 made it clear that the RPP no longer had the consent of the governed. İnönü resigned, and President Gürsel invited Ragıp Gümüşpala, head of the Justice Party, to form a new government. Although he was unable to do so, the evident willingness of the army to consent to an administration headed by the JP contributed to a feeling of greater optimism for the future. İsmet İnönü, now eighty years old, once again cobbled together a coalition and assumed the prime ministry. A weak union of the RPP and independent deputies, this government managed to survive for fourteen months mainly because throughout 1964 everyone became preoccupied with the Cyprus issue. It too finally collapsed, on a budget vote in February 1965, and the country limped to general elections in October 1965.

The principle issues of public policy dividing the parties were socio-economic, and thus the first casualty of the elections of 1961 had been the very reforms that were vital to the success of the constitution. An example of this can be seen in the issue of state planning. After the disintegration of the first coalition, when İnönü was forced into concessions, strident opponents of planning ended up in the cabinet. When the five-year plan, prepared by the SPO went to the High Planning Council for the discussion in August 1962, the section on agrarian reform never reached the table because of cabinet objections, and measures to make the state economic enterprises more competitive were rejected. The cabinet also refused to accede to proposed tax reforms needed to finance the plan. The technical advisors to the State Planning Organization resigned. The absence of political commitment to its work, increasing politicization of appointments, and high turnover weakened the effectiveness of the SPO.

The 1965 elections saw the rise of a new political figure, Süleyman Demirel, who became chairman of the JP after the death of Rağıp Gümü-şpala. A peasant's son with a degree in engineering from Istanbul University, Demirel represented a new generation of Turkish politician. He was a common man and a skilled orator who spoke the language of the ordinary people. He had technical training and experience working with the Americans, having lived in the United States for short periods before entering government service in the 1950s. He was religiously observant and conservative, but a secularist. Though inexperienced, he was a congenial man and an able negotiator, and he unified the right by rebuilding the coalition of industrialists, big landowners, small merchants, and artisans and peasants reminiscent of the DP of the early 1950s.

Demirel took the Justice Party to victory with an outright majority of the votes and 240 seats in the lower chamber. Demirel assured the generals that he would follow his own program, independent of the old Democrats, and smoothed the way to reconciliation by granting them nearly complete autonomy in military affairs and the defense budget. After his victory, Demirel's biggest political problems came not from the opposition, which had been left in disarray, but from within his own party. The lopsided economic growth of the 1960s gradually alienated some parts of his constituency, especially the lower middle class of small urban shopkeepers and artisans. The right wing of the JP began to fragment despite Demirel's frequent tactical use of anticommunist and religious rhetoric, some following Alparslan Türkeş into extreme nationalism, others following Necmettin Erbakan into religious pietism.

Türkeş, one of the key figures of the 1960 junta, had returned from exile abroad in February 1963 and entered politics. He joined the Republican Peasants' National Party (RPNP), and in 1965 he took over the party chairmanship. Under his direction the RPNP took a radically nationalist and racist tone, espousing a doctrine of what Türkeş called "the Nine Lights": nationalism, morality, social responsibility, scientific-mindedness, support for freedom, support for the peasants, developmentalism, industrialization, and technology. In 1969, the party changed its name to the Nationalist Action Party.

Necmettin Erbakan, an electrical engineer who had been an undergraduate at Istanbul Technical University with Demirel in the late 1940s, had taken up an academic career. Entering politics through the Union of Chambers of Commerce and Industry, he won a seat in parliament in 1969. Erbakan gained a reputation as a maverick because of his outspoken advocacy of a role for Islam in public and political life, and a tendency to let fly with intemperate public remarks, as when he accused Demirel of collusion with Zionists and Masons. In January 1970, Erbakan formed the National Order Party, the first of a series of Islamist parties in Turkish politics.

The RPP began a thorough soul searching. Convinced that Demirel's economic and social policies had forsaken the principles of Atatürk and would ruin the common Turkish peasant and worker, in the early 1960s the young leadership of the RPP had persuaded İnönü that the party should adopt a "left of center" agenda for the campaign. Many blamed the new approach for the party's crushing defeat of 1965, but for the time İnönü continued to support the man who was its main author, Bülent Ecevit. İnönü had brought Ecevit into the government in the three RPP-led coalitions of 1961–1965 as Minister of Labor.

Ecevit interpreted the politics of the entire era since 1945 quite differently than most in the RPP, believing that for the party of Atatürk to survive, it must shed its elitist image and trust the Turkish people to know what was best for themselves. He understood that the voters had supported Menderes, and now supported Demirel, not primarily because those parties exploited their ignorance but because they felt alienated by the RPP's smugness and because the opposition had convinced them that its program was better. The RPP, said Ecevit, needed to win back the common Turkish men and women, whose livelihood was directly threatened by JP economic policy. Ecevit's "left of center" theme drove Turhan Feyzioğlu and some other disgruntled members to a break with the RPP and from the Reliance Party.

ECONOMY AND SOCIETY IN THE 1960s

By the early 1970s, Turkey faced a mounting crisis, the origins of which lay partly in the deteriorating economic conditions of the country, partly in the massive social changes that had occurred since the 1950s, partly in a loss of confidence in the Turkish state by certain groups in Turkish society and partly in the circumstances of the Cold War.

Demirel's government had overseen rapid economic growth, almost 20 percent annually between 1963 and 1969. But the growth was very uneven, and the JP steadfastly resisted centralized planning and the structural reforms necessary for healthy long-term growth. Because Turkey lacked sufficient native capital, the overall purpose of economic policy was to develop national industry through a program of import substitution. High tariffs and import restrictions were employed to protect Turkish industry from foreign competition except under certain strictly controlled conditions. Foreign firms were permitted to enter the Turkish market through joint ventures with Turkish companies. Thus the economic expansion in these years was fueled by imports of foreign raw materials, financed largely by foreign loans, and came to depend on a favorable foreign exchange situation. The emphasis was on the manufacture of consumer goods for the domestic market, rather than aiming at production for the export market in order to build foreign currency earning. Without central planning, this foreign capital was used inefficiently and without regard for overall national economic and industrial priorities.

There were some successes. Türk Petrol, the state-owned oil company, inaugurated a pipeline between the fields at Batman and the southern Mediterranean port of İskenderun in January 1967. The Seyhan Irrigation Project, a large dam project in the Çukurova plain that would provide hydroelectric power, flood control, and irrigation, was begun with funding from the World Bank and the U.S. Agency for International Development. Work on another major U.S.A.I.D. project, the Integrated Agricultural Services Project near Denizli in the Aegean region, began in 1968. Turkey had finalized negotiations and joined the European Economic Community as an Associate Member in October 1964, bringing preferential tariffs and quotas for its agricultural products. Some of the greatest economic successes were accomplished through joint Turkish-foreign industrial ventures.

Turkey lacked the structural means, however, to begin amassing native capital out of small family savings. There were few joint stock companies and no significant private life insurance industry. The state monopolies on alcohol, matches, tobacco, and salt continued to be marginally profitable. The recently founded OYAK was quite successful, and by the end of the decade, had become a huge and diverse economic enterprise; and the civil servant pension fund and the social insurance agency for industrial workers were well subscribed. These, and the publicly owned banks, were about the only profitable state economic enterprises, whose collective debts doubled between 1960 and 1969.

The unbalanced growth exacerbated the impact of pressures such as population growth and rising expectations on Turkish laborers. The trend toward mechanization continued to push agrarian labor to the big cities. Some workers went abroad, mostly to western Europe. In fact, beginning in the mid-1960s, Turkey's most important export was its surplus labor. These workers' cash remittances back home increased eight-fold in one year between 1964 and 1965, becoming one of Turkey's most important sources of foreign exchange.

Those who stayed home used the new freedoms granted by the constitution to demand better pay and improved working conditions, and exercised their newly won right to bargain collectively and to strike. Radicalism showed in strikes at the Zonguldak coal mines in 1965 and at Istanbul glass factories in 1966, where rank and file workers rejected the compromises negotiated between the administration of the SEEs and their own union leadership. A group of unions broke from Türk-İş to form the Confederation of Revolutionary Workers' Unions, (*Devrimci İşçi Sendikarları Konfederasyonu*, or DİSK) in 1967. This federation was anti-capitalist and politically activist, encouraging street demonstrations to achieve political and economic objectives. Its president was Kemal Türkler, a founding member of the Turkish Workers' Party.

Another factor contributing to social tensions was the growing economic importance of women, in the professions as well as in the working class. The number of practicing women physicians tripled between 1953 and 1970, and the number of women lawyers quintupled. By 1973, 5 percent of all judges and 14.9 percent of lawyers were women. Melâhat Ruacan became the first woman elected to the Supreme Court of Appeals in 1954. The percentage of administrators in the state economic enterprises who were women increased from 10 percent at the time of Atatürk's death in 1938 to 19 percent in 1970. By 1970, nearly one-third of the administrators in the Ministry of Education were women. Progressive laws passed in the early 1970s prevented women from doing certain dangerous jobs and from working extra hours at night, and prohibited night work for six months after childbirth. Workplace nurseries and child care facilities improved. Some in Turkish society found this increased presence of women threatening, particularly in times of difficult economic circumstances.

As the economic growth favored some segments of the population and hit others hard, the Turkish voting public fragmented. The constitution made room for small political parties, granting them proportional representation in parliament. As a consequence, Turkish public life came to be increasingly influenced by the activities of small extremist groups of both the left and the right of the political spectrum. The leftist Turkish Workers' Party and the rightist Republican Peasants' Nation Party both won parliamentary representation in the 1965 elections and exerted an influence on Turkish politics beyond their numbers throughout the late 1960s and 1970s. Erbakan's National Order Party appeared in 1970.

The prevailing milieu in Turkish universities encouraged the free exchange of ideas. Students formed discussion groups and "idea clubs" on university campuses with a fascinatingly diverse array of perspectives. Political tracts were printed and distributed; world literary classics were translated, read, and discussed; and social agendas were proposed, accepted, changed, and abandoned in an atmosphere of openness and in anticipation of the imminent radical transformation of Turkish society.

Beginning perhaps with the universities, Turkish society gradually became polarized between leftists and rightists, and virtually no area of Turkish culture escaped the pervasive politicization. Certain newspapers were known as leftist papers and others were rightist, even among the national dailies. Music became politicized. The annual Istanbul Festival of Arts and Culture prominently featured Western classical music, including the works of Turkish composers such as Cem Mansur, and was heavily attended by leftist intellectuals and state officials. Leftists also favored Turkish folk music and interesting new genres of popular music using folk instruments and forms as its foundation. Rightists favored Ottoman and Middle Eastern classical music because of its association with the Islamic heritage. The popular genre known as Arabesque, which came to Turkey via Egypt beginning in the 1950s, took over the radio airwaves and nightclubs (*gazinos*) and produced huge stars. Language itself became increasingly politicized, as the Turkish Language Society continued the work of cleansing Turkish of its Arabic and Persian vocabulary and grammatical constructions. A person could be literally identified on the political spectrum by the vocabulary he or she used in daily speech.

On both the left and the right, extremist groups emerged by the late 1960s. One of the most notorious leftist revolutionary groups grew out of an effort to link the "idea clubs" of university campuses nationally under Marxist leadership. This group, *Dev Genç*, or "Revolutionary Youth," advocated the violent overthrow of the Turkish state. The Turkish Communist Party had little influence in Turkey. The real rise of the Turkish left can be traced to the declaration of principles published in the new socialist journal *Yön* and signed by 500 intellectuals in December 1961. The left gained momentum when Mehmet Ali Aybar became chairman of the Turkish Workers' Party in 1962. A speech by Aybar at the beginning of the national election campaign in 1965 stressed opposition to imperialism and to the presence of American military bases in Turkey, and bitterness about the failure of the West to support Turkey's side in the Cyprus conflict as major themes.

Similar circumstances shaped the Turkish right, which coalesced around a common anticommunism, in many cases though not always, advocacy of conservative Islamic piety and values as normative for Turkish society. The JP benefited from this kind of instinctual social and religious conservatism, shared by a large portion of the Turkish populace. Demirel was not above occasionally manipulating traditional Islamic social values or Turkish fears of the Soviet Union for political purposes. But in the atmosphere of open political exchange on the university campuses, more virulent forms of nationalism, anticommunism and religious devotion emerged in the late 1960s.

The main figure on the Turkish far right was Alparslan Türkeş. Although Türkeş publicly stressed the Atatürkist character of his philosophy of the "Nine Lights," the real emphasis of his ideology was on nationalism. For Türkeş the rights of individuals and groups must be subordinate to the nation, whose interests were guarded by an authoritarian state and its charismatic, above-the-law leader. He advocated a state-controlled, national socialist economy. "Anti-nation" elements—especially ethnic minorities—must be suppressed. Beginning about 1968, Türkeş established a paramilitary commando organization called the Gray Wolves within the party's youth movement, arming them and training them at secret camps for attacks against suspected leftists.

CIVIL UNREST AND THE 1971 "COUP BY MEMORANDUM"

Demonstrations by leftist and rightist groups turned more violent in late 1967. On the left, Americans and American interests often became the targets because they represented Turkish subservience to international capitalism and militarism in Turkish society. On the right, Turkish leftists and outspoken secularists became the target. Student protesters accused Demirel and the JP of being "American stooges," and Demirel, chaffing at the constitutional restrictions on executive authority, announced a government and police crackdown on "communists." But more than anything else, the publication in January 1966 of correspondence between American President Lyndon Johnson and then-Prime Minister İnönü over the Cyprus crisis of 1964, in which Johnson threatened to not back Turkey in the event of a Soviet attack, turned public opinion dramatically against the United States. To Turkish leftists, this letter confirmed that the United States had no real interest in Turkey outside a cold calculation of its place in the international power matrix.

By 1967, the numbers of American military personnel and their families stationed in Turkey had reached a peak of about 24,000, and their presence was felt especially in the cities of Ankara, İzmir, and Adana. The American military held leases for more than thirty facilities scattered throughout Ankara, including offices, apartments, warehouses, an exchange, and a hospital. The headquarters of the United States Logistics Group (TUSLOG) occupied two eleven-storied buildings in the main Kızılay section. On the western edge of the city at Balgat, the U.S. military owned land on which it built schools for military dependents. A network of more than thirty distinctly colored blue busses crisscrossed the city twice daily, carrying about 2,000 students to classes. Similar conditions prevailed in İzmir, though the numbers were not as great. At Adana, the Americans occupied a large airbase, separated from the city by several miles, but since not all personnel could be housed at its facilities, a small quarter of Adana became known as "little America" because of the heavy concentration of American families living there.

In addition to these military personnel, smaller groups of American Peace Corps volunteers and American scholars also came to Turkey. The first group of thirty-nine Peace Corps volunteers arrived in September 1962, and 100 more joined them a year later. These young men and women lived in small towns and in villages scattered throughout Turkey.

The American Research Institute in Turkey was established in 1964 with small libraries and hostel facilities for visiting scholars and researchers in Ankara and Istanbul. Each year, a small number of American university teachers came to Turkey through the Fulbright scholarship program.

Sporadic anti-American violence broke out. In November 1966, rioters attacked and stoned the U.S. consulate, the office of the U.S. Information Agency, and the Red Cross in Adana. In October 1967, Turkish employees at the İncirlik airbase went on strike. Anti-American demonstrations accompanied the U.S. Sixth Fleet when it anchored for shore leave, and turned increasingly violent. The reading room of the United States Information Agency in Ankara was bombed.

Politically motivated violence was not, however, only or even mainly directed at foreigners. In June 1968, students seized the administration buildings at Ankara University, demanding reform of the examination system and the fee structure. The following May, the rector and eleven deans resigned over the government's failure to enact reforms. In August 1969, about 1,500 workers occupied the iron and steel works at Ereğli demanding higher wages; riot police called to the scene were unable to evict the demonstrators, who were joined by 3,000 more workers. Demirel finally intervened and brought the issue to negotiations. In September, the airport employees went out on strike.

Election Day fights were reported all over the country in October 1969. Though its share of the popular vote declined to 46.5 percent in the general elections of October 1969, Demirel's JP maintained a shaky parliamentary majority. The RPP, in the throes of its identity crisis, slipped to 27.4 percent of the popular vote. Six other parties won representation in the lower chamber, though none won even 7 percent of the popular vote. Mounting economic problems obliged Demirel to consider unpopular corrective measures. When Demirel presented the budget three months later, JP dissidents joined the opposition to defeat the motion and force Demirel to resign in February 1970. President Cevdet Sunay, who had succeeded General Gürsel in 1966, immediately asked him to form a new government, but his position was obviously weak. Throughout 1970, Demirel's government was unable to accomplish much, with all its efforts seemingly confounded by growing civil unrest.

DİSK, the leftist trade union federation, organized a general strike in the heavily industrialized Istanbul-İzmit region in spring 1970, when the government announced new union regulations. The RPP and the JP traded accusations of responsibility for the unrest. In August 1970, ominous news of a shakeup leaked from the Turkish general staff. In December, rightist and leftist students clashed at Ankara University, the headquarters of the Turkish Labor Party were bombed, and students firebombed Demirel's car. The prime minister was uninjured. A meeting of political parties leaders, convened by President Sunay, produced no solutions. More than 200 students were arrested after a five-hour gun battle at Hacettepe University in Ankara in February 1970, and on March 4, four American soldiers were kidnapped and held for ransom. When police broke into a dormitory at Ankara University searching for the Americans, a battle broke out in which two students died. The police did not find the soldiers, who were later released unharmed.

Finally in March 1971, the chief of the general staff and the commanders of the army, navy, and air force sent Demirel an ultimatum demanding "a strong and credible government" to "neutralize the current anarchical situation" and "implement the reformist laws envisaged by the constitution." Demirel had little choice but to resign. Thus the Turkish military seized control of the state a second time in what has become known as the "coup by memorandum."

RETURN TO CIVILIAN RULE AND THE NATIONAL ELECTIONS OF 1973

The generals who brought down Demirel's government on 12 March 1971 did not have a clear program to lead the country out of its economic difficulties. Acting to forestall another coup by junior officers, they publicly blamed the political parties for the crisis and sought a government that would implement the reforms envisioned in the 1961 constitution. They neither dismissed President Sunay nor prorogued parliament. They selected Nihat Erim as prime minister, appointed a reformer, Attila Karaosmanoğlu, to direct economic policy, and gave their attention to combating terrorism.

Under cover of martial law, the military cracked down on violent groups. Thousands of people were arrested, including leaders of the Turkish Workers' Party, which was dissolved, and trade unions, and numerous university professors—among them personal friends and colleagues of Prime Minister Erim—and writers, including Yaşar Kemal. Erbakan's NOP was closed. Several newspapers and journals were closed, especially the publications of radical leftist and rightist organizations but also some of the mainstream press. Even *Cumhuriyet* received a ten-day suspension. The feared National Intelligence Organization (*Millî İstihbarat Teşkilatı*, or MİT), whose reputation had developed since it succeeded the earlier NSO in a restructuring in 1963, employed repressive means, including torture, to extract confessions from suspects.

Although Erim's cabinet made no progress on socioeconomic reform and was forced to resign, constitutional amendments scaling back civil liberties passed parliament. Universities lost their autonomy with the creation of the University Supervisory Council, the broadcast media lost their autonomy, and restrictions were placed on the freedom of the press. The autonomy of the Constitutional Court was limited. Significant changes were introduced in the national security apparatus. Parliament now found the advice of the National Security Council binding. A system of State Security Courts (*Devlet Güvenlik Mahkemesi*, or DGMs) was introduced, which tried hundreds of cases of national security during the next several years.

During 1972, the political parties began anticipating national elections to be held in the coming year. Necmettin Erbakan organized a new party with the same leadership, the National Salvation Party. At the RPP congress, Bülent Ecevit succeeded İsmet İnönü as party chair. In the elections of October 1973, Ecevit was a surprise winner, but the RPP failed to win a clear majority, taking 33.3 percent of the vote and 185 seats in the lower chamber. Demirel's JP won 29.8 percent and 149 seats. Five other parties divided the remaining seats: the former JP dissidents who had formed the new Democrat Party won 11.9 percent and 45 seats, Erbakan's National Salvation Party took 11.8 percent and 48 seats, Turhan Feyzioğlu's former RPP dissidents in the Republican Reliance Party took 5.3 percent and 13 seats, Alparslan Türkeş's NAP, 3.4 percent and 3 seats, and the Turkish Workers' Party reentered Parliament with 1 seat on the strength of 1.1 percent of the vote. There were also six independent deputies. Ecevit formed a coalition with Erbakan, who shared his distrust of foreign capital and big business, although in other respects the two men and their parties had very little in common. The arrangement was the first of several coalitions that governed Turkey with diminishing levels of success as the decade of the 1970s wore on. Though Ecevit sought chances to break this pattern, he never escaped it. His first opportunity came in the form of an international crisis over Cyprus.

THE CYPRUS CRISIS

The Republic of Cyprus, declared on 16 August 1960, resulted from a compromise between the ideal of union with Greece (*enosis*), favored by most Greek Cypriots, and partition of the island, favored by the Turkish

Cypriots, who made up about 18 percent of the population. Independence, proposed by the Archbishop Makarios II of Cyprus and finally accepted by Britain, Greece, and Turkey with a complex constitution for the island, meant a defeat for powerful local guerillas led by General George Grivas, a veteran of the 1921 Anatolian campaign who had fought for enosis.

The president of Cyprus was a Greek and the vice-president, a Turk, each elected by their respective communities, each with veto power over legislation. Seven Greeks and three Turks comprised the cabinet, and the legislature was 70 percent Greek and 30 percent Turkish. Each community also elected a communal chamber of deputies to govern religious, educational, cultural, and personal matters. The national civil service, the national guard, gendarmerie, and police were to be 70 percent Greek and 30 percent Turkish. Archbishop Makarios was elected the first president of Cyprus, and Fazıl Küçük, an attorney, the first vice-president. Great Britain, Greece, and Turkey became international guarantors of the "independence, territorial integrity and security" of the Republic of Cyprus, and agreed "to cooperate to ensure that the provisions of the Constitution shall be respected."

In the first months of independence, conflicts arose between the Greek Cypriots and Turkish Cypriots over the Turkish right to civil service posts, over the administration of a national income tax and the funding of the communal chambers of deputies, and over the issue of integrated units of the national army. A dispute over the national budget and constitutional amendments proposed by President Makarios degenerated into violence in December 1963 between Greek and Turkish Cypriots in Nicosia, resulting in the division of the city by a "Green Line" between the communities. When fighting spread to other cities, Turkey prepared for military intervention to protect the Turkish Cypriot minority. A cease-fire was arranged in March 1964, and a UN peacekeeping force arrived. In May 1964, President Johnson informed İnönü that he could not promise American support if a Turkish invasion of Cyprus prompted a Soviet attack on Turkey.

Intercommunal warfare broke out again in November 1967. Behind the conflict lay Turkish Cypriot resentment of their relative poverty and ongoing economic weakness, and the conditions of discrimination and harassment experienced by the Turkish Cypriot population. War between Greece and Turkey was prevented when the military junta in Athens acceded to Turkish demands that General Grivas be permanently barred from the island, that 10,000 Greek troops stationed on Cyprus be redeployed, and that the National Guard of Cyprus, which had become virtually an arm of the Greek army, be disbanded. In the aftermath of the 1967 conflict, Turkish Cypriots established the Provisional Cyprus Turkish Administration, which had the semblance of a Turkish Cypriot government despite Turkish insistence that it merely facilitated more efficient administration of the Turkish community.

During the spring of 1974, Turkey and Greece clashed over the issue of Greece's claims to oil rights in the Aegean. Crowds staged public demonstrations in major Turkish cities in April, and the Greek armed forces went on alert as NATO brought Ecevit and the Greek prime minister met for talks in Brussels in late June. Simultaneously, the Ecevit government was acting to fulfill a campaign promise, supported by all the Turkish political parties, to resolve a dispute with the United States over opium production. Thus, when on July 15 the Cypriot National Guard overthrew Archbishop Makarios in Cyprus, declared *enosis*, and installed as president the pro-enosis guerilla Nikos Sampson, the Ecevit government faced the crisis having just gone to the brink of armed conflict with Greece over the Aegean, having just defied the American government over opium, and in full awareness that since the Johnson letter it could not count on American support even in the event of a Soviet response.

Ecevit nonetheless moved decisively to confront the Cyprus crisis. Turkish troops landed on the beaches of northern Cyprus on July 20 and in three days of fighting occupied about a third of the island. Cities along the Turkish Mediterranean coast went under blackout in anticipation of possible retaliatory Greek bombing raids, but the fear proved unfounded. The Greek military junta in Athens, completely discredited, collapsed, handing over power to a civilian government under former President Konstantin Karamanlis. A cease-fire was called and negotiations begun between the two countries. When talks broke down a month later, a second military campaign secured strategic points in the eastern and western sections of the island, as the Turkish army permanently occupied 38.5 percent of the territory of Cyprus. There the Turkish Cypriots organized a "Turkish Federated State of Cyprus," which in 1983 became the Turkish Republic of Northern Cyprus. Only Turkey recognized its legitimacy. The Turkish public responded enthusiastically. "August has once again proven to be a month of victory for Turkishness," gushed one columnist in *Tercüman*, alluding to Atatürk's defeat of the Greek army at Sakarya in August 1921.

Turkey paid a high cost for its commitment to defend the Turkish minority in Cyprus. It forced an estimated 50 percent increase in the defense budget and obligated Turkey to substantially assist the new Turkish Republic of Northern Cyprus. The affair also damaged Turkey's standing in the European Community and caused a serious rupture in Turkish-American relations, leaving the country diplomatically isolated. In February, the U.S. Congress cut off American military assistance to Turkey. In retaliation, the Turkish government closed American military installations in Turkey, keeping only İncirlik open and only for NATO purposes, and placed restrictions on American use of Turkish ports and on American overflights of Turkish air space. Agreements with Germany, France, and NATO partially replaced American assistance, but the embargo contributed to Turkey's grave economic position in the late 1970s.

The embargo was eased slightly in October 1975, and in March 1976, Turkey signed a new four-year defense agreement with the American administration. The agreement languished without the approval of the U.S. Congress, which found it nearly impossible to overcome extremely negative public perceptions of Turkey, fed not only by the political efforts of powerful Greek Americans, but also by other intangible factors. A healthy Armenian nationalism had emerged during the late 1960s in the United States, bringing a wider public awareness of the Young Turk ethnic cleansing campaigns of World War I. Extremists of the Armenian Secret Army for the Liberation of Armenia (ASALA) killed thirty people in attacks on Turkish diplomats around the world, especially in the United States. It is probably difficult to overestimate the impact of Alan Parker's film *Midnight Express* (1978), which reminded American filmgoers of the narcotics controversy of a few years before. The film, which received six Academy Award nominations, was a sensationalized and grossly distorted adaptation of the memoir of Billy Hayes, a young American who had been jailed in Turkey for drug smuggling. The American bases in Turkey remained closed until July 1978. Only then was the ban on American aid finally lifted.

THE LATE 1970s: THE COLLAPSE OF PUBLIC ORDER

Sensing an opportunity to rid himself of the frustration of a coalition with his party's ideological rivals, Ecevit resigned at the height of his popularity in September 1974. This was a serious political miscalculation. He had expected the move to lead to new elections, elections he thought the RPP could win by riding the wave of the triumphant Cyprus campaign. Demirel, however, worked carefully with the leaders of the other parties to prevent this. Instead of new elections and a clean majority, Ecevit's rash move brought legislative stalemate. For the next six years, Turkey was governed by a series of weak and unstable coalition governments.

Independent deputy Sadi Irmak formed a government in November that lasted three months, until early 1975. In March 1975, Demirel established the first of two "Nationalist Front" coalitions, joining his JP, Erbakan's NSP, Türkeş's NAP, and the Republican Reliance Party, with Ecevit and the RPP going into opposition. This government held together for more than two years, until June 1977, when the nation finally went to the polls. Ecevit and the RPP won these elections, falling some 20 seats short of a majority in the lower chamber, and Demirel's JP ran second. No other party reached 10 percent. Despite this, cooperation between the RPP and JP was impossible both for ideological and personal reasons, and the political stalemate continued while each party convinced itself that a real majority was just an election away. The small parties held the balance of power, and Ecevit's efforts to form a government failed when his minority coalition could not win a vote of confidence. Instead, Demirel formed the second "Nationalist Front" coalition, this time with the NSP and the NAP, and once again Erbakan and Türkeş became deputy prime ministers. This coalition unraveled rather quickly, and in January 1978, Ecevit pieced together a majority when his RPP was joined by the lone deputy of the Democrat Party, the two deputies of the Republican Reliance Party, some independents, and eleven JP dissidents. This patchwork government held for a remarkable 22 months, until the end of 1979. Under the circumstances, none of these coalitions possessed the strength to manage the country's critical economic problems nor could they control the increasing political violence.

An initial period of economic expansion had followed the military coup of 1971. Some large enterprises, which because of success during the 1950s were poised to take advantage of foreign capital, grew tremendously during the 1960s. Keen to maintain their position, 114 industrialists and businessmen, owners of some of the largest firms in Turkey, formed the Association of Turkish Industrialists (TÜSİAD) in 1971 to promote private enterprise in Turkey and to lobby the government for support. But problems left over from 1960s became more acute when, beginning with the Arab-Israeli War in the fall of 1973, the cost of the imports Turkey depended on rose sharply due to the quadrupling of petroleum prices. At the end of the 1970s, this consumed about two-thirds of Turkey's foreign currency income. Remittances from Turkish workers abroad, the country's most important source of foreign exchange, peaked in 1974 and then declined as a result of the same events. By 1978–1979, there were shortages of basic commodities: butter, kerosene, gasoline, and sugar. Inflation and unemployment, under control in the early 1970s, climbed steadily after 1977.

Civil unrest escalated in spring 1977. After the 1971 military coup, the harsh crackdown on leftists by the military and security forces began a slow spiral of offense, retaliation, and retribution between radical leftists, the police, and rightists, to which there seemed to be no resolution. An extremely negative development was Demirel's appointment of Türkeş as minister of state in the Nationalist Front coalitions of 1974–1977. Türkeş filled the ministry with his political clients, and the police and security forces became thoroughly infiltrated by neo-fascists loyal to Türkeş. They carried out a violent campaign against leftists of all kinds, contributing substantially to the collapse of public order and bringing about conditions of virtual civil war by 1980.

In 1977, the first May Day celebration since the 1920s, a demonstration by labor unions and leftist political parties, turned into a gun battle with the police in which 39 people died and more than 200 were wounded. Leftists, blaming the killing on far-right elements in the Istanbul police force, retaliated with a wave of bombings, killing several people in attacks at Yeşilköy airport and at the Sirkeci railway station. From this point, a state of virtual war existed in Istanbul between DİSK, the Turkish Workers' Party, and other powerful leftist groups on the one hand and the Istanbul police force on the other. The head of the force was wounded by gunmen in March 1978, and the deputy prosecutor, investigating an illegal strike, was killed. In October 1978, four members of the Turkish Workers' Party were murdered and two others kidnapped and slain.

Periodic clashes between far-right Sunnite Muslim groups and Shiite Alevis, who typically were affiliated with the political left, expressed the same conflict. Twelve people died in violence between rightists and Alevis in Sivas in September 1978. In December 1978, a terrible battle broke out in the southeastern city of Kahramanmaraş when Sunnite hoodlums interrupted the Alevi funeral of two murdered vocational teachers. In five days of chaos, more than 100 people died and thousands were wounded. Ecevit, never eager to use force, declared martial law, saying that the violence represented "a rebellion against the Turkish state."

The disorder and violence was most pronounced on university campuses. In the middle of the academic year 1974–1975, fascist students disrupted classes at Istanbul University, leading to demonstrations and riots that claimed one student's life. The following year, violent protests forced the temporary closing of four universities in Ankara and Istanbul. The battles began to move off campus as well. A number of attacks and killings occurred at cafés, coffee shops, and other venues frequented by students. In October 1978, the former rector of Istanbul Technical University was murdered. It was at Ankara University in 1978 that a Kurdish student named Abdullah Öcalan formed the Kurdish Workers' Party.

The country slipped toward anarchy. A professor at Istanbul University was killed in December 1979. Later that month, four Americans returning from a NATO facility were murdered by a leftist guerilla force, and nine people died in demonstrations in Ankara. Public May Day observances were banned, but demonstrations by organized labor continued. More clashes between Sunnis and Alevis in Çorum left thirty people dead. Abdi İpekçi, editor of the respected İstanbul daily *Milliyet*, was murdered by the young Gray Wolf terrorist Mehmet Ali Ağca. Three weeks later leftists killed the owner of a right-wing paper in retaliation. An official of Türkeş's NAP was murdered in İzmir in April 1980; Gün Sazak, the Minister of Customs and Monopolies in the second Nationalist Front coalition, was assassinated on 27 May 1980; on June 17, a former RPP deputy was killed in Nevşehir. On 19 July 1980, former Prime Minister Nihat Erim was assassinated in an Istanbul suburb; three days later strikes by hundreds of thousands of workers followed the murder of Kemal Türkler, founder and former president of the leftist labor federation DİSK.

By the latter part of the summer of 1980, the Second Republic had plainly failed. Demirel's economic advisor Turgut Özal presented an ambitious austerity plan suggested by the IMF, but the divided legislature did not have the will to take it up, let alone the consensus required to implement the reforms. When President Fahri Korutürk's term expired in February, parliament was unable to elect a successor and the presidency remained vacant for months. Repeated warnings sounded that Sunnite fundamentalists were preparing to forcefully take control of the local government in Konya. Kurdish separatists had begun a war of liberation in the southeastern provinces. Sunnites and Alevis and leftists and rightists continued their murderous confrontations. The government announced that more than 2,500 persons had died in the two-year period prior to January 1980 and at least that many more in the first nine months of 1980.

The constitution of 1961 had restructured Turkish government and society in important ways, but responsibility for fleshing out the details of the new structure, and for implementation, was given to parliament. Fulfillment of the tremendous promise for Turkish society of the personal and political liberties outlined in the constitution depended on fundamental economic and social reforms, including land reform, tax reform, and reform of the system of state economic enterprises. A major cause of the political and social degeneration of the 1960s and chaos and anarchy of the late 1970s was the failure to carry through these reforms. It left the Turkish economy incapable of surmounting the enormous difficulties brought on by the world petroleum crisis after 1973 and unable to formulate adequate revisions of the prevailing political culture for the needs of an open society. Deep fissures opened in Turkish society between those who had benefited from the rapid and haphazard social and economic development since 1945 and those who found themselves victimized by the inflation, unemployment, and urban migration it engendered, between those who had benefited from political liberalization and multiparty democracy through their links of patronage with powerful officials and those who still lived with the residue of the single-party era with its authoritarian model of leadership, the equation of dissent with disloyalty, and party control of state offices. Turkey's participation in the Cold War contributed to the polarization of society, masked the sources of its problems, and made it impossible to achieve the political consensus necessary to adopt reforms. In the end the nation's armed forces, which parliament had failed to fully subordinate to civilian rule, put an end to the Second Republic.

10

The Military Republic, 1980–1993

In the 1982 film *Yol*, five prisoners receive permission to visit their families on a seven-day pass. The film follows the five men on their road home, detailing in the experience of each of them Yılmaz Güney's vision of Turkish life at the beginning of the 1980s. When *Yol* won the Cannes film festival award in 1982, the film and its creator gained notoriety in Europe because the film was made under conditions of martial law and was actually banned (with all Güney's films) by the military rulers in Turkey.

Güney, a Marxist who had served two prison terms in the 1960s, wrote *Yol* while serving another term for killing a judge in a restaurant brawl. Güney enjoyed comparative personal freedom in prison and continued scripting films, among them *Yol*, until the military coup of 12 September 1980. He smuggled directions for filming out to Şerif Gören, who directed the project. Later Güney escaped from prison while on a leave, slipping out of Turkey to France and then to Switzerland, where he oversaw the final editing of the film. Güney's almost unrelievedly grim vision takes in the full sweep of contemporary Turkey, moving from the prison island of İmrali, in the Marmara Sea in the country's far west, to the little town of Sancak, in the mountains southwest of Erzurum, in eastern Anatolia. Though the men are on leave, they never seem to leave their prisons, which are sometimes socially imposed and sometimes of their own making. Martial law forms part of the backdrop against which the stories of the prisoners are told, but the men are entangled in a complex web of kinship relations, social expectations and obligations, personal failings, and pure contingency. Islam too, forms part of the prisoners' lives, but is seen neither as especially a problem nor as a solution.

The film built on Güney's earlier work, which increasingly explored universally human themes, especially the ultimate weakness of the individual to escape the prisons of social convention and tradition. The relations of husbands and wives, including sexual relations, provide especially sensitive grounds for Güney. In one scene, a young bride-to-be unselfconsciously admires her husband's eloquence as he lays out the authoritarian rules of their relationship. Standing on a Gaziantep street corner in front of an equestrian sculpture of Atatürk, the suitor demands that his bride demonstrate her true devotion by not even speaking to him in public. "Where did you learn to talk like that?" she asks wonderingly. "In prison," he responds ironically. In these scenes, the artist bares the contradictions of modernity in Turkey. The film, and Güney's career, provide very powerful examples of the tensions and the enduring issues in Turkish life as the military once again took power in Turkey at the beginning of the decade of the 1980s.

THE MILITARY COUP OF 12 SEPTEMBER 1980

During the early hours of Friday morning, 12 September 1980, tanks rolled through the streets of Ankara, Istanbul, and other major Turkish cities. The leaders of the major political parties, including Prime Minister Süleyman Demirel of the Justice Party, Bülent Ecevit of the Republican People's Party, and Necmettin Erbakan of the National Salvation Party, were arrested and placed in protective custody. Alparslan Türkeş, leader of the Nationalist Action Party, who nearly twenty years earlier had broken the news of the first military coup to the nation in a radio announcement, turned himself in two days later. Parliament was dissolved and about 100 of its members arrested, and the constitution was suspended. Martial law was extended to all of the provinces of the nation. For the third time in twenty years, the Turkish military had seized direct control of the state.

The generals had planned the coup meticulously. Two incidents on the same day in early September may have influenced its precise timing. One was the forced resignation of the foreign minister, which dashed

Demirel's hopes of an early national election to secure a strong majority in parliament. The other was a mass demonstration in Konya, where the crowd called for Islamic law and refused to sing the national anthem.

In his first radio broadcast to the nation, at 4:30 A.M., General Kenan Evren, chief of the general staff and leader of the coup, reviewed the political, economic, and social chaos in which the country found itself. His remarks were translated and reported in *The New York Times* the next day. Bombings, assassinations, and street battles between leftists and rightists had taken 5,241 lives since the beginning of the year (more than double the number admitted by the Demirel government). By contrast, Evren noted, only 5,713 had died in the Turkish War of Independence between 1919 and 1923. The economy was in tatters, with inflation running at 130 percent and the unemployment rate at 20 percent. Paralysis had overcome the political system. Parliament had been unable to elect a successor to President Fahri Korutürk, whose term had expired the previous February. The paralysis gripping the state endangered the very existence of the country.

Although General Evren emphasized that the military would return the nation to civilian rule, he was determined that it would not do so hastily but only after fundamental revisions of Turkey's political order had been accomplished. The coup leaders—the commanders of the armed forces—formed the five-member National Security Council, named General Evren head of state and appointed a 27-member cabinet composed mostly of retired officers and state bureaucrats. Martial law commanders in all the provinces were given broad administrative authority over public affairs, including education, the press, and economic activities. In the first week after the coup, the number of arrests reached several thousand, all political parties were closed, and political activity forbidden. In October, the generals announced a seven-point provisional constitution giving themselves unlimited power indefinitely. Where it did not contradict these points, the 1961 constitution would remain in effect until a new constitution could be written. General Evren stated that Turkey's foreign policy, and its economic policy, would remain unchanged under military rule. Turkey was barred from the Council of Europe, and the European Community suspended aid. NATO urged a timely return to democracy.

General Evren's reference to the Turkish War of Independence in his initial radio broadcast provided an early clue to one significant theme of this period of military rule. The military rulers considered the country to have passed through a national crisis comparable to the violent years of the War of Independence, and in the military takeover of September 12 to have come to a point of new beginnings. Kemalism had gradually been forgotten, they believed, and the country left leaderless. Now the excesses of the past few years would be corrected, a new constitution would be written, the junta would enforce a new commitment to Kemalism and patriotism, and General Evren would provide national leadership. For similar reasons, the new regime exhibited a concern for historical interpretation and for historical memory reminiscent of the early republican years. The coup leaders banned all political activities. In early 1982, the leaders of the old political parties were forbidden to speak about politics—past, present, or future. Later that year, the old political parties were finally permanently dissolved, and their archives of the past thirty years seized. These records subsequently disappeared. All former political parties were outlawed, and more than 700 former members of parliament and party leaders were forbidden from participation in politics for a period of ten years. The regime wanted to create a new political order.

Another way the military regime seemed to consciously invoke the historical memory of the early Republic was to warn that separatist forces threatened the integrity of the country. Alluding to Atatürk's famous "Address to Turkish Youth" that every child memorized, Evren spoke of enemies within and enemies without, implicitly calling citizens to the duty of defending the nation. Turkish life had witnessed a spiraling whirlwind of civil violence since mid-1977, and much of the country viewed the coup with a sense of relief, expecting that near civil war conditions would soon be brought under control. This the army successfully achieved within a few months of the coup. In doing so, it began a crackdown on Kurdish resistance movements that gradually escalated into war by 1983. Expressions of Islamic political activism were also suppressed.

The economic policy already begun under the previous government was continued under military rule. When the cabinet was formed after the coup, the only figure of the old regime the generals kept was Turgut Özal, whom they named deputy prime minister and minister for economic affairs. As Demirel's undersecretary and head of the State Planning Organization, Özal had been the architect of the economic austerity program announced by the Demirel government in January 1980. The new cabinet pledged to continue to implement these austerity measures. In this way, the Turkish state under military rule began a transition that other states of east central Europe would also face in the 1980s—Poland,

Hungary, Czechoslovakia, and later other East bloc countries—a transition from an economy directed from above by state planning to an economy open to penetration by and integration with world capitalism.

Özal had acted as principal representative of the government in negotiations with the IMF, the World Bank, and the European Community. His policy aimed to make Turkey competitive on world markets, especially European markets, by developing those sectors that would be prominent exporters. The absence of a stable consensus among the major parties had proved an impediment to implementation of the austerity program. In late September, the IMF signaled its support three weeks after the coup by releasing $92 million in new credits to Turkey, and in October, the United States permitted Turkey to reschedule $350 million in debts. By the end of January 1981, Özal also renegotiated Turkish debts totaling more than $3 billion.

TOWARD A NEW POLITICAL ORDER

The regime's first order of business was to reestablish public order. Striking workers were ordered back to work and all union activity was forbidden. Imposing a strict curfew, the army swept the country, arresting thousands of people with suspected ties to terrorist organizations. By May 1981, the number of arrests surpassed 100,000 in the first eight months of military rule. A general amnesty was offered to all who voluntarily surrendered their weapons; those who refused faced a stiff thirty-year prison sentence for possession of an unregistered weapon. Spectacular acts of terrorism sometimes still made the headlines of Turkish newspapers, as when the deputy chief of police was ambushed by leftist gunmen in an Istanbul suburb in February 1981. Leftists also targeted American military personnel stationed in Turkey. In a guerilla war essentially unrelated to the military takeover, the Armenian Secret Army for the Liberation of Armenia (ASALA) attacked targets in Turkey and killed more than a dozen Turkish diplomats in Europe and the United States between 1981 and 1983.

In general, however, acts of political violence declined dramatically in the first months after the coup. Martial law authorities attempted to be evenhanded, arresting rightist as well as leftist gang members. In January 1981, the army declared victory over the revolutionary leftist organization Dev Sol. The leftist labor federation DİSK and rightist labor federation MİSK were disbanded. Hundreds of members of the right-wing NAP and the Islamist NSP were arrested with their leaders, Alparslan

Türkeş and Necmettin Erbakan. Kurdish nationalist groups also were targeted. Several newspapers were closed at one time or another for publishing articles critical of the regime, including the respected national daily *Hürriyet* and the venerable old *Cumhuriyet*. Prominent, public trials occupied the national attention for months. By early 1983, about 2,000 prisoners had been executed or faced the death penalty. The trial of Mehmet Ali Ağca, who tried to assassinate Pope John Paul II in Rome in March 1981, revealed the extent of interactions between some extremist groups of the Turkish left and right and organized crime both in Turkey and abroad. Ağca had once been a member of the Gray Wolves.

The blow fell more heavily, however, on the Turkish left. What legitimate leftist movement there had been in Turkey before 1980 was left completely demoralized by the army takeover and never recovered. It had been discredited by its association with labor and with the Kurdish cause. It had advocated an economic policy aimed at protecting national Turkish industry against laissez-faire international capitalism that in the 1980s appeared increasingly obsolete. Turkish universities were soon "depoliticized" by being placed under the supervision of a newly created Higher Education Authority (*Yüksek Öğretim Kurulu*, or YÖK), and faculty members were forbidden from membership in political parties. The government, now holding the power to directly appoint university rectors and deans, dismissed hundreds of university faculty in two purges aimed at the political left. Meanwhile, the number of existing universities was expanded from nineteen to twenty-nine in the decade of 1980s and the right of university admission was widened, effectively diluting the power of the old university faculties and the traditional elite classes whose children filled the student bodies. The right—secular, religious, and nationalist—survived this era in comparative strength to exercise a tremendous influence on Turkish politics in the next two decades.

Of the former politicians now banned from political participation, Ecevit and Erbakan were the most insistent in defying the muzzle. Erbakan was tried for remarks advocating an Islamic state in public speeches. Ecevit returned to his original career in journalism, publishing a magazine of public affairs. Arrested more than once, he eventually served a four-month jail term for statements critical of the military regime.

General Evren's public prominence gave a deliberately distorted impression of him as a military strongman, when in fact decisions were reached among the top leadership with a considerable degree of mutuality and consensus. The generals, however, deemed it important to project an image of strong, personal leadership. Beginning in May 1981, the country celebrated the "Year of Atatürk," in commemoration of the 100th anniversary of his birth. A new Atatürk cultural center was built on Taksim Square in Istanbul, academic conferences were sponsored, commemorative volumes of books published, and numerous municipal parks, schools, and even a university received the name "100th Anniversary" in his honor. Appearing alongside Atatürk's, Evren's face on banners at parades and public ceremonies linked Evren to the national hero and connected the new military regime to the regime of the founders.

After about a year, in the fall of 1981, the generals named a consultative assembly of 160 members to draft a new constitution. Forty members of the consultative assembly were appointed directly by the National Security Council, and the rest were named by the martial law governors of the provinces. In carrying out its mandate, the consultative assembly did much to purge the country of the effects of the 1960 coup, including the 1961 constitution. That constitution was partly blamed for the fragmentation and polarization of parliament, political parties, the judiciary, bureaucracy, and universities that had needlessly politicized all of Turkish public life and contributed to the violence of the late 1970s. Significantly, the army abolished Freedom and Constitution Day (May 27), an annual holiday commemorating the 1960 coup.

The consultative assembly presented a draft constitution in the early fall of 1982. It emphasized that "The Turkish state is an indivisible entity. Its language is Turkish." The first fundamental aim and duty of the state was "to safeguard the independence and integrity of the Turkish Nation, the indivisibility of the country, the Republic and democracy." The most significant structural revisions it brought to government were a strengthened presidency and a formalized role for the military leadership. In the 1961 constitution, the president had functioned as a mere figurehead. Now the president of the Republic, who was charged with ensuring "the implementation of the constitution and the steady and harmonious functioning of the state organs," would become guardian of the state, serving a single seven-year term with potentially wide powers. He appointed the Constitutional Court, the Council of State (that is, the cabinet), the military Court of Cassation, the Supreme Council of Judges and Prosecutors, and the High Court of Appeals. He chaired the National Security Council, which was made a permanent body with the right to submit its views on state security to the Council of Ministers. The Council of Ministers was required to give its views priority.

The constitution strengthened the position of the prime minister as regards the other ministers and the cabinet, and strengthened the cabinet over the parliament, which again became a unicameral legislature. The prime minister could fire a minister without necessitating the resignation of the entire cabinet. A new discretionary fund was created and put at the personal disposal of the prime minister, outside of the parliamentary budgetary process. The cabinet would enjoy stronger latitude in making laws by executive order. Restrictions were placed on the press and on labor unions. State Security Courts would have the power to adjudicate strikes, lockouts, and collective bargaining disputes. Unions were strictly depoliticized. The new constitution stated that the economy of Turkey was based on free enterprise, but the role of the state in the economy was limited to supervision; the government lost its mandate to restrict private enterprise in the public interest. On 7 November 1982, the voters approved the constitution in a national referendum by a majority of 91 percent. By a "temporary article" appended by the NSC to the draft constitution, General Evren became president of the Republic for a seven-year term.

After the referendum, a period of intense political discussion and activity began as the country prepared for general elections. President Evren and the NSC insisted that no politicians from the precoup period would be permitted to participate in the elections, scheduled for November 1983. The former political parties were officially dissolved, and 672 former parliamentarians and party activists were banned from the elections. The regime shut down several newspapers for short periods of time for failing to observe severe restrictions on political articles. In the spring of 1983, the NSC permitted the formation of new political parties. To encourage the creation of parties with broad popular appeal, the new election law required that a party receive at least 10 percent of the national vote in order to win seats in parliament. Any party falling short of the threshold would not receive parliamentary representation.

When some new parties appeared to be reincarnations of the old parties, or when they appeared to be directed from behind the scenes by former party leaders, they were closed. Thus the Great Turkey Party was condemned as being nothing but the Justice Party resurrected, and Süleyman Demirel was placed under house arrest for three months. Likewise, the founders of the new Social Democratic Party (SODEP), including Professor Erdal İnönü, the son of İsmet İnönü and a newcomer to political life, were barred from the elections and their party closed. Ironically, had the military authorities used their power to limit the election to a contest between these two parties, they might have achieved one of their objectives for the new political order, a stable two-party system. These two new parties, Demirel's representing a broadly right-of-center political program and İnönü's a broadly left-of-center program, summarized the views of the great majority of the Turkish electorate since the late 1940s. But under Evren's influence, the NSC remained adamantly opposed to allowing former politicians any opportunity to recreate the dysfunctional political atmosphere of the late 1970s.

Eventually, three political parties received approval to participate in the elections. One was the Nationalist Democracy Party, led by retired General Turgut Sunalp; the second was the Populist Party headed by Necdet Calp, a former private secretary of İsmet İnönü; and the third was the Motherland Party, formed by Turgut Özal.

Özal had left the cabinet in July 1982, even before public release of the draft constitution. A bank crisis—an early sign that not all was well with the Turkish economic recovery—had forced his resignation. Taking advantage of the average Turkish citizen's desperation to overcome the debilitating impact of ongoing inflation, brokerage firms sold junk bonds and used deregulation of the banking industry to offer extremely high rates of interest on bank deposits. Hundreds of brokerage firms went bankrupt during the first half of 1982 when the government imposed restrictions on the industry and worried consumers caused a bank run. When the brokerage firm Banker Kastelli collapsed in June, the scandal forced Özal and two other cabinet ministers to resign. Özal, however, bounced back, filing an application to form a political party as soon as it was permitted to do so in spring 1983.

President Evren did little to hide his annoyance with Özal, whose ambition he evidently had not anticipated. The Motherland Party clearly could not be said to continue a precoup political party, and the generals themselves had brought Özal into their cabinet, so the new party would have to be permitted to enter the elections. As it turned out, Evren's obvious dislike for the Motherland Party made it an early favorite with a voting public that was so tired of military rule it quickly forgave the Banker Kastelli scandal. Evren's stated preference for Sunalp's NDP probably condemned it to a third-place finish. When the results were tallied, Özal's Motherland Party had won 45 percent of the vote and an absolute majority in the first postcoup parliament.

THE ÖZAL YEARS: ECONOMIC LIBERALIZATION

From the elections of 1983 until his death ten years later, Turgut Özal dominated the politics of Turkey. Born in Malatya, Özal was an engineer by training and had studied economics in the United States. During the late 1960s, he had served as Demirel's head of the State Planning Organization. After the military coup of 1971, Özal had positions in academe and industry, and at the World Bank. Demirel brought him back to the government in 1975 as an undersecretary to the prime minister and acting head of state planning. After an unsuccessful parliamentary campaign, he was back at Demirel's side in 1979 as his primary advisor before the coup.

Özal's decision to create a new political party in 1983 was a fateful one for Turkish political life. It had the effect of splitting the Turkish right, arguably the largest voting bloc, between those who followed Özal and those who, either out of old loyalties or because they disliked Özal or resented his cooperation with the military authorities, refused to support him and instead looked forward to Demirel's return. The two groups became increasingly unable to cooperate, with reverberations occurring throughout Turkish life in the late 1980s and 1990s.

After his electoral victory, Özal continued to pursue his program of liberalizing the Turkish economy. He aimed at a fundamental shift of approach to economic development, from protecting national industry and limiting imports to instead encouraging exports and forcing Turkish products into a competitive position on the world market. Özal's tactics did not change much throughout the period: rapid devaluation of the Turkish lira to make Turkish goods more competitive, high interest rates to combat inflation by discouraging consumer demand, gradual privatization of inefficient state economic enterprises, wage controls, price increases, and an end to state industrial subsidies. Throughout the mid-1980s, these policies showed promising signs of success. The economy grew steadily before leveling off. Exports expanded dramatically. Especially, Turkey increased its exports to the countries of the Middle East, but exports to the European Community increased as well. These included a wide variety of products: Whereas in 1979, 60 percent of Turkish exports were agricultural products, by 1988 80 percent came from industry. Textiles in particular proved an outstanding success. The government invested in large-scale infrastructural development projects, including the second Bosphorus bridge in Istanbul completed in 1987, petroleum excavation in the Aegean, and the Southeast Anatolia project, a massive network of dams and hydroelectric plants on the upper Tigris and Euphrates Rivers. The annual inflation rate hovered around 40 percent—still worrisome, but not as high as it had been during the late 1970s.

In other areas of the economy, however, progress was incomplete. The privatization program proceeded only very slowly during the 1980s, although the government had success in breaking up state monopolies, such as tobacco. The state continued to take the largest role in expanding the economy, and it seemed impossible to really curtail the size of the bureaucracy. In the late 1980s, the state still employed 30 percent of all nonagrarian workers. Public sector borrowing continued to rise, with the result that interest payments on the public debt tripled as a percentage of GNP between 1984 and 1988.

This unstable economic growth pattern contributed to notable social trends in the 1980s. While the population of Turkey grew by 26 percent during the decade, the growth rate in all of the major cities was higher, and in some far higher, as industry drew surplus agricultural labor off the farm. The population of Istanbul, the largest city in the country, and of İzmir, the third largest, more than doubled in the 1980s. Istanbul, a city of about 2.8 million in 1980, had grown to more than 6.6 million by the time of the 1990 census. Because new housing construction could not keep up with the human migrations, vast squatter settlements ringed the main cities, straining the urban infrastructure. At the same time, the positive results of economic liberalization came most rapidly to a few of the largest industrial conglomerates like the Koç, Sabancı and Eczacıbaşı groups, all big, diversified holding companies. Some of the biggest state economic enterprises, which themselves were huge conglomerates, also fared well—the five largest state economic enterprises were still bigger than even the biggest private holding company at the end of the 1980s. Small business felt the benefits of liberalization only much more slowly. As a consequence, the gap between the richest and the poorest in Turkey grew steadily. In the major cities, the contrast between the conspicuous consumption of the rich in their glass office high-rises, suburban single-family dwellings and expensive, imported automobiles, and the poor whose cement block and plaster dwellings with tin roofs stood sometimes just a few blocks away, were reminiscent of Aziz Nesin's mansion children and street kids.

The mixed results of the economic transition do not fully explain the disappointing rejection of Turkey's formal application for full membership in the European Economic Community, which Özal championed in 1987. Özal, who had risen to power under military rule, determinedly pursued political liberalization, but his statement in December 1985, that Turkey was "already a full democracy," was clearly an example of wishful thinking. The European Community continued to point to this as the basic problem holding up a positive decision for Turkey. Martial law was gradually lifted, beginning with thirteen provinces in early 1984. Fifty of Turkey's sixty-seven provinces were free of martial law by mid-1985, but Istanbul was not until late in 1988, and eight provinces of the Kurdish southeast remained under a state of emergency throughout Özal's term as prime minister. A series of "antiterrorism" laws, moreover, remained in place throughout the country.

The issue pointed to a paradox of Özal's leadership: Economic liberalization did not necessarily bring with it political liberalization. While Özal introduced many new faces to political life in Turkey, he seemed reluctant to completely normalize political life, to permit old political rivals to return and to exert political control of the military. Özal's Motherland Party won the 1984 local elections in spite of increased competition. In the months following, much discussion concerned the possible return to political life of the banned leaders of the pre-1980 parties, especially Demirel, Ecevit, and Erbakan. It was already widely believed that the new True Path Party was run behind the scenes by Süleyman Demirel, and in 1985 Rahsan Ecevit, the wife of Bülent Ecevit, registered the Democratic Left Party. Erbakan, too, was heavily involved in the Welfare Party. After a nationwide referendum approved their return, Özal called early general elections for November 1987. In these elections, Özal's Motherland Party again came out ahead with just over 36 percent, but took advantage of revised election laws it had pushed through parliament to win an absolute majority, 292 of the 450 seats. Erdal İnönü's Social Democratic Populist Party finished a strong second with just under 25 percent of the vote, winning 99 seats. Demirel's True Path Party, third with 19 percent, took the remaining 59 seats. Neither Ecevit's Democratic Left Party nor Erbakan's Welfare Party, nor any other party, managed to climb over the 10 threshold. The manner of Motherland Party's electoral victory attracted increasing criticism of the prime minister's authoritarian management style.

As prime minister, Özal skillfully built and managed client relationships, creating a reputation as a master of the tradition of political patronage so crucial to the operation of Turkish politics. He manipulated the discretionary fund at the disposal of the prime minister's office into a major budget item, unregulated by parliament. By 1987, this fund, divided into more than a hundred separate expenditure items paid for by various kinds of special taxes, absorbed more than 40 percent of the budget. Özal used it to attract and support his protégés, beginning with members of his own family. His brothers Korkut, who had gained cabinet experience with Erbakan's National Salvation Party in the coalition governments of the mid-1970's, and Yusuf, his wife Semra, and his son Ahmet became close advisors. Yusuf was brought into the cabinet in 1987 as economy minister, and a nephew served as defense minister for several months. Semra Özal served as provincial chair of the local Istanbul branch of the Motherland Party in the early 1990s. But the resentment of Özal went deeper.

An important dimension of Özal's political leadership in this period of liberalization was his encouragement of an increased role for Islam in public life. Özal had run unsuccessfully for parliament on the slate of Erbakan's NSP in 1977, and his brother Korkut had ties to the Nakshibendi dervish order. Though he had distanced himself from religious fanatics by such symbolic actions as holding hands with his wife in public, Özal understood that Islam, as the source of the belief system and the values of most Turkish citizens, was excluded from Turkish politics only with increasing awkwardness and artificiality. "Restrictions on freedom of conscience breed fanaticism," he said in a speech in December 1986, "not the other way around." In 1984, Özal's government provided for religious instruction in public school classrooms, Özal supported a huge increase in the number of *İmam-Hatip* schools, religious secondary academies organized ostensibly for the training of mosque leaders, during the 1980s. Graduates of these schools were now permitted to enter universities. Members of Özal's party and cabinet made more prominent their attendance at mosque worship services and observance of religious rituals and holy days.

The appearance of politically active fundamentalists was a sensitive one because it presented a constitutional challenge and a profound dilemma: Was Turkey a secular state or was it a democratic republic? Nothing seemed to focus the issues more sharply than the controversy over the government's decision to permit university students to cover their heads in the classroom.

For advocates of the headscarf, or *hicab*, the issue became one of civil liberties. In a modern democracy, the individual ought to be free to wear any clothing, within the limits of public decency. The Turkish constitution, moreover, guaranteed freedom of religion. Thus laws forbidding the wearing of headscarves violated the Turkish citizens' civil liberties. For opponents, however, the headscarf was a reference to the veil that Atatürk had made the most famous symbol of the Islamic order. Wearing it amounted to a political gesture directed against the secular Turkish state guaranteed by the constitution. In March 1989, President Evren himself petitioned the constitutional court for a repeal of the new law permitting headscarves. Thousands of university students demonstrated throughout 1989 as the issue went into litigation, first being banned and then permitted again by an act of parliament.

The location of the headscarf controversy on university campuses is a clue that the headscarf issue, and the larger question of the role of Islam in Turkish public life, needs to be seen among the wider social ramifications of Özal's political and economic liberalization program. Industrialization had raised the prestige of engineering and other scientific and technical fields, and the prominence in public life of men trained in these fields. Demirel, Erbakan, and Özal were all trained engineers. The more open business climate of the post-1980 coup years had also witnessed the emergence of a new class of wealthy entrepreneurs. At the same time, the new universities and broadened educational opportunities assisted the rise of a more diverse professional class. Many of the new technocrats and businessmen came from outside the traditional classes of republican elites, were personally religious and conservative, and more willing than their predecessors to give open expression to that aspect of their personalities. Mass migrations of peasants from the countryside, meanwhile, swelled the biggest cities with hundreds of thousands of conservative villagers turned urban laborers, some of them gaining a new political consciousness. These people, too, responded positively to political ideas expressed in a religious idiom.

There was probably little chance of a movement to establish an Islamic state gaining wide popularity in Turkey in the 1980s. Islamic fundamentalists occasionally staged dramatic acts of violence, as when respected *Cumhuriyet* columnist Uğur Mumcu was killed by a car bomb in January 1993 or when later that year rioters in Sivas burned down the hotel where Aziz Nesin was staying, killing forty people, though Nesin escaped. (Nesin had translated parts of Salman Rushdie's *Satanic Verses* into Turkish.) Yet trials of Islamic revolutionaries made up only a small percentage of the cases brought to the attention of the State Security Courts. A poll of the general population conducted in 1986 found that only about 7 percent of Turks favored the establishment of a political and legal order based on the sharia, Islamic law. Throughout the 1980s, electoral returns gave Erbakan's Welfare Party no more than 10 percent of the popular vote nationally. Sometimes the specter of an Iranian style Islamic revolution was raised, but Turkey was not Iran. Even at its most repressive, the Turkish police and army could not be compared to SAVAK, the former Shah's secret police, nor did Necmettin Erbakan in any way resemble the Ayatollah Khomeini. In other words, in Turkey there existed neither the immoral target that might galvanize a national Islamic movement nor a charismatic leader who might direct one. Most significantly, Turkey's conservative and religious citizens had all grown up in a secular, democratic tradition and accepted its fundamental premises. Turkey's Islamic movement was a democratic movement, committed to and indeed deriving its strength from the democratic tradition of the republic.

An unmistakable class element showed in the concern about fundamentalism, as there had always been a class dimension to the Kemalist revolution. During the decade of the 1980s, the Motherland Party had introduced new groups of people into the patronage system, including scientists and technicians, newly successful businessmen and professionals, with whom the traditional privileges of patronage had to be shared. Kemalism was the ideology and the way of life of an educated elite, who shared a worldview, a set of common assumptions about what was valuable in life. These were the people who had gone to secondary schools and perhaps universities, and who filled posts in government offices, the military officer corps, school faculties and who had always believed that they knew what was best for Turkey. Access to these groups spread only slowly to other sectors of the Turkish population. Beginning in the 1980s, secularists grew increasingly wary of a different ethos they detected in these new conservatives, that they did not speak the same political language, that among them there did not prevail the same commitment to secularism and the goals of Kemalism.

ÖZAL BECOMES PRESIDENT

After the 1987 elections, the accumulated allegations of corruption and scandal and continued economic difficulties, especially inflation, which surpassed 80 percent for 1988, seriously eroded support for Özal. In the local elections of March 1989, the Motherland Party lost control of several large cities and polled only 22 percent of the vote, behind both Erdal İnönü's SDP and Süleyman Demirel's TP. Several Motherland Party deputies deserted the party, but Özal rejected suggestions that he resign or call general elections. Instead, declaring that he would never lead the opposition, he ran for president on the expiration of General Evren's term. In October 1989, parliament elected him the eighth president of the Republic of Turkey.

Taking office in the middle of the tumultuous fall of 1989, just days before the dismantling of the Berlin Wall, Özal seemed to sense equally the risk and the opportunity of the cascading fall of events. Özal had resided in the president's mansion less than a year when, on August 2, 1990, Iraq invaded Kuwait. He used his position to redefine Turkey's role in regional and world politics. Firmly directing a pro-American foreign policy, he believed that the best hope for long-term solutions to Turkey's fundamental economic problems lay in close cooperation with the United States and in gaining full membership in the European Community. Özal used his trips to America for medical care to form a cordial relationship with President George Bush, to meet with other American officials, and to appear repeatedly on CNN and on American network newscasts, articulating Turkey's perspective while communicating staunch loyalty to the Atlantic alliance and the anti-Iraq coalition. President Bush reciprocated with a visit to Turkey in July 1991. Özal also thought he saw in this a potential opportunity of a political resolution of the Kurdish problem.

Initially, Özal's efforts paid off. In return for use of the İncirlik base and its participation in the embargo of Iraqi oil, Turkey was compensated by increased American imports of Turkish products, especially textiles, and by aid from the Arab Gulf states to offset Turkey's lost pipeline revenue. In the aftermath of the Gulf War, however, Turkey faced an enormously complicated relationship with Iraq and with the Kurds. The regime of Saddam Hussein was left intact in Baghdad. When a Kurdish rebellion against Baghdad failed, the United States and its allies created a de facto Kurdish autonomous zone under their protection in the "no fly zone" in northern Iraq. The Turkish government, and the Turkish military, which had been fighting Kurdish separatists in southeastern Turkey in an increasingly repressive war since the early 1980s, viewed these developments with dismay, for they saw in the Kurdish zone of northern Iraq a potential model for Kurdish autonomy that might be attractive to the Kurds of Turkey.

Since 1989, when Özal had publicly stated that he himself was part Kurdish, he had sought a nonmilitary resolution of the Kurdish conflict, advocating greater cultural liberty for Kurds. Circumstances after the Gulf War ended in 1991 seemed to indicate it might be a propitious time for a political solution. Even as Turkish military campaigns against Kurdish separatists in the southeast continued, at Özal's direction, the cabinet repealed the 1983 law forbidding the use of languages other than Turkish. President Bush arrived in Ankara in July for a state visit. Two prominent Iraqi Kurdish leaders, Jalal Talabani and Muhsin Dizayi, who had met with Turkish Foreign Ministry officials in the spring, returned in August and September for talks with the Turkish military, and were hosted by Özal at the presidential palace in Ankara. General elections brought Süleyman Demirel to power in October at the head of a coalition government with the Social Democrats of Erdal İnönü. Nearly one-fourth of the SD's parliamentary bloc were members of a small Kurdish party, which had been barred from the election on a technicality. In March 1992, Demirel publicly stated that he recognized the reality of Kurdish ethnicity in Turkey.

But the truth was that after the 1980 military coup, Turkey's civilian politicians had never succeeded in gaining control of the Turkish military's actions in the southeast. Through the mechanism of the NSC, the generals had repeatedly intimidated Turkish politicians, including Özal and his successor as the Motherland Party's chair, Mesut Yılmaz, who became prime minister in 1991. In demonstrations celebrating Nowruz, the Kurdish New Year in March 1992, more than ninety people were killed by Turkish security forces. The Kurdish deputies in the SDP resigned in protest, and the chance of a negotiated solution faded. Meanwhile, the number of "unsolved" murders in Kurdish areas climbed. These killings were carried out by clandestine paramilitary groups. Although some of these groups probably operated independently of the Turkish military, evidence began to mount that they were funded by the Turkish state.

Far from permitting a political solution to the Kurdish rebellion, Turkey's generals escalated the conflict in 1992 and 1993, pouring nearly 250,000 troops into the region and implementing scorched earth tactics that wiped out some 2,000 villages, displaced an estimated 2 million people, and resulted in more than 20,000 Turkish casualties. Kurdish refugees bloated major Turkish cities, especially Diyarbakır, Adana, Mersin, İzmir, and Istanbul. The Turkish army crossed the Iraqi border a number of times in minor incursions and then staged a massive invasion of Iraq in October 1992 in an effort to wipe out Kurdish bases there that were being used against Turkey.

In March 1993, Kurdistan Workers Party (PKK) leader Abdullah Öcalan announced a unilateral cease-fire. Demirel and the generals were surprised, but Özal may have been directly involved. Deciding that the PKK must have been weakened by the campaign of the previous autumn, and sensing final victory, the generals stepped up military operations. Negotiating with Özal through Jalal Talabani, Öcalan renewed the cease-fire at a press conference attended by Kurdish former members of parliament. At this critical juncture, President Özal suffered a heart attack and died suddenly on 17 April 1993.

11

Turkey after Özal

In the years after the death of Turgut Özal, Turkey struggled to reconcile the changes of the 1980s and early 1990s that were the legacy of the late president with the traditions of the Turkish Republic and with the circumstances of life in a modern democracy. A strong, stable government seemed illusive as Turkey was beset by economic difficulties, political scandals, the ongoing war against Kurdish rebels, and politicized Islamic revivalism. Although each of these issues was in many ways as old as the Republic itself, their particular manifestation after the death of President Özal owed much to the policies the late president had pursued.

Süleyman Demirel, Özal's successor as president of the Republic, began a seven-year term in May 1993. The True Path Party picked the Minister of Economy Tansu Çiller to replace Demirel as party chief. In June 1993, Çiller, American-educated and a former economics professor, became Turkey's first female prime minister. Within a month, the Kurdish cease-fire broke down and military operations against the PKK continued as before. PKK guerillas ambushed a commercial bus near Bingöl and murdered thirty-four people, of whom thirty-three were off-duty soldiers. Heavy new fighting erupted, the cease-fire was canceled, and hope of a political solution to the conflict seemed lost. Despite a reputation as a tenacious political operator, the inexperienced Çiller seemed no more capable of standing up to Demirel, her patron, or opposing the wishes of the generals, than had her predecessor in that position, Motherland Party's Mesut Yılmaz. The brutal conduct of the war brought serious economic problems, led to estrangement from the European Community, and compromised the integrity of the state through the influence of organized crime and rightist death squads.

Worried about Turkey's inability to control spending and its consequently high public debt, in January 1994, international credit rating agencies downgraded Turkey's status, prompting a devaluation of the Turkish lira that cost Turkey an estimated $1.2 billion. The Istanbul stock market plummeted. An austerity package including new taxes, worker layoffs, wage freezes, the closing of some inefficient state economic enterprises, and price increases on certain commodities, especially gasoline, tobacco, and sugar did little to help. The lira lost half its value in six months.

One consequence was that in the local elections of March 1994, the Welfare Party of Necmettin Erbakan suddenly captured nearly 20 percent of the vote nationally and took control of major Turkish municipalities including both Istanbul and Ankara. Erbakan had once again put fundamentalist Islam on the national political agenda.

THE ELECTIONS OF 1995 AND POLITICAL ISLAM

After Çiller's government lost a vote of confidence, the country went to the polls on 24 December 1995 in national elections. Seven parties split the vote, with five gaining representation in parliament. The Welfare Party won the largest share of the popular vote, only 21.4 percent, followed closely by Çiller's True Path Party and the Motherland Party of Mesut Yılmaz. The Democratic Left Party of Bülent Ecevit and the Republican People's Party headed by Deniz Baykal also won seats. Among the parties failing to meet the national threshold were the new far-right Nationalist Movement Party of Alparslan Türkeş and the leftist People's Democracy Party, which showed strongly in the Kurdish regions—winning more than 50 percent of the vote in Hakkari—but less well among Kurdish populations in the major cities of western Turkey.

Offered the prime ministry, Erbakan was unable to attract coalition partners. A minority coalition of Motherland and True Path parties seemed desirable, since the two parties shared the strong center-right of the Turkish political spectrum and together controlled 267 delegates. Despite their similarities, however, the two parties seldom cooperated. The

differences between them went deeper than the personal animosity between Çiller and Yılmaz. The Motherland Party was the party of Özal,
who in the 1980s had cooperated with the military authorities. Mesut
Yılmaz was Özal's protégé. The True Path Party was in many ways the
successor to the Justice Party of Demirel, whom the military had barred
from politics. Demirel had, moreover, severely criticized Özal for abuse
of power when he continued to influence the Motherland Party as president after 1989. So when at length, in the spring of 1996, Çiller and
Yılmaz were able to set aside their personal and political differences to
form a government, their grand "Motherpath" coalition lasted only
eleven weeks. Çiller, overcoming her distaste for entering an agreement
with the Islamists, joined a coalition with Erbakan that finally brought
the Welfare Party to power in June 1996.

The following year in which Erbakan served as prime minister and
led the Welfare Party government saw an extended public debate about
the role of religion in the life of the Turkish Republic and the meaning
of political Islam. The extent to which Erbakan, as the partner in a coalition, could expect to carry through the social revolution his speeches
seemed to allude to was unclear. Once during the 1994 municipal elections, he had promised that the Welfare Party would bring about a religious regime, "even by the shedding of blood if necessary." During the
national campaign in December 1995, Erbakan praised Iran for resisting
the power of the West, and in a speech, pledged to take Turkey out of
NATO, set up an Islamic NATO, an Islamic UN, an Islamic version of
the European Union, and to create an Islamic currency. Other Welfare
Party deputies, and mayors of cities, made similar or more inflammatory
statements, widely reported in the press.

It seemed difficult to determine whether the Welfare Party victory was
a thing to be feared or whether it was merely the sign of a healthy
Turkish democracy. Arguments both for and against the Welfare Party
government could be stated as a matter of principle. "If we believe in
democracy, we have to test Refah (Welfare) in government," said industrialist Sakıp Sabancı on the one hand. On the other, Bülent Ecevit, parliamentary deputy and former prime minister, noted "Secularism is the
most sensitive aspect of the [republican] regime in Turkey—if it collapses, the whole regime collapses." The electoral victory of the Welfare
Party seemed also to have resulted from simple, political factors. The
Welfare Party articulated a vision of the just society in Turkey through
the use of a commonly understood Islamic religious idiom. The Welfare
Party also benefited from an "anti-Ankara" sentiment, as voters reacted

against a government apparatus riddled by scandal and out of touch with common people. The program agreed on by Erbakan and Çiller contained few of the initiatives advocated by Erbakan during the campaign.

Nevertheless, opposition party members, and a sizable portion of the Turkish voting public, remained suspicious about the Welfare Party's motives, taking note of Erbakan's efforts to recruit Islamists in a variety of lower level government, police, and military positions. The distribution of political power in the Turkish system emphasized relationships between people; electoral success had now given the Welfare Party access to the privileges of power as never before. The Welfare Party brought a new class of people into public life. It had been supported by a rising group of newly urbanized laborers, shopkeepers, small businessmen, and industrialists who did not fit the traditional Kemalist mold of the Turkish state servant. Nor did these voters fit the unfairly stereotyped image of the ignorant and conservative village folk. Rather, they tended to be devout, well educated, urbanized, fashion conscious, and deeply shaped by Turkey's tradition of secular political give and take. Some segments of Turkish society resented and feared the uncertainty of a future in which this new class of people would have a growing role to play.

Erbakan's efforts to chart an independent foreign policy course for Turkey brought mixed results. He made a series of visits to Muslim countries. In Iran, he signed a $23 billion, 23-year agreement to purchase natural gas via a pipeline to be constructed from Tabriz to the Turkish border. This marked the Turkish entry into the competition for access to the promising new petroleum and natural gas fields of the Caspian Sea basin. During a trip to Libya, Erbakan sat meekly through a public tirade against Turkey's Kurdish war delivered by Libyan leader Colonel Muammar Qadhafi, refusing to challenge the remarks. He narrowly survived a no-confidence vote in an indignant house of parliament on his return to Ankara.

Although the demise of Erbakan's coalition came as much from its failure to lower the budget deficit, curb inflation, and act on various government scandals, it was precipitated by an incident in Sincan in early February 1997. At a rally hosted by the mayor of the town in honor of "Jerusalem Day," a holiday first declared by the Ayatollah Khomeini in Iran in 1980, the Iranian ambassador called for the political rule of sharia in Turkey, saying, "We can wait no longer . . . God has promised

... the victory." The crowd chanted slogans against Israel and against Yasir Arafat and displayed posters promoting the violently anti-Israel, Islamic fundamentalist groups Hamas and Hizbullah. Within a few days, army tanks on maneuvers rumbled through the streets of Sincan, and the Turkish army began an investigation of the Welfare Party. Widespread public speculation anticipated an imminent military coup.

Instead of a coup, on 28 February 1997, the National Security Council released a public statement that "destructive and separatist groups are seeking to weaken our democracy and legal system by blurring the distinction between the secular and the anti-secular. . . . In Turkey, secularism is not only a form of government but a way of life and the guarantee of democracy and social peace . . . it is impossible to step back from our understanding of the social and legal principles which form the structural core of the state . . . out-of-date measures which are taken without regard for these principles do not coincide with our legal system." The military commanders forced Erbakan's agreement to a twenty-point plan to reduce the influence of fundamentalism in Turkey. The ban on certain Islamic sects would be enforced, the Welfare Party would cease recruiting fundamentalists for government posts and stop the spread of religious secondary schools, and restrictions on politically symbolic garments like womens' head scarves would be maintained. Erbakan was forced to sign an order purging 160 officers for Islamic political activities and sympathies. Perhaps one reason that a military coup did not occur was that it was unnecessary. Through the NSC, the Turkish military possessed a constitutionally defined executive authority that it used since the 1980s to exert its power on a range of important issues.

In June 1997, Erbakan resigned and Mesut Yılmaz formed a new government. In January 1998, the Turkish Constitutional Court closed the Welfare Party "because of evidence confirming its actions against the principles of the secular republic." Six Welfare Party leaders, including Erbakan, were banned from political leadership for five years, and individual members also faced criminal charges of subverting the constitution. Bekir Yıldız, the mayor of Sincan, received a sentence of four years, seven months for "inciting religious hatred"; former Kayseri mayor Şükrü Karatepe received ten months; and Tayyip Erdoğan, the mayor of Istanbul, received a ten-month prison sentence on similar charges. Within a few weeks, most of the Welfare Party's parliamentary deputies had joined a successor party, the Virtue Party, which subsequently became the largest party in parliament. In the end, for all its accomplishments at the municipal level, the Welfare Party had fared no better than the other parties at finding solutions to the basic economic and political problems of the country.

The new prime minister, Mesut Yılmaz, pressed forward the "February 28 Process," efforts to limit Islamic influence in public life. Parliament required students to complete eight years of primary education before becoming eligible for admission to Islamic academies. These academies, popularly called *imam-hatip okulları*, or prayer-leader and preacher schools, were first permitted during the period of military rule in the early 1980s. In fifteen years, however, their numbers had grown to more than 600, and they enrolled fully one-tenth of the eligible secondary education students in the country. They were places where a simplistic, fundamentalist Islam was taught to students, who after graduation could go on to enroll in universities, law faculties, police academies, and other postsecondary institutions. Yılmaz also instructed the Ministry of Education to enforce regulations banning headscarves from public schools and universities. Public protests broke out immediately all over Turkey, the largest being in Istanbul. The administration also moved against Islamic influence in other areas. Police detained twenty leading Islamist businessmen on charges they had provided funding for activists, and in May 1998, the chief prosecutor in Ankara's State Security Court asked for the closure of MÜSİAD, the Independent Industrialists' and Businessmen's Association, and filed charges against its president, Erol Yarar, for inciting hostility based on religion.

Yılmaz's attacks on government corruption were primarily aimed against Tansu Çiller, his political rival, whose Welfare Party coalition partners had shielded her from prosecution. But before long, Yılmaz himself was implicated in revelations of corruption on such a massive scale that the foundations of Turkish democracy were threatened. The sordid tale began to come out with a car accident.

THE SUSURLUK CRASH AND GOVERNMENT CORRUPTION

In the accident near Susurluk in November 1996, a speeding Mercedes-Benz carrying four passengers crashed into a semi-tractor-trailer, killing three occupants of the car and injuring the fourth. When the identity of the crash victims and the story of how they happened to be riding together in the car came out, the truck driver, who survived, was hailed as a national hero.

The three dead included Abdullah Çatlı, a criminal right-wing hit man and mafia kingpin wanted in connection with the murders of seven leftist students and an attack on leftists at a coffee house in Ankara in 1978–1979. Çatlı had also been involved in the Istanbul jailbreak of Mehmet Ali Ağca, the Pope's assailant. At the time of his death, Çatlı held a gun permit and, among his thirteen passports in various names, a Turkish diplomatic passport. The second passenger was Çatlı's girlfriend Gonca Us, a former beauty queen and mistress of gangsters. The third passenger was Hüseyin Kocadağ, a senior security officer and deputy police chief of Istanbul. He had commanded police units in missions against Kurdish rebels. The lone survivor in the Mercedes, Sedat Bucak, was a True Path Party member of parliament with close connections to Tansu Çiller, who led a Kurdish clan militia receiving government funding to fight Kurdish rebels. Guns and silencers were also discovered in the car.

At first, President Demirel denied government involvement in criminal activity. The Minister of the Interior, Mehmet Ağar, resigned when it became clear that his initial statements about the crash were not only wrong, but that in fact he had a long relationship with Çatlı. Leading Turkish newspapers published reports, based on police and military intelligence documents, showing that the Turkish government had been hiring death squads to murder Kurdish rebels and other enemies of the state since the mid-1980s, and that these death squads had evidently received a strengthened mandate in 1991. Before his death, Alparslan Türkeş, the aging leader of the far-right Nationalist Movement Party, publicly acknowledged that Çatlı had been employed by the government to carry out clandestine missions on behalf of the police and the army. Former Interior Minister Mehmet Sağlam admitted that the NSC had approved the use of illegal means to dispose of enemies. Their weapons were in some cases traced back to police sources. Funding for the death squads was raised through bank presidents, who in return received kickbacks from the drug trade that the squads were allowed to run; the profits were laundered through casinos licensed by the Ministry of Tourism.

The published versions of official reports on the affair, directed by Yılmaz, were incomplete and misleading, aiming at the period of Tansu Çiller's premiership, but rumors of missing persons and mysterious murders dated back earlier than that, to 1991, during Yılmaz's first term as prime minister. And Yılmaz's statements, that outside the gendarmerie the Turkish armed forces were unaware of and uninvolved in the activities of the death squads, seemed unbelievable. New information became

available almost daily, revealing the depth and complexity of interrela-
tionships between state security forces and the police, the banking institution, the government privatization process, cabinet ministries and
members of parliament, organized crime, and far-right gangs of violent
thugs. It pointed to two ultimate sources of the problem. The first was
fanatical pursuit of the war against Kurdish rebels in southeastern Turkey, and the second was corruption of the ongoing strategy to privatize
state-owned businesses. Both the True Path and Motherland Parties were
implicated in the escalating spiral of scandals. But the issue went even
deeper than that. It appeared possible that the tacit arrangement of the
1980s, between former prime minister and then President Özal and the
military, allowing Özal to pursue economic liberalization and privatization and leaving the generals a free hand to prosecute the war against
Kurds and leftists, had turned uglier in the aftermath of the Gulf War.
Far right nationalist and fundamentalist Muslim groups had apparently
been secretly armed and used as paramilitary death squads with the
knowledge of the highest officials of the Turkish state.

Investigations of Çiller's abuse of the prime ministry slush fund suggested that she had used the account to pay hit men and death squads
against suspected Kurdish terrorists both in Turkey and abroad. Three
True Path Party associates were convicted while Çiller and her husband
spent most of 1998 defending themselves against charges involving their
personal finances. Yılmaz's government finally collapsed at the end of
1998, as parliament investigated his connections to organized crime.

The scandals of the 1990s were not necessarily evidence of anything
wholly new in Turkish politics. Insofar as they might be described as
influence peddling, they resembled the ways that the Turkish political
system had worked for decades, as the elaboration of systems of patronage. What was new, however, was that the national economic policies
implemented since the early 1980s had made it possible for political patrons to deliver access to dramatic sources of wealth in the form of control of former government-owned industrial ventures and businesses.
Beginning in the early 1980s, a very large portion of Turkey's industrial
capacity went up for sale. The stakes were enormous, and it is hardly
surprising that in the struggle for control of this huge financial potential
some of the darkest forces in Turkish society came out into the open, in
ways similar to what has been seen all over east central Europe since
the breakup of the USSR and the fall of the old Stalinist regimes. The
ugliest aspect of the problem was that murderous gangs of criminal terrorists operated with the apparent acquiescence, if not approval, of the

Turkish military, which found them useful against Kurdish separatists and other political dissidents. These included not only neo-fascist groups but even Islamic fundamentalists. A police shootout with an illegal Islamic group called Hizbullah (unrelated to the group of the same name in Lebanon and Palestine) in eastern Anatolia in early 2000 led to the discovery of huge caches of weapons and the remains of dozens of persons murdered by the group who, it was alleged, received state support for its opposition to the PKK.

THE RETURN OF BÜLENT ECEVİT: THE PAST AND THE FUTURE

Bülent Ecevit, head of the Democratic Left Party and Yılmaz's coalition partner, returned to the premiership for the first time since the mid-1970s. Ecevit, virtually the only prominent political leader untouched by scandal, led the nation to early elections in April 1999. His victory in those elections was helped by his successful management of the spectacular capture of Abdullah Öcalan, leader of the PKK. Ecevit formed a coalition with the Nationalist Movement Party, which finished a surprising second in the balloting, and with Yılmaz's Motherland Party. Turkey's first prime minister of the third millennium, Ecevit confronted issues, some as old as the Republic and others unexpected by earlier generations, that illustrated the degree to which the life of the nation had become integrated with global issues at the beginning of the new millennium.

Forced out of hiding in Syria and tracked by Turkish intelligence as he tried to gain political asylum in several European countries, Öcalan was seized by Turkish authorities in Kenya in February 1999. He was tried, convicted, and sentenced to death for treason for his role in leading the Kurdish resistance war against the Turkish military. Öcalan's conciliatory public statements, however, seemed to offer the hope of a conclusion to the long war and a reconciliation between the Turkish state and the Kurdish population. While thousands of Turks, carrying photographs of loved ones whose lives were lost in the long war in Kurdistan, demonstrated publicly for Öcalan's execution, other voices counseled patience. Öcalan himself, reminding his public audience that his mother was Turkish, called for an end to the separatist war, pleading that the two peoples, Turkish and Kurdish, were in the end indivisible. The Turkish military interpreted these remarks as evidence of PKK weakness, but Öcalan had said similar things publicly since 1990, when for the first time he had suggested that a solution to the Kurdish problem need not necessarily mean a separate Kurdish state. The increasing Kurdish migration to cities in western Turkey since the mid-1980s led Öcalan to doubt the possibility of ever achieving Kurdish independence and to seek instead some form of Kurdish cultural autonomy within the Republic of Turkey as an acceptable alternative.

Not only in the concern for the civil and human rights of all persons, but also in the global economic system, in environmental problems, in the phenomenon of mass migrations of peoples and in other issues of transnational importance, it was evident that the context of Turkish history had shifted from that of the early Republic. The barriers behind which a nation attended to its internal affairs had become more permeable. It had become more apparent that a nation's identity and view of itself was not a fixed thing, permanent for all time and in all circumstances, but was subject to new influences. Using a proactive and communicative management style, Ecevit delicately balanced popular sentiment for Öcalan's execution with European calls for clemency, carefully keeping the crucial allegiance of the junior partners in his coalition and stressing the importance to Turkey's economy of membership in the European Union (EU).

Meeting in Luxembourg in December 1997, EU member states invited eleven countries, ten East European nations and Cyprus, to apply for membership. Six of these were invited to apply for full membership, while the other five were put on a slower timetable. All were given "pre-accession partnerships," a status which gave them access to financial aid and placed them under annual reviews of progress. And although the European Council confirmed Turkey's eligibility for accession to the EU, it did not offer Turkey a preaccession partnership. The decision stunned Turkey, which had held associate membership status since 1964. Having joined the Customs Union in 1995, Turkey had anticipated that full EU membership would quickly follow.

Turkish membership, some EU member states feared, would have a significant negative economic and financial impact on the EU. Turkey's population of about 64 million is greater than any other EU member or preaccession partner except Germany. Member states worried that extension of the EU common agricultural policy to Turkey would swamp its financial capacity. Led by Germany, where the largest numbers of Turkish migrants lived, they also expressed the fear that, frontier barriers removed, cheap Turkish labor would migrate throughout Europe and outbid the comparatively high-priced European laborer. The EU also raised political objections to Turkey's membership. Paramount among these were its notoriously poor relationship with its neighbor Greece, a member state in the European Union, and Turkey's abuses of the civil rights of political dissidents and minorities and the use of torture in its prisons. In view of the EU decision, the budding relationships between Turkey and the Caucasus republics of the former Soviet Union took on greater significance.

The Turkish EU relationship improved, ironically, as Turkey coped with a vast natural disaster. A devastating earthquake struck the most populous and heavily industrialized region of the country, the Istanbul-İzmit corridor, in August 1999. The earthquake, measuring 7.8 on the Richter scale, was one of the worst anywhere in the world in the twentieth century. The aftermath of the quake showed both the weaknesses and the strengths of Turkey. Aware of the new climate emphasizing private initiative, and hoping to maintain a low profile for the state, the government hesitated to call on military assistance too hastily after the quake. But the disaster was of such a scale that it swamped all relief efforts, private and public, and the state response was completely inadequate and ineffective. More than 17,000 people died. Corruption in contracting procedures had allowed construction companies to build shoddy structures and ignore construction codes. Among the countries contributing foreign assistance, which allowed a cleanup to begin, was Greece. The genuinely humanitarian aid provided by Greece was reciprocated a couple of months later when Athens, too, suffered an earthquake. The icy relations between Turkey and Greece began to thaw in the months following, as Greece modified its strong opposition to Turkish membership in the EU. One result was the return of Turkey to candidate status in the EU in December 1999.

Some of the issues Turkey faced at the beginning of the new millennium were unknown to its founders, different from those the Republic had faced a half-century earlier, when the Turkish state was first opened to democratic processes, or seventy-five years before, when the Republic was new. The dominance of international capitalism was unforseen at that time. In the midst of a transition to the market, the underlying strengths of the Turkish economy, its strong agricultural base and vibrant industrial and manufacturing sector, compared well to the problems being faced by other national economies in the region. The collapse of the USSR and the East bloc, and the end of the Cold War, made Turkey's international position somewhat less certain than it had been at the height of the Cold War, when its geographical position assured it great value as an ally of the United States. Turkey's statesmen worked to establish close working commercial and political relations with the Balkan states as well as with the new states of the Caucasus and Central Asia.

At the beginning of the new millennium, it was apparent that a political transition was taking place in Turkey. The generation of men who had led the country since 1961 was passing from the scene. Bülent Ecevit, seventy-five years old, remained prime minister, at the head of a coalition government. His careful efforts to amend the constitution and enable Süleyman Demirel, his rival during the 1960s and 1970s, to serve a second term as president of the Republic failed. Rebellious parliamentary deputies urged the retirement of Demirel, who was even older than Ecevit, in spite of the potential for political and economic destabilization. Necmettin Erbakan, long the leader of the Islamic right, was barred from participation in politics; Alparlsan Türkeş, ideologue of the far right, was dead. Even in Cyprus, Rauf Denktaş, who belonged to the same generation, faced the possibility of electoral defeat.

To succeed Demirel, Supreme Court judge Necdet Sezer, 51, an outspoken advocate of democracy and human rights, became the tenth president of the republic in May 2000. A younger generation of Turkish people seemed to join its voices to the chorus of the rest of the world's peoples, calling for a more democratic, more open, more liberal, and more humane public regime. The task facing the emerging younger generation of their leaders was to translate the nation's enduring myths, symbols, and rituals into a form that communicated meaningfully in new conditions.

Notable People in the History of Turkey

Abdülhamid II (1842–1918). Ottoman Sultan 1876–1909. Son of Sultan Abdülmecid. Raised to the throne on the breakdown of Murad V. A modernizer who oversaw the economic and technological development of the empire. Promulgated the first Ottoman constitution, but suspended it a year later and closed the parliament. The Young Turk revolution forced him to restore the constitution and call elections. Deposed after the failure of the counterrevolution of April 1909, he was exiled to Salonika, where he stayed until the outbreak of the First Balkan War. He lived in retirement in the Beylerbeyi Palace in Istanbul until his death.

Adıvar, Halide Edib (1884–1964). Nationalist journalist, novelist, and orator. Born and raised in a traditional Islamic household in Istanbul; learned to read, write, and recite the Qur'an. Attended a Greek kindergarten and had English governesses and private tutors. The first Turk to graduate from the American College for Girls (1901). Married Salih Zeki and had two sons, but divorced her husband when he took a second wife. Later she married the noted scholar Dr. Abdülhak Adnan Adıvar. Published several novels, the most famous of which were *Ateşten Gömlek* (Shirt of Fire), *Sinekli Bakkal* (Grocery of Flies), and *Vurun Kahpeye* (Strike the Whore). She and her husband disagreed with the radical secularism of the early Republican years. While she was abroad in 1925, the Independence Tribunals began arresting Atatürk's political enemies, and she and her husband decided not to return to Turkey. Except for a short visit, they returned only after Atatürk's death. While in exile, Halide Edib published in English two volumes of her personal remembrances, *Memoirs* (1926) and *The Turkish Ordeal* (1928), and wrote and spoke extensively as a goodwill ambassador for the Turkish revolution.

Ahmet Rıza (1858–1930). Ottoman intellectual and politician. Interested in bringing about the advancement of modern, scientific, and rational society, his thought was influenced by the French positivist Auguste Comte. Founded the Association for the Union of Ottomans in 1889, which became the Committee of Union and Progress in 1895. In the same year, he began publishing the dissident journal *Meşveret*, whose editorial stance advocated a synthesis of modern science and Islamic civilization. A believer in constitutional monarchy, Ahmet Rıza thought that loyalty to the Ottoman dynasty could unite the different ethnic and religious groups of the empire.

Alp Arslan (1030–1073). Seljuk Sultan 1063–1073. Son of the Seljuk chieftain Chaghri Beg, he demonstrated military leadership early in his youth. Succeeded to the Seljuk throne in 1063 and was recognized as Sultan by the Caliph in Baghdad. Campaigned in Armenia and the Caucasus in order to control the Turkoman forces in his army. Defeated the Byzantine army at the Battle of Manzikert, August 1071, taking the emperor prisoner. As a result of this victory, all of Anatolia was opened to Turkish raiding, migration, and settlement.

Atatürk, Mustafa Kemal (1881–1938). General and politician, first president of the Turkish Republic (1923–1938). Born in Salonika and graduated from the military staff college in 1905. In Damascus in 1907, he founded a secret society, the Fatherland and Freedom Society. Began to work with the CUP when he was stationed in Salonika with the Ottoman Third Army. He participated in the Action Army that put down the counterrevolution in 1909. Before World War I, served in Libya and in Sofia. First achieved fame for his leadership in the defense of the Dardanelles in 1915. Directed the Ottoman retreat from Syria in 1917. In May 1919, was appointed to direct the demobilization in eastern Anatolia, but instead joined the growing resistance movement, immediately becoming one of its most important leaders. He led the unification of the various Anatolian Societies for the Defense of Rights at two nationalist congresses in July and September 1919, at which he was elected president. During the next three years, he served as president of the nationalist parliament and coordinated and led the military campaign that repelled the Greek invasion of Anatolia. He was elected first president of the Republic when it was proclaimed on 29 October 1923. During the next fifteen years, he oversaw the beginnings of the modernization of Turkey through a series of reforms. Took the family name Atatürk in 1934. He died of cirrhosis of the liver on 10 November 1938. His remains were buried in the archaeological museum in Ankara and transferred to a mausoleum at Anıtkabir when it was completed in 1953. Married to Latife in 1923–1925. Atatürk left no heirs.

Ayla, Safiye (1907–1998). Popular singer. Born in Istanbul, attended the Girls' Teaching School in Bursa, and taught school in Istanbul. Received musical and theoretical training from Yesari Asım Arsoy, the greatest composer of the era. Debuted in 1930 at the famous Moulin Rouge theater in Istanbul. Made more than 500 records in her career, performing both in Turkey and abroad, on the radio and in films. The most famous singer of her generation.

Bayar, Celal (1883–1985). Banker, government administrator, politician, prime minister, and third president of the Republic (1950–1960). Born in a village near Bursa; worked for the Deutches Orient Bank branch there. He joined the CUP in 1907 and the Ottoman Association for the Defense of Rights in 1918. Elected to the last Ottoman parliament that met in Istanbul in 1920, then fled to join the nationalist parliament in Ankara. Became the nationalist Minister of the Economy in 1921 and Minister of Reconstruction and Settlement in 1924. Directed the Business Bank (İş Bankası) from its founding in 1924 until he became Minister of the Economy again (1932–1937). Oversaw the economic development of the SEEs during the 1930s in balance with support for private enterprise. During 1937–1938, served as prime minister. One of the founders of the Democrat Party in 1946. Became third president of the Republic after the DP victory of 1950. After the military coup of 1960, was arrested and convicted of violations against the constitution, but his death sentence was commuted to life imprisonment by the National Unity Committee. Released because of advancing age and ill health in 1964, he lived another twenty years.

Cebesoy, Ali Fuat (1882–1968). General and politician. A classmate of Mustafa Kemal at the military academy, he became a CUP member. In the War of Independence, commanded the nationalist troops on the western front and entered the nationalist parliament. Became nationalist envoy to the Bolsheviks in 1920–1921. With Kâzim Pasha, he opposed Mustafa Kemal's increasing dictatorialism, and with him was arrested, tried, and acquitted in the İzmir conspiracy trials, 1926. Reentered parliament before Atatürk's death; appointed to İnönü's cabinet in 1939. After the death of Kâzim Karabekir, he was speaker of parliament.

Çiller, Tansu (1944–). Professor, economist, politician and prime minister. Born in Istanbul; educated at Boğaziçi University, received an M.A. from the University of New Hampshire and a Ph.D. from the University of Connecticut (1978). After postdoctoral work at Yale University and teaching a year at Franklin and Marshall College, she returned to Turkey and taught economics at Boğaziçi University. Became an economic advisor to Süleyman Demirel, joined his True Path Party; elected party vice president in 1990. Entered the cabinet as Minister of Economy in 1991. After Özal's death and Demirel's election to the presidency, she became True Path Party chief and Turkey's first female prime minister in 1993–1995. Served as deputy prime minister in a coalition government with the Welfare Party, 1996–1997. She and husband Özer Uçuran, who married her and took her name in 1963, amassed a considerable personal fortune, which became the object of criticism and a legal investigation, and of parliamentary investigations for corruption.

Demirel, Süleyman (1924–). Engineer, politician, prime minister, and president. Born in the village of İslamköy near İsparta. Earned an engineering degree from Istanbul Technical University in 1949. Studied in the United States as an Eisenhower fellow, 1954–1955. Returning to Turkey, he directed the Department of Hydraulic Works, 1955–1960. After the fall of the Menderes government, he taught at the Middle East Technical University, Ankara, before joining the Justice Party in 1962. Became party chair after the death of Rağıp Gümüşpala in 1964; served as prime minister between 1965 and 1971. Resigned after the "coup by memorandum" of 12 March 1971. Became prime minister again as head of two "Nationalist Front" coalitions in 1975–1977 and 1979–1980. The latter government was unseated by the military coup of 12 September 1980. After the ban on political participation of former politicians was lifted in 1987, he became chair of the True Path Party and entered parliament again. When the TP won the general elections of 1991, he became prime minister a seventh time. After the death of Turgut Özal, parliament elected Demirel the ninth president of the Republic (1993–2000).

Ecevit, Bülent (1925–). Journalist, politician, and prime minister. Born in Istanbul, he graduated from Robert College (1944) and studied Sanskrit literature at Ankara University. Leaving university, he began a career as a journalist. Served as assistant to the press attaché at the Turkish Embassy in London. After returning to Turkey and working for two newspapers, Ecevit spent a year at Harvard University (1957–1958). Though a published poet and known as one of Turkey's most intellectual statesmen, he did not obtain a university degree. Entered parliament as a member of the RPP in 1957. After the first military coup, he served on the Constituent Assembly (1961) and as Minister of Labor entered the cabinet of the İnönü coalition governments (1961–1965) while continuing to write a daily newspaper column. Authored the "left-of-center" program of the RPP after the mid-1960s and took a principled stance against cooperation with the military government in 1971. In 1972, he became the third president of the RPP (after Atatürk and İnönü). Served as prime minister in a coalition government (1973–1974, during which time he directed the Turkish invasion of Cyprus) and in 1978–1979. After the military coup of 1980, he and other politicians were barred from political participation until 1987. Led the Democratic Left Party, founded by his wife Rahsan (1987–1989). Returned to parliament in 1991, becoming deputy prime minister in a coalition government with Mesut Yılmaz's Motherland Party (1998) and prime minister again (1998–2001).

Enver Pasha (1881–1922). Ottoman army officer and politician. Touched off the 1908 Young Turk revolution when he defied orders to return to Istanbul and fled to the Macedonian hills. Occupying Köprülü with his troops, he forced Sultan Abdülhamid to restore the Constitution of 1876 and convene parliament. Led the coup d'état of January 1913 that brought the CUP faction to power. Acting on his dream of a unified Eurasian Turkish state, he led Ottoman troops in an invasion of the Russian Empire in the Caucasus after the Ottomans entered World War I in 1914. After the war, he fled to Berlin. Failing to obtain Bolshevik backing, he attempted a comeback with troops marching into eastern Anatolia against the nationalists in 1921. The nationalist victory at Sakarya dashed his hopes. He died leading central Asian Turks against Bolshevik armies in the Russian civil war in 1922.

Erbakan, Necmettin (1926–). Professor, engineer, politician, and prime minister. The political leader of Islamic fundamentalism in Turkey. Born in Sinop, son of a judge. Took an engineering degree from Istanbul Technical University in 1949 and a doctorate in mechanical engineering at Aachen Technische Hochschule, Germany. As president of the Union of Chambers of Commerce and Industry in 1969, Erbakan clashed with Prime Minister Demirel in defense of small business against international capitalism and the European Community. After entering parliament as an independent deputy from Konya in 1969, he created the National Order Party in 1970 and led its several subsequent manifestations, becoming the leading voice of politicized revivalist Islam in Turkey. Served as deputy prime minister in a coalition with Ecevit and the RPP in 1974 and in the two Nationalist Front coalitions of the 1970s. After the military-imposed ban on political participation by former politicians was lifted in 1987, he became head of the Welfare Party (1987) and reentered parliament in 1991. After the Welfare Party won the most votes in the 1995 elections, Erbakan was at first shut out of the government, but served as prime minister in 1996–1997. Charged with advocating the fall of constitutional secularism in Turkey, the Welfare Party was closed by court order in 1998, and Erbakan was barred from party politics for life.

Evliya Çelebi (1611–1682). Pen name of Dervish Mehmed Zilli, Ottoman writer, born in Istanbul. His father was chief court jeweler, his mother an Abkhazian slave girl who was the cousin of the Ottoman statesman Melek Ahmed Pasha and grew up in the palace. Evliya was educated as a Qur'an reciter and then received a palace education, becoming a member of an elite palace guard corps. Melek Ahmed became Evliya's patron; Evliya lived in the household of Melek Ahmed and accompanied the pasha on his various assignments until Melek Ahmed's death in 1662. Evliya is famous for the ten-volume *Seyahatname*, or Book of Travels, which he wrote. The work, the product of more than forty years of travel and observation, is a monumental description of Ottoman life and culture, full of linguistic and historical trivia, folklore, social analysis, and humorous anecdotes. It qualifies Evliya as perhaps the greatest travel writer of world history, surpassing Marco Polo and Ibn Battuta.

Evren, Kenan (1918–). General and president. Graduated from the military academy in 1939. Became a four-star general in 1974 and chief of general staff in 1978. Led the 1980 coup d'état and became head of state, chairing the National Security Council. By the national referendum of

November 1982 approving the new constitution, he automatically became the seventh president of the Republic and resigned his commission. Retired at the end of his term in 1989.

Güney, Yılmaz (1937–1984). Actor and filmmaker. Born in a village near Adana, he began working in the Turkish commercial film world in the early 1960s. Became a popular actor and in 1968 established his own film company. Served two prison sentences in the 1960s for his political activities. Released in the general amnesty of 1974; imprisoned again for killing a judge in a brawl in a restaurant. Among his films, *Umut* (Hope) and *Yol* (The Road) stand out for their cinematic style and for their themes of the struggle of the individual against social convention and the force of tradition. After escaping from prison in 1978, he oversaw the final editing of *Yol* in Switzerland. The film won the highest award at the Cannes film festival. He died of cancer in Paris in 1984.

Hurrem Sultan (1500?–1558). Wife of Ottoman Sultan Süleyman I (r. 1520–1566) and mother of Sultan Selim II (r. 1566–1574). Probably Polish by birth, her name may have been Alexandra Lisowska. Called Haseki Hurrem, Hurrem the "favorite concubine," in Turkish sources, and Roxelana in Western sources. Taken in a Tatar slave raid, she was probably presented to Süleyman by his mother shortly after his accession. She revolutionized Ottoman politics first by her marriage to Süleyman and then by her permanent residence in the Topkapı palace in Istanbul, where she deeply influenced public affairs. Her mosque in Istanbul (1539) was the first commission of the court architect Sinan. Some of her correspondence survives, including her letters to Süleyman.

İnönü, İsmet (1884–1973). General and politician, prime minister, and second president of the Republic (1938–1950). After graduating from the Army Staff College in 1906, he joined the CUP in Edirne. Worked with Mustafa Kemal in Syria in 1917; appointed undersecretary of the Ministry of War, 1918. Joined the nationalists in 1920 and entered the nationalist parliament and became first Minister of War. As commander of the nationalist forces on the western front, he twice defeated the Greek armies at İnönü, hence the family name he was given by Atatürk (1934). Headed the Turkish delegation at the Lausanne conference. Resigning his commission, after October 1923 he became RPP chief and first prime minister of the Republic (1923–1924, 1925–1937). When Atatürk died, parliament elected İnönü the second president of the Republic (1938–

1950). After World War II, guided the transition to a multiparty system, going into opposition in parliament when the RPP was defeated in the 1950 elections. He again served as prime minister in coalition governments between 1961–1965. Resigned from the RPP in 1972 when opponents of his policy of cooperation with the military government, led by Bülent Ecevit, defeated him. He kept his seat in the Senate until his death.

Karabekir, Kâzim (1882–1948). General and politician. Graduated from the military academy in 1905; joined the CUP in Edirne in 1907. Promoted to brigadier with command of the armies in the Caucasus in 1918. His support for Mustafa Kemal, and his commitment of troops under his command, were critical to the success of the nationalists. Helped coordinate the calling of the first nationalist congress at Erzurum in 1919. Defeated the Armenians in 1920. Became a member of the nationalist parliament, but disagreed with Mustafa Kemal after the War of Independence, forming the opposition Progressive Republican Party in 1924. Arrested and tried by the Independence Tribunals in 1926 but acquitted. After the death of Atatürk, he reentered politics, becoming speaker of parliament in 1946, which post he held until his death.

Koç, Vehbi (1901–1996). Businessman, industrialist, and philanthropist. Began in business at the age of fifteen, opening a grocery store in Ankara. Entered contracting after Ankara became the capital of the Republic and, in the 1930s, was Turkey's leading private investor in imports of American and European manufactured goods. Produced Turkey's first automobile, the Anadol in 1967. Founded Turkey's largest private conglomerate, Koç Holding, with holdings in motor vehicles, home appliances and electronics, information technology, processed food, and tourism; it employs 32,000 people. The Koç foundation established one of the first private universities in Turkey.

Köprülü, Mehmed Fuad (1890–1966). Historian, professor, politician, and cabinet minister. The leading historian of the early Republican era. Appointed director of the Turkish Historical Society in 1927, but the Society fell out of favor with Atatürk and was replaced in 1932. Was largely responsible for the introduction of professional methodology, emphasizing the identification and interpretation of primary sources, in historical studies in Turkey. His work was broadly interdisciplinary and influenced by insights from anthropology and literary criticism. Entered politics and was elected to parliament in 1935. After World War II, became one of the founders of the Democrat Party and, with the party's victory in the 1950 elections, became foreign minister. Resigned from the cabinet and the party in 1957. Helped found the short-lived New Democrat Party in 1961.

Kösem Valide (1589?–1651). Popular name of Mahpeyker Sultan. Favorite concubine of Ottoman Sultan Ahmed I (r. 1603–1617) and Ottoman *Valide Sultan*, or Queen Mother, from 1623–1651, when her sons, Murad IV (1623–1640) and Ibrahim (1640–1648), and her grandson Mehmed IV (1648–1687) reigned as Ottoman sultans. Greek by birth, she became probably the most powerful woman in Ottoman history. She was the effective ruler of the empire during the reign of the incompetent Mustafa I (1617–1618 and 1622–1623), and the regent for her minor son Murad IV in the early years of his reign. She saved the dynasty by preventing the murder of Ibrahim by Murad IV, who had executed his other brothers. Later she permitted the deposition of Ibrahim in favor of Mehmed IV. That led to her demise, because Mehmed's mother, Turhan, ordered Kösem's assassination. Kösem's vast fortune was dedicated to charitable and humanitarian causes.

Mahmud II (1784–1839). Ottoman Sultan 1808–1839. Born in Istanbul, the youngest son of Abdülhamid I and Nakş-i Dil Sultan. He was raised to the throne on the deposition of Sultan Mustafa IV and assassination of Selim III in July 1808. He reigned during a critical period in Ottoman history, when conservative opposition made rapid institutional and financial reform difficult to accomplish, and when the Napoleonic wars necessitated a revision of the balance of power in Europe. In spite of this, Mahmud II carefully built a coalition of interest groups in support of reforms, succeeded in destroying the Janissary corps in 1826, and reasserted Ottoman central control of western and central Anatolia. His efforts lay the foundation for the period of Tanzimat reforms, which followed his death.

Mehmed II (1432–1481). Ottoman Sultan in 1444–1446 and 1451–1481. Son of Murad II and Hüma, a slave concubine. Born in Edirne. Placed on the throne as a youth by his father, but an international crisis forced Murad's return. Returned to the throne in 1451. Conquered Istanbul 29 May 1453. Rebuilt and resettled the city, making it the Ottoman imperial capital. He conquered Albania, the Morea, and Bosnia, establishing the northern Ottoman boundary at the Danube, conquered Karaman, and defeated Uzun Hasan. His conquests established Ottoman domination of the Black Sea. A man of culture and a skilled administrator, his work on the codification of imperial law (Kanun) defined the fundamental institutions of Ottoman government and restructured the basic taxation system of the empire.

Mehmed V Reşad (1844–1918). Ottoman sultan 1909–1918. Son of Sultan Abdülmecid. Elevated to the throne on the deposition of his brother Abdülhamid. Ruled as a constitutional monarch during the Young Turk era, having little influence on public affairs.

Mehmed VI Vahideddin (1861–1926). Son of Abdülmecid. Last sultan of the Ottoman Empire. Succeeded to the throne on the death of his brother, Mehmed V, shortly before the end of World War I. Followed a policy of cooperation with the victorious allies after the armistice of Mudros, opposing the nationalists. Accepted the Treaty of Sèvres in 1920 and was deposed by the nationalists in 1922. He fled the empire and lived out his life in exile.

Menderes, Adnan (1899–1961). Politician, prime minister, 1950–1960. Born into an old landholding family in the region of Aydın. Served in World War I and the War of Independence; studied law at the Ankara Law Faculty. Joined the Free Republican Party in 1930; after its closure, joined the RPP and represented Aydın in parliament from 1931 on. Led opposition to the land reform act after World War II; became one of the founding members of the Democrat Party with M. Fuad Köprülü, Celal Bayar, and Refik Koraltan (1946). Healed divisions among the Democrats, became party chief, and with the party's victory in the 1950 elections, he became prime minister. Led the government throughout the decade of the 1950s. His government was brought down by a military coup on 27 May 1960. Arrested, tried, and convicted of treason; he was executed on 17 September 1961. His remains, buried on İmrali, were reburied in Istanbul in a public ceremony in 1990.

Nesin, Aziz (1915–1995). Pen name of Mehmet Nusret Nesin, humorist and satirist, journalist, short story writer, and novelist. Born in Istanbul; graduated from the military academy in 1937. Discharged from the army for "abuse of authority," arrested in roundup of leftists in 1946 and jailed for the first time. First satirical book, *Azizname*, published 1948. Was arrested during the Istanbul riots of 1955 and several other times. Founded the Aziz Nesin Trust (1972); became one of Turkey's leading philanthropists. Elected general secretary of the Turkish Writers' Union in 1977. Several volumes of his short stories are available in English, as are his memoirs, *Istanbul Boy*.

Nursi, Said (1873–1960). Popular religious leader, writer, and Islamic modernist. Had good relations with the Young Turks leadership. One of the founders of the Mohammedan Union in 1909, he did not condone the violent counterrevolution. Became an advisor of Sultan Mehmed V and served as a propagandist for the Special Organization during World War I. After the war, supported the nationalists and addressed the nationalist parliament. Arrested and tried by the Independence Tribunals in the aftermath of the Shaykh Said rebellion of 1925. Lived out his life between prison and exile in various villages and towns of western Anatolia, writing extensively. His major work, *Risale-i Nur*, (Epistle of Light) circulated in unpublished form. Sought an accommodation between modern rational, scientific society, and Islam. Exercised a decisive impact on the emergence of political Islam in Turkey.

Orhan (d. 1362). Ottoman Sultan 1324?–1362. Son of Osman, who founded the Ottoman dynasty. Although according to popular tradition his mother was Sheikh Edebali's daughter, Orhan's mother was probably Mal Hatun, the daughter of a local Turkish lord. Conquered Bursa (1327) making it the first capital of the Ottoman state, and İznik (1331). His alliance with John VI Cantecuzenos, sealed through Orhan's marriage to John's daughter Theodora, secured the Byzantine throne for John. Armies sent by Orhan under the command of his son Süleyman raided Thrace and took Gallipoli (1354) and Edirne (1361).

Öcalan, Abdullah (1948–). Leader and one of the founders of the PKK (Partiye Karkaran Kurdistan, or Kurdish Workers' Party) and its military commander. Born in Siverek in eastern Anatolia. While a student at Ankara University, organized a meeting in Diyarbakır in 1977, at which a group of Kurdish rebels adopted a document called "The Path of the Kurdish Revolution." The document laid out a plan for the violent liberation of Kurdistan from rule by Turkey and collaborators within the Kurdish feudal classes. It became the official program of the PKK when it was founded in November 1978. He fled Turkey before the 1980 military coup, directing PKK operations from bases in Lebanon and Syria. Began a war for the political liberation of Kurdistan in 1984, which cost an estimated 30,000 lives over fifteen years. Öcalan was captured in Kenya in 1999 after being expelled from Syria. When brought back to Turkey, he was imprisoned and tried on İmrali Island and sentenced to death.

Özal, Turgut (1927–1993). Engineer, economist, politician, and president of the Republic. Born in Malatya; graduated from Istanbul Technical University in 1950; studied engineering and economics in the United States. After his return to Turkey, served for a time as deputy director of the Electrical Studies and Research Administration. Entered Demirel's cabinet as head of the State Planning Organization in 1967–1971. After the coup of 1971, taught at Middle East Technical University in Ankara before becoming special projects advisor at the World Bank. On his return, he joined the Sabancı Holding company. Reentered the government, March 1975, as undersecretary to Prime Minister Demirel as well as acting Head of State Planning. Ran for parliament, 1977, but was not elected. In 1979, became deputy prime minister and minister for Economic Affairs. Architect of the economic austerity program announced by the Demirel government, January 1980. After the 1980 coup, remained in government until forced to resign in a banking scandal in 1982. Founded the Motherland Party and led it to victory in the 1983 general elections, serving as prime minister until 1989. Succeeded Kenan Evren to become eighth president of the Republic, 1989. Died of a heart attack, 17 April 1993.

Sabahettin (1877–1948). Called Prens Sabahettin or Prince Sabahettin. Member of the Ottoman royal family, dissident politician. His father, Damad Mahmud Celaleddin Pasha, was the son of a vezir and a grandson of Sultan Mahmud II. Prince Sabahettin's mother was a daughter of Sultan Abdülmecid and sister of Sultan Abdülhamid II. Joining the CUP in Paris, Sabahettin became the main rival of Ahmet Rıza. Influenced by Edmond Desmolins, he believed that the best route to modernization lay in individualism and support of the family unit. He advocated economic development through classical liberalism, free trade, and encouragement of an entrepreneurial spirit. Advocated freedom of religion in a multiethnic empire, and supported foreign intervention on behalf of Ottoman Armenians. Accused of plotting the assassination of Mahmud Şevket Pasha, he left the empire in 1913 but returned in 1918. He was exiled in 1924 with other members of the Ottoman dynasty.

Sabancı, Hacı Ömer (1906–1966). Businessman, industrialist and philanthropist. Received a village education before moving to Adana for work in his youth. Entered the cotton business, opening the first modern cotton factory in 1938. Diversified into other sectors and founded Akbank (1947). Adana-based investments were unified in Sabancı Holding in 1967 by his son and heir, Sakıp Sabancı. During the 1980s, it became the second leading private conglomerate in Turkey.

Selim I (1466–1520). Ottoman sultan 1512–1520. Son of Bayezid II and Ayşe Hatun, the daughter of Ala al-Davla, of the rival Anatolian Muslim dynasty of Dulkadir. Born in Amasya, where his father was provincial governor. Selim's nickname *Yavuz*, usually translated "the Grim" in order to rhyme in English, is better translated "tough," or "resolute." His short reign was pivotal in Ottoman history because of his victories over Shah Ismail in Eastern Anatolia, Armenia, and Azerbaijan, which effectively limited the influence of Shiism in Anatolia, and over the Mamluks, which unified Anatolia and added Syria and Egypt to the empire's dominions.

Selim III (1761–1808). Ottoman sultan 1789–1807. Born in Istanbul, son of Mustafa III and Mibrişah Sultan. Corresponded with French King Louis XVI before acceding to the Ottoman throne. Carried out a thorough reform of Ottoman military administration and finance. Was overthrown by a Janissary coup, May 1807, imprisoned, and assassinated in July 1808 before the faction that supported him could restore him to the throne.

Süleyman I (1494–1566). Ottoman sultan 1520–1566. Known as "Kanuni Süleyman," or Süleyman the Lawgiver, in Turkish literature, and as "Süleyman the Magnificent" in the West. Born in Trabzon, where his father, later Sultan Selim I, was provincial governor. Conquered Rhodes (1520) and Belgrade (1521). Defeated Hungarian kingdom at Battle of Mohács (1526) and occupied Hungary (1541). Captured Baghdad and Iraq (1534). His legislative activity reorganized the central Ottoman bureaucracy and military-administrative institutions. Died on campaign at Szigetvár.

Talat Pasha (1874–1921). Ottoman administrator and Young Turk politician, Grand Vezir. As a postal clerk in Edirne, founded the dissident Ottoman Freedom Society, later merging it with the Committee of Union and Progress. Became acting speaker of the first Young Turks parliament, after the elections of December 1908. Held several cabinet posts, becoming especially influential as interior minister (1913–1918) and simultaneously finance minister and Grand Vezir (1917–1918). Organized the mass deportation of Armenians in April 1915 and was the government figure ultimately responsible for the campaign of ethnic cleansing and mass murder that the operation became. Resigned from the government in October 1918 and fled the empire. Assassinated in 1921 in Berlin by an Armenian terrorist.

Türkeş, Alparslan (1917–1997). Army officer and politician, one of the leaders of the nationalist far right in Turkey. Born in Cyprus. In 1944 his conviction for anti-Republican activities and racist, pan-Turkic views was overturned on appeal. Held the rank of colonel and was among the junior officers who staged the 1960 military coup. During the early months of the National Unity Committee, he was undersecretary to the prime minister and widely regarded as leader of the radical faction and the most powerful man in the cabinet. Dismissed in the purge of November 1960 and sent to the Turkish embassy in India. Returned to Turkey in 1963 and became a member of the Republican Peasant's Nation Party, taking over its chairmanship in 1965. As chair, made his philosophy of the "Nine Lights" the program of the party; the name was changed to the Nationalist Action Party in 1969. Became deputy prime minister and minister of state in the two Nationalist Front coalitions of the 1970s. After the 1980 military coup, was tried for organizing the violent actions of the NAP commandos during the 1970s. Regained a seat in parliament in 1991 as leader of the new Nationalist Movement Party.

Yalman, Ahmed Emin (1888–1973). Born in Salonika into a Sabbatean family. Obtained a PhD degree from Columbia University (1914); took up an academic position in Istanbul during World War I. Exiled by the British in 1920–1921. Founded the newspaper *Vatan* in 1923, introducing an innovative, American-style journalism. When the paper was closed by Mustafa Kemal in 1925, he entered business. Reopened *Vatan* in 1940; it became the leading voice of the opposition Democrat Party after World War II. Spent time in prison after he broke with the Menderes government in the late 1950s. His memoirs were published in English.

Yaşar Kemal (1923–). Pen name of journalist and novelist Kemal Sadık Gökçeli. Born into a mixed Kurdish and Turkish family in a village in the Çukurova. Introduced to the circle of socialist activists and writers in Adana in the late 1930s, publishing his first poem in the journal of the Adana People's House in 1939. Tortured in prison in 1950. He began writing for *Cumburiyet* in 1951, reporting on the life of the common people of Anatolia. His first published novel, *İnce Memed* (Slim Memed, translated into English as *Memed, My Hawk*) won the Varlık Press prize for the best novel of 1955. Of his dozens of novels, about ten are available in English translation, including *They Burn the Thistles* (part 2 of the Slim Memed series), *The Wind from the Plain, The Legend of Ararat*, and *The Legend of the Thousand Bulls*.

Yılmaz, Mesut (1947–). Politician. Took a degree in political science from Ankara University; received graduate training in Germany. After working in industry and in SEEs, was one of the founders of the Motherland Party and entered the first post-coup parliament in 1983, as a deputy from Rize. Entered the government under the patronage of Turgut Özal during the mid-1980s, holding several posts before becoming foreign minister (1987–1991). Succeeded Yıldırım Akbulut as leader of the Motherland Party and Prime Minister for a few months, 1991, after Akbulut quarreled with Özal. Formed a coalition government with Tansu Çiller and the True Path Party in 1996, according to which the two party leaders would alternate as premiers over a five-year period. The coalition collapsed within weeks. After the fall of Necmettin Erbakan's Welfare Party, served again as prime minister in 1997–1998, and deputy prime minister in the coalition government in 1999–2000.

Ziya Gökalp (1876–1924). Sociologist and essayist. Born in Diyarbakır, he was part Kurdish. Became active in the dissident movement before the revolution of 1908. Through his theoretical writings about the existence and characteristics of the Turkish nation, he became the most influential theorist of the Turkish nationalist movement. He envisioned a modern, westernized nation in which Turks would retain their native culture. His major works were *Türkleşmek, İslamlaşmak, Muasırlaşmak* (published in English as *Turkish Nationalism and Western Civilization*), and *Türkçülüğün Esasları* (The Principles of Turkism). Elected to parliament in 1923.

Glossary

Akhi: Masters of guild associations in medieval Anatolia. The akhis supervised both the commercial production of the guild and the devotional exercises of the members and their families.

Alevis: The name by which the Shiites in Turkey are known. The name means "of Ali," those who are followers of or devotees of Ali, the son-in-law of the Prophet Muhammad.

Beg (Bey): Turkish military title. Its meaning has changed gradually over time. In medieval Turkey a *beg* was a commander or prince. In the classical Ottoman Empire, the title was given to provincial military commanders and senior officers below the rank of vezir. In the later empire the title, pronounced *bey*, meant a military officer. In modern Turkey, the word *bey* is a title of respect, used after the first name, for older men or adult men.

BMM: *Büyük Millet Meclisi*, Grand National Assembly, the parliament of Turkey.

Caliph: The title of the supreme ruler of the medieval Islamic world. It derives from the Arabic word *khalifa*, meaning "successor," referring to the origin of the title in the early successors to the Prophet Muhammad. The office of the caliph is called the caliphate in English. After the first four "Rightly Guided" caliphs of the first Islamic century, the caliphate became hereditary in the Umayyad dynasty. In 750, the Umayyads were overthrown by the Abbasids, who held the office of the caliphate until the Mongol conquest of Baghdad in 1258.

Capitulations: Agreements between the Ottoman government and foreign commercial communities, granting privileges such as tax exemptions and low tariffs, and allowing them to fall under the legal jurisdiction of their own consuls rather than the Ottoman courts. The first of these agreements was reached with France in 1536. In the nineteenth century, the merchants and their consuls, backed by their home governments, manipulated and exploited the old agreements to their commercial and political advantage, extending their rights of extraterritoriality to Christian Ottoman clients and creating powerful financial enterprises outside Ottoman political control.

Committee of Union and Progress (CUP): The Ottoman dissident group of expatriates organized by Ahmet Rıza in Paris in 1889. After the revolution of 1908, begun by officers loyal to it, the CUP became the most important group in the Ottoman government. It remained a secret organization until the growth of opposition forced it to begin operating as a quasi political party in 1911. Officers of the CUP carried out a cabinet coup d'état in 1913 and governed the empire until the end of World War I.

Democrat Party (DP): Political party founded in 1946 by Celal Bayar, Refik Koraltan, Adnan Menderes, and Fuat Köprülü after their ouster from the Republican People's Party. Its Turkish name was *Demokrat Partisi*. The party won the elections of 1950 and ruled Turkey throughout the decade of the 1950s. After the military coup of 27 May 1960, the party was outlawed and its leaders jailed. Menderes and two former cabinet members were hanged in September 1961.

Democratic Left Party (DLP): Political party founded in 1985 by Rahsan Ecevit. Its Turkish name is *Demokratik Sol Partisi* (DSP). It is currently led by Bülent Ecevit, the husband of Rahsan Ecevit.

Dervish: Member of a mystical Islamic (*sufi*) order. Important orders in Turkey included the Bektashis, the Nakshibendis, and the Mevlevis (the "Whirling Dervishes").

Devşirme: The Ottoman institution of the child levy. Christian youths mostly from the Balkans were taken as state slaves, converted to Islam, taught Turkish, and trained in the palace system for service in the military-administrative hierarchy of the empire. By this means, most of the ruling class of the classical Ottoman Empire was of slave origin. The devşirme was discontinued in the seventeenth century.

DGM: *Devlet Güvenlik Mahkemeleri*, State Security Courts. Extraordinary courts established in 1972 to try political crimes against the nation. Abolished in the late 1970s, they were reestablished after the 1980 military coup.

DİSK: Turkish acronym of *Türkiye Devrimci İşçi Sendikaları Konfederasyonu*, the Confederation of Revolutionary Labor Unions of Turkey, a Marxist-oriented labor union association. Formed in 1965, it was closed by the military authorities after the 1980 coup. It reopened in 1991.

Divan: The Ottoman Council of State. The council was headed by the Grand Vezir and included the governors-general (beglerbegis) of the two greatest provinces, Rumelia and Anatolia, other officers with the rank of vezir, the *kadıaskers* of the provinces of Rumelia and Anatolia, the Head Treasurers, the Chancellor (*nisancı*), the commander of the Janissary corps (*Yeniçeri ağası*) and the Admiral fleet (*Kapudan Paşa*).

Etatism: Term for centralized economic planning and supervision in the Turkish Republic. State planning of the economy, expanded in the 1930s in response to the worldwide economic depression, was institutionalized as one of the "Six Arrows" of ideological Kemalism, and enshrined in the constitution by amendment in 1937.

Futuwwa: Philosophy and ethics of the craft guild associations in medieval Anatolia that were also dervish orders.

Ghazi: Warrior in the *ghaza*, the sacred struggle against the enemies of God. Muslim fighters in medieval Byzantine and Armenian Anatolia called themselves ghazis. The term was also occasionally used informally as a title for victorious commanders throughout the Ottoman period.

Grand Vezir: English translation of the Ottoman title *Sadr-ı Azam*. The Grand Vezir was appointed by the sultan to be deputy head of state and chair of the council of state (*divan*). He carried the sultan's seal as the mark of his authority. During the classical age, the Grand Vezir was typically of *devşirme* origin and a successful military commander and administrator. Informal "afternoon" meetings of the council, in the residence of the Grand Vezir, gradually became the most important meetings of the council. In the nineteenth century, the office evolved into a kind of prime ministry and was not necessarily held by military commanders.

Gray Wolves: The paramilitary arm of the youth organization of the Nationalist Action Party.

İmam-Hatip Okulları: Popular name of secondary academies for the training of preachers, prayer leaders, and other mosque leaders in the Republic of Turkey.

Janissary corps: The elite infantry corps of the classical Ottoman army. In the classical age, janissaries were of devşirme origin. The janissaries were destroyed by Sultan Mahmud II in 1826.

Justice Party (JP): The political party founded in 1961 as the main successor to the banned Democrat Party. Its Turkish name was *Adalet Partisi*, AP. The first chair was Rağıp Gümüşpala. After his death, the party was chaired by Süleyman Demirel until it was closed down by the military authorities after the coup of 12 September 1980.

Kanun: Sultanic law. In the Ottoman Empire kanun, comprising the corpus of decrees of the sultan, was considered a legitimate source of law, alongside the sharia and custom, to regulate the life and institutions of the Islamic state.

Karakol: A nationalist organization created by the CUP officials in 1918 in anticipation of the end of the war, Ottoman defeat, and occupation of the empire. Its purpose was to protect the CUP party members from arrest and to support a nationalist resistance movement in Anatolia.

Kemalism: *Atatürkçülük*, the worldview and ideology of the Republican People's Party, and the military and bureaucratic elites of modern Turkey. It is encapsulated in the "Six Arrows," Republicanism, Secularism, Nationalism, Populism, Etatism, and Revolutionism.

Kurush: The Ottoman silver coin and basic currency of the late Ottoman classical age. First minted in 1690, the kurush replaced the earlier Ottoman silver coin, called the akcha.

Lira: The basic unit of currency in the Turkish Republic. The Ottoman gold lira, introduced in 1844, was made the equivalent of 100 silver kurush. The lira (*Türk Lirası*) was retained as the name of the currency of the Turkish Republic after the revolution and War of Independence.

Malikane: A lifetime contract giving the holder rights to collect specified revenues on behalf of the Ottoman central treasury and the responsibility to remit the revenues according to an agreed upon timetable.

Medrese: An Islamic college. Its traditional curriculum stressed exegesis of the Islamic sacred texts, and the study of theology, rhetoric, Arabic grammar, philosophical logic, and astronomy.

Millet: One of several religiously defined national communities in the Ottoman Empire and also the system of semiautonomous self-government of these communities. Christian and Jewish community life in the empire was organized through the institution of the millet system.

MİT (*Millî İstihbarat Teşkilatı*): National Intelligence Organization. Founded in 1963 to reorganize and replace the older National Security Agency, its purpose was to uncover and track conspiracies in the armed forces and to monitor radical, especially leftist, activities in the general population.

Motherland Party: The political party founded in 1983 by Turgut Özal. Its Turkish name is *Anavatan Partisi*, abbreviated ANAP. It is currently led by Mesut Yılmaz.

Mukataa: A short-term tax form contracted between the Ottoman central government and an agent for the purpose of collecting and remitting specified imperial revenues.

National Pact (*Misak-ı Millî*): Document originally drawn up by the national congress at Erzurum (July 1919) as the basis for the establishment of the post-World War I Turkish nation. It was expanded and ratified by the Sivas congress (September 1919) and accepted by the last Ottoman parliament (February 1920).

Nationalist Action Party (NAP): The name of the right-wing political party controlled by Alparslan Türkeş. Its Turkish name was *Millî Hareket Partisi* (MHP) The former name of the party was the Republican Peasants' Nation Party. Türkeş took over the party in 1965 and renamed it in 1969. The party was closed by the military government in 1980.

Nationalist Front: Popular name of two coalition governments of the 1970s, led by Süleyman Demirel and the Justice Party. The first, from

March 1975 to June 1977, included the NSP of Necmettin Erbakan, the NAP of Alparslan Türkeş, and the Republican Reliance Party. The second, from July 1977 to January 1978, included the Justice Party and the first two of the junior partners.

NOP: The National Order Party, founded by Necmettin Erbakan and others in 1970. Its Turkish name was *Millî Nizam Partisi*, MNP). It was the first explicitly religious political party in Turkey. After the NOP was closed by court order in 1971, Erbakan started another Islamic party, the National Salvation Party (NSP; Turkish *Millî Selâmet Partisi*, MSP). When it, too, was closed after the 1980 military coup, its successor was the Welfare Party (its Turkish name, *Refah Partisi*, is best translated Prosperity Party). *Refah Partisi* was closed by court order in 1998 and succeeded by the Virtue Party (*Fazilet Partisi*, FP).

NSC: National Security Council. Its Turkish title is *Millî Güvenlik Kurulu (MGK)*. Established in 1962 following the failed coup attempt of Colonel Talat Aydemir, it comprises the president; the prime minister; the ministers of defense, foreign affairs, and internal affairs; the chief of the general staff; and the commanders of the military branches, the army, navy, air force and gendarmes.

NUC: National Unity Committee. Its Turkish name was *Millî Birlik Komitesi (MBK)*. Headed by General Cemal Gürsel, the NUC was a council of thirty-eight members that governed the country after the military coup of 27 May 1960.

OYAK: The Turkish acronym of *Ordu Yardımlaşma Kurumu*, the Army Mutual Assistance Association, founded in 1960. It is one of the largest conglomerates in Turkey.

Pasha: Senior officer in the Ottoman military. In the classical age, the title was given to the governors-general of the most important provinces and the vezirs of the dome. It was gradually extended to senior nonmilitary administrators. In the late empire, the rank was essentially that of a general. The title was abolished by the republican parliament but is still popularly used to refer to the senior military brass.

PDA: Ottoman Public Debt Administration. A European financial bureau created in 1881 for the purpose of administering the repayment of the Ottoman debt and brokering new loans for the Ottoman government.

People's Houses (*Halk evleri*): Public cultural and educational organizations established in cities and towns of Turkey beginning in 1932 for the purpose of communicating and encouraging loyalty to Republican ideals. In small towns and villages, their equivalent were called People's Rooms (*Halk odaları*).

PKK: Kurdish acronym of the *Partiye Karkaran Kurdistan*, the Kurdish Workers' Party, a Maoist revolutionary party founded by Abdullah Öcalan in Ankara in 1978.

Qur'an (Turkish Kur'an): The Koran, the sacred scriptures of Islam. It contains the revelations of God to the Prophet Muhammad (d. A.D. 632).

Republican People's Party (RPP): The political party founded by Mustafa Kemal Atatürk in 1922. Its original name was *Halk Fırkası*, the People's Party, becoming the Republican People's Party (*Cumhuriyet Halk Fırkası*, later *Partisi*, abbreviated CHP), in 1924. Like all political parties, it was closed by order of the military government in 1980. It was reestablished in 1992 and is currently headed by Deniz Baykal.

Second Republic: A popular term referring to the period of the second republican constitution, between 1961–1980.

SEEs: State Economic Enterprises. Government-owned conglomerates created in the 1930s for the purpose of carrying out the planned industrialization and economic development of Turkey.

Seljuks: A medieval southern Turkish tribe that took control of Baghdad and dominated the caliphate from the mid-eleventh to the mid-twelfth century. A branch of the Seljuk ruling dynasty established a kingdom in central Anatolia (Rum) between the late eleventh century and the Mongol invasions of the mid-thirteenth century.

Sharia (Turkish *şeriat*): Islamic canonical law, comprised of material distilled from the Qur'an, the tradition of the prophet, jurisprudential commentaries, and the wisdom of community consensus. There are four accepted schools (*mezheb*) of orthodox Sunni Islamic jurisprudence: the Hanafi, Maliki, Shafii, and Hanbali. The Ottoman Empire practiced the Hanafi tradition.

Shaykhulislam (Turkish *şeyhülislam*): Title of the highest ranking ulema official in the Ottoman Empire, appointed by the Sultan. He gave authoritative juridical rulings and administered a large governmental department that oversaw religious affairs.

Shiites: Members of one of two major denominations in Islam. The name derives from the Arabic term *Shi'atu'Ali*, the Party of Ali. Shiites in Turkey are known as Alevis.

Southeast Anatolia Project: A major hydroelectric system under construction in the upper Euphrates region of southeastern Turkey.

SPO: State Planning Organization (*Devlet Planlama Teşkilatı*). An advisory council created in 1960 under the authority of the prime minister to determine and implement state economic strategy and policy.

Sublime Porte: Translation of *Bab-ı Ali*, the residence of the Grand Vezir that came to be synonymous with the Ottoman central government.

Sultan: Islamic ruler of a territory who received investiture from the Caliph in Baghdad. The term came to mean any Muslim king, queen, prince, or princess.

Sunnites: Member of one of the two major Islamic denominations (the other being Shiites). The name derives from the *Sunna*, the tradition of the Prophet Muhammad.

Susurluk: Site in northwestern Anatolia of an auto-truck accident in November 1996 that led to the uncovering of a web of government corruption.

Tanzimat: The period of centralizing governmental reforms between the Rose Garden Rescript of 1839 and the Constitution of 1876.

Timar: The Ottoman feudal military revenue grant. Typically, cavalry soldiers living in the provinces received a grant of the right to collect the revenues of an estate, called a timar. In return, they owed the Ottoman central government the obligation of military service.

Topkapı: The Ottoman imperial palace in Istanbul, residence of the sultans and seat of the central government in the classical age. The palace was built by Sultan Mehmed II in the 1470s and expanded by later sultans. It served as the residence of the sultans until the construction of the Dolmabahçe Palace in the nineteenth century.

Treaty of Lausanne: The treaty, signed in July 1923, that established Turkey as an independent nation.

Treaty of Sèvres: The treaty, signed in August 1920, that formed the settlement of World War I for the Ottoman lands. It partitioned the Ottoman Empire between the victorious allies.

True Path Party: A political party founded in 1983. It became the successor to the Justice Party, banned by the military government. Süleyman Demirel, former chair of the Justice Party, became chair of the True Path Party in 1987, when the ban on political participation by former politicians was lifted. Its Turkish name, *Doğru Yol Partisi*, abbreviated DYP, might better be translated the Party of the Right Way, or the Straight Way. It is currently led by Tansu Çiller.

Turkoman: Semi-nomadic Turkish clans who fought and raided on behalf of the Seljuk dynasty on the Byzantine and Armenian frontiers of the Islamic world in Anatolia.

Türk-İş: *Türkiye İşçi Sendikaları Konfederasyonu*, Confederation of Labor Unions of Turkey, the country's largest and most influential organized labor association. It was founded in 1952.

Ulema: The scholars, jurists, and liturgical leaders of Islam. Strictly speaking, the term *clergy* should not be used to translate ulema, because unlike Christian clergy, the ulema do not receive ordination.

Vakıf: Islamic financial institution. A registered foundation in which the profits from a source were earmarked to the support of a specified charitable or religious purpose, and thereby became tax exempt. A charter defined the purpose and conditions of the *vakıf*, spelled out its management structure and appointed its trustees.

Vezir: The rank of an Ottoman military commander. The highest ranking vezirs were called "vezirs of the dome" (*kubbealtı vezirleri*) because they were assigned oversight of affairs of the council of state and stationed in the capital. Other vezirs were provincial governors-general.

Village Institutes (*Köy Enstitüleri*): A national system of schools to train teachers for village-level literacy and vocational education. Developed by İsmail Hakkı Tonguç in the late 1930s, the system began operations throughout Turkey in 1940. They were closed in 1953.

Virtue Party: The Islamic political party, founded in 1998 after the court-ordered closure of the Welfare Party. Its Turkish name is *Fazilet Partisi*, abbreviated FP. See also NOP.

Young Turks: English translation of *Jeune Turques*, the name given in Paris to the group of Ottoman dissident expatriates led by Ahmet Rıza and to the junior officers who staged the revolution of 1908.

YÖK (*Yüksek Öğretim Kurulu*): Higher Education Council. Founded in 1982 as the organ of centralized control of universities, it is responsible for long-range planning and policy making in national higher education and makes all appointments of deans and rectors (university presidents).

Bibliographic Essay

The books, articles and other materials mentioned below are intended as a guide for the interested reader who wishes to know more about specific aspects of Turkish history. Although this essay gives only materials published in English, it should be emphasized that much of the historical research on Turkish history is published in Turkish, and the overwhelming majority of the primary sources exist only in Turkish.

Turkologischer Anzeiger, an annual compilation originally published as a supplement to the journal *Wiener Zeitschrift für die Kunde des Morgenlands*, and after 1977 as a separate volume, is the most complete bibliography for specifically Turkish subjects. *Turkey*, Revised ed., published in the World Bibliographical Series by Çiğdem Balım-Harding (London, Santa Barbara and Denver, 1999), is selective and annotated. Metin Heper's *Historical Dictionary of Turkey* (Metuchen, N.J., 1996) is a handy, short reference work.

It is possible now to keep up on current events in Turkey through the websites maintained by all important Turkish daily newspapers and many news magazines. The best of the English sites is maintained by the excellent *Turkish Daily News*, edited by İlnur Çevik (archived since 1996), at www.turkishdailynews.com.

Seton Lloyd, *Turkey: A Traveller's History of Anatolia* (Berkeley and Los

Angeles, 1989) is a readable introduction to the history of ancient Anatolia. Ekrem Akurgal's guide *Ancient Civilizations and Ruins of Turkey from Prehistoric Times Until the End of the Roman Empire* (Istanbul, 1985) is a handy single-volume reference. On the mother goddess cult, see Lynn E. Roller, *In Search of God the Mother: The Cult of Anatolian Cybele* (Berkeley, Los Angeles and London, 1999), an excellent and careful study of the available data. John Freely, coauthor with Hilary Sumner-Boyd of the best guidebook for the city of Istanbul, *Strolling Through Istanbul: A Guide to the City* (Istanbul, 1972), also wrote the excellent, brief *Classical Turkey* (London, 1990) in the Architectural Guides for Travellers series. The best history of the Byzantine Empire is George Ostrogorsky, *History of the Byzantine State* (New Brunswick, N.J., 1969).

Further study of the Seljuks and their contemporaries in Anatolia before the Ottoman conquest should begin with Claude Cahen's *Pre-Ottoman Turkey* (New York, 1968) and the work of Speros Vryonis, Jr., *The Decline of Medieval Hellenism in Asia Minor and the Process of Islamization from the Eleventh through the Fifteenth Century* (Berkeley and Los Angeles, 1971). The work of Clive Foss, *Byzantine and Turkish Sardis* (Cambridge, Mass., 1976), and *Ephesus After Antiquity: A Late Antique, Byzantine, and Turkish City* (Cambridge, 1979), on the period of transition, is exemplary. Ibn Battuta's travels were translated by H. A. R. Gibb and published in three volumes of the Hakluyt Society series as *The Travels of Ibn Battuta A.D. 1325–1354*. Volume two contains the parts on Anatolia (Cambridge, 1962).

The foundation of the Ottoman Empire and the problems of interpreting the contemporary sources is one of the most intriguing problems of the historiography of medieval Europe and southwestern Asia. Cemal Kafadar provides an excellent discussion of the entire issue in his *Between Two Worlds: The Construction of the Ottoman State* (Berkeley and Los Angeles, 1995). The history of Ottoman Anatolia as a discrete piece of the Ottoman Empire has been neglected. Historians of the Ottoman Empire have tended to regard the project of an Anatolian history as anachronistic, while historians of the Republic have tended to take the entire Ottoman Empire as the background to Republican history. The place to start might be the *Book of Travels* of Evliya Çelebi, now being published in a multivolume series by the Dutch press E. J. Brill, at Leiden. Robert Dankoff, the leading scholar and translator of Evliya Çelebi, has also compiled the highly entertaining *The Intimate Life of an Ottoman Statesman; Melek Ahmed Pasha (1588–1662) As Portrayed in Evliya Çelebi's Book of Travels* (Albany, N.Y., 1991). The older translation of the Anatolian section, *Narrative of Travels in Europe, Asia and Africa, in the Seventeenth Century, by Evliy á Efendí,* by Joseph von Hammer [-Purstall] (London, 1834), is rare, even in its 1968 New York reprint.

There is unfortunately no equivalent of Ostrogorsky for Ottoman history. The closest equivalent in quality and elegance is Halil İnalcık, *The Ottoman Empire: The Classical Age 1300–1600* (New York and Washington, D.C., 1973), but it covers only the early period. İnalcık also coedited, with Donald Quataert, and wrote the first volume of the two-volume *An Economic and Social History of the Ottoman Empire* (Cambridge, 1994). The second volume, covering the period 1600–1914, includes contributions from Quataert, Suraiya Faroqhi, Bruce McGowan and Şevket Pamuk. Justin McCarthy's *The Ottoman Turks: An Introductory History to 1923* (London, 1993) surveys the entire history of the empire. See also Stanford J. Shaw and Ezel Kural Shaw, *History of the Ottoman Empire and Modern Turkey*, 2 vols. (Cambridge, 1976). Cemal Kafadar's chapter "The Ottomans and Europe," in volume one of the *Handbook of European History, 1400–1600*, ed. Thomas A. Brady, Jr., Heiko Oberman, and James D. Tracy (Grand Rapids, Mich., 1994), is a good short summary. For maps, see Donald Edgar Pitcher, *An Historical Geography of the Ottoman Empire from Earliest Times to the End of the Sixteenth Century* (Leiden: E. J. Brill, 1972).

Interpretations of the period after 1600, long dominated by the concept of a declining empire, are being reshaped by recent scholarship. Rifa'at 'Ali Abou-El-Haj, *Formation of the Modern State: The Ottoman Empire; Sixteenth to Eighteenth Centuries* (Albany, N.Y., 1991) is a provocative essay. Leslie Peirce's *The Imperial Harem: Women and Sovereignty in the Ottoman Empire* (Cambridge, 1993) presents a significant revision of the first four centuries of Ottoman political history. Ariel Salzmann's influential article, "An Ancien Régime Revisited: 'Privatization' and Political Economy in the Eighteenth-Century Ottoman Empire," *Politics and Society* 21 (1993): 393–423, broke through stubborn interpretive problems. On women in the Ottoman period, see the collection of articles edited by Madeline C. Zilfi, *Women in the Ottoman Empire: Middle Eastern Women in the Early Modern Era* (Leiden, 1997).

For an overview of the late Ottoman period, see M. E. Yapp, *The Making of the Modern Near East 1792–1923* (London and New York, 1987), William L. Cleveland, *A History of the Modern Middle East* (Boulder, Colo., 1994), Şevket Pamuk, *The Ottoman Empire and European Capitalism, 1820–1913: Trade, Investment and Production* (Cambridge, 1987), and Roger Owen, *The Middle East in the World Economy 1800–1914* (London and New

York, 1993). Stanford J. Shaw studied the period of Selim III in *Between Old and New: The Ottoman Empire Under Sultan Selim III 1789–1807* (Cambridge, Mass., 1971). The collection edited by L. Carl Brown, *Imperial Legacy: The Ottoman Imprint on the Balkans and the Middle East* (New York, 1996), examines the Ottoman impact in a number of areas, including nationalism and politics, administration, education, language, the economy, the military and others. The demographic context was examined by Justin McCarthy, *Death and Exile: The Ethnic Cleansing of Ottoman Muslims 1821–1922* (Princeton, N.J., 1995), and by Kemal H. Karpat, *Ottoman Population 1830–1914; Demographic and Social Characteristics* (Madison, 1985).

On the Tanzimat, see Roderic H. Davison, *Reform in the Ottoman Empire, 1856–1876* (Princeton, N.J., 1963) and two model studies of the bureaucracy by Carter V. Findley, *Bureaucratic Reform in the Ottoman Empire: The Sublime Porte, 1789–1922* (Princeton, N.J., 1981) and *Ottoman Civil Officialdom. A Social History* (Princeton, N.J., 1989). Şerif Mardin, *The Genesis of Young Ottoman Thought: A Study in the Modernization of Turkish Political Ideas* (Princeton, N.J., 1962) is good intellectual history of the era. On the constitution, see *The First Ottoman Constitutional Period: A Study of the Midhat Pasha Constitution and Parliament* (Baltimore, 1963; second ed. 1964). The best study of the diplomatic history of the period is M. S. Anderson's exhaustive *The Eastern Question 1774–1923: A Study in International Relations* (New York, 1966). Selim Deringil's book, *The Well-Protected Domains: Ideology and the Legitimation of Power in the Ottoman Empire 1876–1909* (London, 1998) provides an outstanding example of the ongoing reassessment of the reign of Sultan Abdülhamid II.

Two excellent recent surveys of the twentieth century are Erik Jan Zürcher, *Turkey: A Modern History* (London and New York, 1993; second ed. 1997), which emphasizes political economy, and Feroz Ahmad, *The Making of Modern Turkey* (London and New York: Routledge, 1993), written from a strongly Kemalist and RPP perspective. The popular book by Nicole and Hugh Pope, *Turkey Unveiled: A History of Modern Turkey* (Woodstock and New York, 1998), is good for the period after 1980, in spite of the cliché in the title.

The classic history of the Turkish revolution by Bernard Lewis, *The Emergence of Modern Turkey* (London, 1961; second ed. 1968), stressed intellectual and social developments. It should be read alongside Niyazi Berkes's richly detailed *The Development of Secularism in Turkey* (Montreal, 1964), which has just been reprinted with a new introduction by Feroz

Ahmad (New York: Routledge, 1998). Both books were written during the Democrat era of the 1950s.

The Young Turk era has been the subject of several books. See Feroz Ahmad, *The Young Turks: The Committee of Union and Progress in Turkish Politics 1908–1914* (Oxford, 1969), and M. Şükrü Hanioğlu, *The Young Turks in Opposition* (New York and Oxford, 1995). Erik Jan Zürcher's research has stressed the continuity between the Young Turk era and the early Republic; see his *The Unionist Factor: The Role of the Committee of Union and Progress in the Turkish National Movement* (Leiden, 1984). E. E. Ramsaur, Jr., *The Young Turks: Prelude to the Revolution of 1908* (Princeton, N.J., 1957), Masami Arai, *Turkish Nationalism in the Young Turk Era* (Leiden, 1992), and Taha Parla, *The Social and Political Thought of Ziya Gökalp 1876–1924* (Leiden: E. J. Brill, 1985) studied ideologies of nationalism. See also Hasan Kayalı, *Arabs and Young Turks: Ottomanism, Arabism and Islamism in the Ottoman Empire, 1908–1918* (Berkeley, Los Angeles, and London, 1997). The social and economic context is the subject of Donald Quataert, *Social Disintegration and Popular Resistance in the Ottoman Empire, 1881–1908: Reactions to European Economic Penetration* (New York and London, 1983). A solid introduction to the literature on the Armenian genocide, now somewhat dated, is Gwynne Dyer, "Turkish 'Falsifiers' and Armenian 'Deceivers': Historiography and the Armenian Massacres," *Middle Eastern Studies* 12 (1976): 99–107. Ronald Grigor Suny, "Empire and Nation: Armenians, Turks, and the End of the Ottoman Empire," *Armenian Forum*, no. 2 (Summer 1998): 17–51, with responses by Engin Deniz Akarlı, Selim Deringil and Vahakn N. Dadrian, initiates a courageous effort to work toward common ground on the divisive issue. Stanford J. Shaw's exhaustive study, "Resettlement of Refugees in Anatolia, 1918–1923," *The Turkish Studies Association Bulletin* 22, no. 1 (Spring 1998): 58–90, reconstructs the attempts of the Ottoman government to confront the demographic disaster immediately following World War I.

Several important figures have published English memoirs of the Young Turk era, including two volumes by Halidé Edib [Adıvar, *Memoirs of Halidé Edib* (London and New York, 1926) and *The Turkish Ordeal* (New York and London, 1928), Djemal Pasha, *Memories of a Turkish Statesman, 1913–1919* (New York, 1922), and Talat Pasha (excerpts only), "Posthumous Memoirs of Talaat Pasha," *Current History* 15, no. 2 (November 1921): 284–295. For Ziya Gökalp's essays, see the translations by Niyazi Berkes in *Turkish Nationalism and Western Civilization: Selected Essays of*

Ziya Gökalp (New York, 1959), and Uriel Heyd, *Foundations of Turkish Nationalism: The Life and Teachings of Ziya Gökalp* (London, 1950).

Andrew Mango's long awaited biography *Atatürk; The Biography of the Founder of Modern Turkey* (London, 2000) appeared when this book was ready to go to press. It replaces the earlier standard biography by Lord Kinross, *Atatürk; A Biography of Mustafa Kemal, Father of Modern Turkey* (London, 1964). The collection edited by Ali Kazancıgil and Ergun Özbudun, *Atatürk: Founder of a Modern State* (Hamden, Conn., 1981), contains articles by leading academics on various aspects of policy and his legacy. See also *Atatürk and the Modernization of Turkey*, ed. Jacob M. Landau (Leiden, and Boulder, Colo., 1994). İsmet İnönü has been neglected by comparison, but see Metin Heper's *İsmet İnönü: The Making of a Turkish Statesman* (Leiden, 1998). See also Selim Deringil, *Turkish Foreign Policy during the Second World War: An 'Active' Neutrality* (Cambridge, 1989), and Edward Weisband, *Turkish Foreign Policy 1943–1945: Small State Diplomacy and Great Power Politics* (Princeton, N.J., 1973).

Much of the early literature on the Kemalist revolution was overly enthusiastic. Richard D. Robinson, *The First Turkish Republic: A Case Study in National Development* (Cambridge, Mass., 1963), however, is very good on the political economy of the period to 1923–1960, and Henry Elisha Allen, *The Turkish Transformation: A Study in Social and Religious Development* (Chicago, 1935; reprint New York 1968) is insightful. On language and the alphabet, see Uriel Heyd, *Language Reform in Modern Turkey* (Jerusalem: Israel Oriental Society, 1954).

The recent scholarship has focused on the diversity of perspectives among the nationalists and their gradual suppression by the one-party state. See Erik Jan Zürcher, *Opposition in the Early Turkish Republic: The Progressive Republican Party 1924–1925* (Leiden, 1991). Important in this regard also are the study of the Kurdish revolt by Martin van Bruinessen, *Agha, Shaikh and State: The Social and Political Structures of Kurdistan* (Leiden, 1992), and Şerif Mardin's *Religion and Social Change in Modern Turkey: The Case of Bediüzzaman Said Nursi* (New York, 1989). See also the study by Walter F. Weiker, *Political Tutelage and Democracy in Turkey: The Free Party and its Aftermath* (Leiden, 1973).

Beginning in 1947 and continuing throughout the 1950s, the quarterly *Middle East Journal* covered Turkey extensively in informative articles. It also publishes a chronology of political and other public events in each issue. The leading opposition journalist and editor of *Vatan*, Ahmed Emin Yalman, published his memoirs, *Turkey in My Time* (Norman, Okla., 1956). Other significant firsthand descriptions of the period include the memoir by the Village Institutes teacher Mahmut Makal, *A Village in Anatolia*, translated by Sir Wyndham Deedes, ed. by Paul Stirling (London, 1954), and anthropologist Stirling's ground breaking *Turkish Village* (New York, 1965), the fieldwork for which was carried out in 1949–1950.

The best study of the transition to democracy in the late 1940s is Kemal Karpat, *Turkey's Politics: The Transition to a Multi-Party System* (Princeton, N.J., 1959). Feroz Ahmad, *The Turkish Experiment in Democracy 1950–1975* (Boulder, Colo., 1977), gives a wealth of detail on the politics of the era. Frederick W. Frey, *The Turkish Political Elite* (Cambridge, Mass., 1965), studied the makeup of the ruling class before and after 1950. On the 1960 coup see Walter F. Weiker, *The Turkish Revolution, 1960–1961: Aspects of Military Politics* (Washington, D.C., 1963). For an evaluation of the constitution and politics of the early second republic, see C. H. Dodd, *Politics and Government in Turkey* (Berkeley and Los Angeles, 1969).

Jacob Landau, *Radical Politics in Modern Turkey* (Leiden, 1974), is a useful reference work on the politics and society of the Second Republic. See also the same author's *Politics and Islam: The National Salvation Party in Turkey* (Salt Lake City, 1976), and Robert Bianchi, *Interest Groups and Political Development in Turkey* (Princeton, N.J., 1984). On the role of Islam in the 1960s and 1970s, see Uriel Heyd, *The Revival of Islam in Turkey* (Jerusalem, 1968), and Binnaz Toprak, *Islam and Political Development in Turkey* (Leiden, 1981).

The leading authority on the Cyprus issue has been C. H. Dodd, whose books *The Cyprus Issue: A Current Perspective* (Huntingdon, England, 1995) and *The Cyprus Imbroglio* (Huntington, 1998) serve as concise introductions to the complex problem.

Mehmet Ali Birand's book *The Generals' Coup in Turkey: An Inside Story of 12 September 1980* (London, 1987), gives a blow-by-blow description of the military intervention. See also the study by C. H. Dodd, *The Crisis of Turkish Democracy* (Washington, D.C., 1983; revised 1990). *Turkey: The Generals Take Over*, a special issue of *MERIP Reports*, no. 93 (January 1981), contains analyses of the political and social background of the coup. Frank Tachau published a study of the military government, *Turkey: Authority, Democracy and Development* (New York, 1984). Birand also published an interesting study of military life, based on interviews, *Shirts of Steel: An Anatomy of the Turkish Armed Forces* (London, 1991). See also William Hale, *Turkish Politics and the Military* (London, 1994).

The 1980 military coup became a turning point in Turkish history for younger intellectuals, who began reassessing the entire history of the

Republic in the light of the continued dominance of the military. Several important collections of studies have been published. An early example is Irvin C. Schick and Ertuğrul Ahmet Tonak (eds.), *Turkey in Transition: New Perspectives* (New York, 1987). Sibel Bozdoğan and Reşat Kasaba edited a valuable collection of papers, *Rethinking Modernity and National Identity in Turkey* (Seattle, 1997); another good collection was edited by Andrew Finkel and Nükhet Sirman, *Turkish State, Turkish Society* (London and New York, 1990). The chapters in Günsel Renda and C. Max Kortepeter (eds.), *The Transformation of Turkish Culture: The Atatürk Legacy* (Princeton, N.J., 1986), cover various aspects of modern Turkish literature, art, and music. Hugh Poulton's *Top Hat, Grey Wolf and Crescent: Turkish Nationalism and the Turkish Republic* (London, 1997) is a valuable interpretation of the nationalist ideology.

Zvi Yehuda Herschlag's *The Contemporary Turkish Economy* (London, 1988) should be read alongside Berch Berberoğlu's *Turkey in Crisis: From State Capitalism to Neocolonialism* for an understanding of the economic transformation after 1980. *The Life of Hacı Ömer Sabancı*, by Sadun Tanju, translated into English by Geoffrey Lewis (Saffron Walden, England, 1988), is a biography of the founder of one of Turkey's largest conglomerates. His son, Sakıp Sabancı, one of Turkey's leading industrialists, has published a memoir called *This Is My Life* (Saffron Walden, England, 1988). The political parties were the subject of a study by Metin Heper and Jacob M. Landau (eds.), *Political Parties and Democracy in Turkey* (London, 1991). Metin Heper has authored a number of important articles about political life in Turkey in the 1980s and 1990s. Ayşe Güneş-Ayata published a study of a crucial aspect of Turkish political culture, "Roots and trends of clientelism in Turkey," *in Democracy, Clientelism and Civil Society* ed. Luis Roniger and Ayse Güneş-Ayata (Boulder, Colo., 1994), pp. 49–64. The papers edited by Richard Tapper, *Islam in Modern Turkey: Religion, Politics and Literature in a Secular State* (London, 1991), cover aspects of religion in the 1980s.

On the status of women in Turkey, see the relevant chapters in Lois Beck and Nickie Keddie (eds.), *Women in the Muslim World* (Cambridge, Mass. and London, 1978). Other important books on the subject include the anthology edited by Şirin Tekeli, *Women in Modern Turkish Society: A Reader* (London and Atlantic Highlands, N.J., 1991), and Julie Marcus, *A World of Difference: Islam and Gender Hierarchy in Turkey* (London, 1992). On the issue of the veil, see the thoughtful book by Nilüfer Göle, *The Forbidden Modern: Civilization and Veiling* (Ann Arbor: University of Michigan Press, 1996).

The standard work on the Kurds in Turkey is now Kemal Kirişçi and Gareth M. Winrow, *The Kurdish Question and Turkey: An Example of Trans-State Ethnic Conflict* (London, 1997). See also David McDowell's general history, *A Modern History of the Kurds* (London, 1996); Servet Mutlu, "Ethnic Kurds in Turkey: A Demographic Study," *International Journal of Middle East Studies* 28 (1996): 517–541; and Michael M. Gunter, *The Kurds in Turkey: A Political Dilemma* (Boulder, Colo., 1990). One of the few studies of Turkish Shiites (Alevis) is Tord Olsson, Elisabeth Özdalga and Catharina Raudvere (eds.), *Alevi Identity: Cultural Religious and Social Perspectives* (Curzon Press, 1999). On Jews, there are Stanford J. Shaw, *Jews of the Ottoman Empire and the Turkish Republic* (New York, 1991); and Walter F. Weiker, *Ottomans, Turks, and the Jewish Polity: A History of the Jews of Turkey* (Lanham, Md., 1992).

Yaşar Kemal was the subject of a special issue of the journal *Edebiyât: A Journal of Middle Eastern Literatures*, 5, nos. 1–2 (1980), edited by Ahmet Ö. Evin. *Yaşar Kemal on His Life and Art*, trans. Eugene Lyons Hébert and Barry Tharaud (Syracuse, N.Y., 1999), the publication of a series of interviews, amounts to an autobiography. The English translation of Aziz Nesin's autobiography, *Istanbul Boy*, published by the University of Texas Press (Austin, Tex., 1977), provides a richly evocative description of Turkey during the early decades of the republic. Evin also has published a study of the history of the Turkish novel, *Origins and Development of the Turkish Novel* (Minneapolis, 1983). A valuable collection of stories by major writers is *An Anthology of Modern Turkish Short Stories*, ed. Fahir İz (Minneapolis, 1978). Kemal Sılay's *An Anthology of Turkish Literature* (Bloomington, Ind., 1996) contains texts and interpretations of Turkic literature from the seventh to the twentieth century. Metin And's *History of Theatre and Popular Entertainment in Turkey* (Ankara, 1963–1964) is still one of the few of its kind. Martin Stokes has led the study of Turkish popular music, including *The Arabesque Debate: Music and Musicians in Modern Turkey* (Oxford, 1992), and "Turkish Urban Popular Music," *Middle East Studies Association Bulletin* 33, no. 1 (Summer 1999): 10–15. Traditional Crossroads has published several CDs of early recorded Turkish popular music.

Index

About the Author

DOUGLAS A. HOWARD is Professor of History at Calvin College in Grand Rapids, Michigan. A specialist in the history of Turkey, he is the author of a number of papers on the topic and the former editor of *The Turkish Studies Association Bulletin*. He is at work on a study of the Ottoman provincial cavalry in the 16th and 17th centuries.

**Other Titles in the
Greenwood Histories of the Modern Nations**
Frank W. Thackeray and John E. Findling, Series Editors

The History of Holland
Mark T. Hooker

The History of Nigeria
Toyin Falola

The History of Brazil
Robert M. Levine

The History of Russia
Charles E. Ziegler

The History of Portugal
James M. Anderson

The History of Poland
M.B. Biskupski

The History of Mexico
Burton Kirkwood

The History of South Africa
Roger B. Beck

The History of France
W. Scott Haine

The History of Iran
Elton L. Daniel

The History of China
David C. Wright

The History of Turkey
Douglas A. Howard